CARS, TRUCKS, AND BUSES

MADE BY TRACTOR COMPANIES

Bill Vossler

Published by

**krause
publications**

700 E. State Street • Iola, WI 54990-0001
Telephone: 715/445-2214

Please call or write for our free catalog.
Our toll-free number to place an order or obtain a free catalog is 800-258-0929
or please use our regular business telephone 715-445-2214
for editorial comment and further information.

Cover Photo Courtesy of Marlin Brubaker

Library of Congress Catalog Number: 98-87288
ISBN: 0-87341-672-4

Printed in the United States of America

Dedication

To my wife, Nikki, beacon of logic and reason flashing over the dark and turbulent waters of book writing. You always guide me home.

Acknowledgments

THANKS to Gary Hoonsbeen, Roy Bernick, and Dan Roen for lending their magazines, time, and expertise—I owe them debts that can never be repaid; to Richard Birklid, for the use of photos from his collection; and finally to all the anonymous workers at the state historical societies and small libraries across the upper Midwest (and a few out East) who went out of their way to help me find what I needed, in person, but mostly by telephone and fax. My deep appreciation and thanks.

Table of Contents

Introduction

This book is about connections: connections between people and farm tractor companies; connections between tractor and car and truck divisions within tractor companies; connections between tractor companies and car companies and truck companies; connections between families and friends and workers.

Many of the connections are obvious: Wichita Falls Motor Company of Wichita Falls, Texas, made Wichita tractors, Wichita trucks, and Wichita cars, for instance.

Some are less obvious: William Galloway Company of Waterloo, Iowa, manufactured Farmobile tractors, Arabian automobiles, and Galloway trucks.

Some of the connections might be tenuous: did Benjamin Lawter, for example, manufacture automobiles and tractors during different years and with different companies in Newcastle, Indiana? When information was sketchy, I decided to err on the side of possibility–in this case, two Lawter-named businesses both manufacturing vehicles in a small town within four years leans toward connecting the two.

But I've made clear when I'm not sure, in a section is called Yes, Maybe, No, and you must be the final judge until more information surfaces–if indeed, it does. If nothing else, speculating is fun.

Some company connections are spread over many years between the manufacture of one type of vehicle and another, and may run through two or three companies, but the connection, however remote, is still there.

Most of the companies have photos representing most of the types of vehicles they made; where there are none, they were simply not available.

The danger in producing a book like this is in its incompleteness: not every word of every history of every company can be included, simply because of space. Nevertheless, you'll find that the most pertinent information for each company and vehicle has been included.

The first two decades of the 20th century–when tractor companies made cars and trucks and all manner of other machines–were vibrant and exciting years, full of the possibility and promise of these new-fangled machines; I hope some of that excitement shines through to you as you read the book.

SECTION I:

Tractor Companies That Made Cars, Trucks, and Buses

Chapter 1

Avery Rises Twice From the Dead

The Avery Company of Peoria, Illinois, was probably the earliest service-oriented tractor company. President J. B. Bartholomew said in a *Motor Age* article ca. 1910 that "Service is a word that seems to have a very elastic meaning. Each person in the trade looks upon this word from a different angle and applies their own sort of reasoning to it.

"From our angle, the word has come to mean everything its elasticity will stand for. The very first service work on a farm tractor is done at the factory...to see that the machine is so constructed that a novice can handle it without making a serious mistake. See to it that when it goes out to the field there is nothing fundamentally wrong in its design and construction."

The foundation for this company, which made Avery tractors, trucks, and cars, was laid during the Civil War, when Robert H. Avery, a Union soldier, languished in dreaded Andersonville Confederate Prison. While there, Avery designed a corn planter; after his release, he and his brother, Cyrus M., organized the R.H. and C.M. Avery Firm in Galesburg, Illinois. In 1882, they moved to Peoria because of better shipping opportunities.

Avery tractors

The Avery Company made large, heavy tractors. That remained the perception even after the company made the tiny 5-10 in 1916 (to compete with the upcoming Fordson.) The 5-10 was priced at $295 and soon raised to $365. This oddity had the seat in the middle, between the front and back wheels. Other small Averys included the 8-16, built in 1914, under 5,000 pounds; the 12-20 at 5,500 pounds; and the 14-28 at 7,540 pounds.

Despite these small tractors, in the eyes of the farmer,

Avery built large and heavy tractors. Part of the reason is clear: it did build large, heavy tractors, like the Avery 40-80, built in 1913 and weighing 22,000 pounds; and the 45-65, built in 1920 and also weighing 11 tons.

The Avery Company began in 1891, with threshers and steam-traction engines, and under varied company names. Avery was a force in American agriculture, with branch offices in Omaha, Des Moines, Kansas City, Indianapolis, Minneapolis, and St. Louis, selling products all over the world.

The greatest coup the company made was hiring J. B. Bartholomew as vice president in 1892. He invented or improved nearly every item made by the company. One invention was the Avery Undermounted Steam Engine, a huge success which further strengthened Avery's position in the market.

The Avery Company was very humane, with a company dispensary employing two doctors five hours a day, and an insurance plan for workers.

In 1917, Avery bought the Kingman Plow Company land, then Davis Manufacturing Company, to build its own gasoline engines. By 1920, Avery employed 2,600 men and produced eight different models of tractors.

A mere year later, only 260 men remained; four years later, the company went bankrupt, partly because of the agricultural depression that struck in 1920, partly because the company had not built smaller tractors earlier, and partly because with so many tractor varieties, it had huge inventories.

The Avery Company returned in 1925 as Avery Power Machine Company; disappeared in the early '30s; and reappeared as Avery Farm Machinery Company in 1936, making combines, separators and cylinder teeth, but World War II, with its shortage of steel and loss of markets, intervened and Avery never recovered.

This North Dakota field scene shows how the Avery steam traction engines dwarfed the people who worked them. The Avery Company of Peoria, Illinois, was a power in steam traction engines long before it started making gasoline tractors, cars, and trucks. This Avery is a 30-hp steam traction engine from 1906 or 1907. (Richard Birklid Collection)

This photo from inside the new Avery Company factory at Peoria, Illinois, ca. 1915, shows one of the company's new under-mounted engines hanging on a 20-ton electric crane. Avery made a wide variety of tractors, which ended up being its downfall when tough times came–the company had too much money tied up in stock and when dealers and farmers couldn't pay, Avery suffered. (Dan Roen Collection)

Avery cars

Little is known about Avery cars; most car-reference books don't mention an Avery car made by the tractor company. However, *The Handbook of Automobiles 1915-1916*, shows the accompanying photo of the Avery Glide 30 automobile, manufactured by the Avery Company of Peoria, Illinois. This five-person roadster sold for $1,195, and had a horsepower rating of 19.6. The price included top, top hood, electric lighting, electric self-starter, windshield, speedometer, and demountable rims.

That Avery would build automobiles is not surprising because an article in *Motor Age* magazine says Avery's long- time President J. B. Bartholomew, "...did a good portion of the machine work on the original Duryea motor car built back in 1893."

Independent of Avery, Bartholomew also built a prototype car in 1901 called the Bartholomew. He also founded the Bartholomew Company, which built the Glide car in Peoria from 1903-1920.

Most reference books about old cars don't even mention the Avery Company of Peoria, Illinois, made a car. This is its Glide Touring Car "30," which was manufactured in 1915 in meteor blue for the body and chassis, while the fenders and hood were black. It was a five-person vehicle, with a 114-inch wheelbase and a 19.6 hp four-cylinder engine. This touring car and the roadster both sold for $1,195 in 1915. (Gary Hoonsbeen Collection)

Avery trucks

In 1910, the Avery Company began building agricultural trucks. Its first, designed by J. B. Bartholomew, was called the tractor-truck, "for city, town, and country hauling," its advertisements said. The company suggested using it to haul grain, hay, livestock, and other loads, as well as pull plows, harrows, discs, binders, road graders, and other farm machinery or loaded wagons. This was a one-ton model with a four-cylinder engine, open cab, and chain drive.

These tractor-trucks had a 9-1/2-inch thick shell on the brass radiator and another 3 inches of radiator under the hood, four individual cylinder blocks, dual rear chain drive, and exterior brake and gearshift levers. The lamps were made entirely of brass. It also had bucket seats like those on a fire engine and right-hand drive.

Its most unique feature was its wheels, however, which were made of wood, with wooden spokes and felloes and steel rims, 1-1/2 inches thick and 5 inches wide.

One old Avery truck had an interesting history, according to *Antique Automobile* magazine of July-August 1980: A 1912 Avery truck on the Hawaiian island of Lanai was used to haul pineapples and supplies until about 1917. "That year, the vehicle was on its way to meet an incoming supply barge, when the mighty four-cylinder engine abruptly stopped. The truck was pushed to the side of the road and a mechanic was summoned. The trouble was diagnosed as being in the magneto. This was removed and shipped to California for repair. It was never returned. Then, with newer trucks coming into use, the Avery remained abandoned at the side of the road and virtually forgotten.

"In time, the road itself was bypassed when a new blacktop road was cut through about three hundred yards to the side. The Avery truck could still be seen from the paved road. ...The Avery remained intact until World War II, when brass strippers removed the huge radiator to sell for scrap. In time, someone also removed the engine to power a skow; next, one of the front wheels disappeared,

In 1910, Avery began advertising its "wonderful new gasoline farm wagon and general farm power machine," as it called its truck. The company said it would do more work than any other farm power machine, that it was entirely original in design. The advertising said, "It carries loads on its own body, pulls plows and other machinery in the field and drives other machines by belt power. You can do road work, field work or belt work, all with this one machine." It was an axiom of the time that every manufacturer tried to get a machine that would cover all farm uses, like a horse. (Roy Bernick Collection)

This old Avery truck was found in the corner of an old shed, and is in its original condition. It is a 1910, 1911, or 1912 model, and has regular tread on the wheels. Its top speed is 12 mph and it still works. It was originally purchased in South Dakota, and was eventually trucked on a flatbed out to California, where it appeared in parades until it was consigned to the corner of the shed. (Gary Hoonsbeen Collection)

This 1909 line drawing of the areas of the Avery farm truck shows how little Americans knew about motoring in those early days. At this time, farmers were fighting with the concept of getting rid of the horses on the farm, animals which took extra time, effort, and expense, and buying a farm truck or tractor. This loyalty issue was very difficult for many farmers. (Roy Bernick Collection)

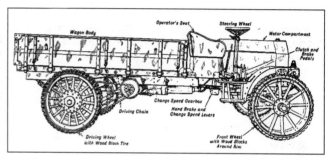

and then the other." Until it was restored in 1976.

It was used as a hunting platform at times, as men would point the vehicle into the corn fields, keep it running without a driver, hop up on back, and shoot pheasants.

In 1912, Avery built 2- and 3-ton trucks with solid rubber tires; C-cabs were made a year later; and in 1917, the cab-over-engine design with enclosed chain drive was fully in use. By 1921, Avery trucks were conventional ones. Its new six-cylinder truck introduced in that year didn't last long because the company went into bankruptcy a couple of years later.

Chapter 2

Bethlehem Motor Truck Corporation

Finances were not ideal for Bethlehem Motor Truck Corporation of Allentown (or East Allentown), Pennsylvania when it built its first automobile in 1920. It had already built Bethlehem trucks and Bethlehem tractors by this time, and bought an engine-building company so it could build its own engines.

Bethlehem tractors

Up until 1920, the financial situation for Bethlehem was solid. During 1919 and 1920, Bethlehem built its only farm tractor, a 3-ton four-wheeled 18-36 using a Beaver four-cylinder 4-3/4 x 6 engine with two forward speeds. Standard equipment included a Stromberg carburetor, Bosch magneto, and Fedders radiator. Hyatt roller bearings were used throughout, 17 in the transmission alone.

Certainly the company's precarious financial position did the Bethlehem tractor in, but doubtless two other items factored in: first, the rabid competition among numerous tractor companies–more than 200 of them during these years alone, which made it very difficult for a new product to get seen and heard; second, the agricultural depression, which struck about 1920. Whatever happened, Bethlehem disappeared.

Bethlehem Motors Corporation of Allentown, Pennsylvania, built its 18-36 tractor in 1918, with a Beaver four-cylinder engine with 4-3/4- x 6-inch bore and stroke. It was a vertical motor mounted lengthwise. It ran at 1,000 rpm and was cooled by a pump, fan, and radiator. It had a single forward speed of 3.3 mph, and weighed 6,200 pounds. Other references say the tractor was built in 1919 and 1920, but it is unclear.

Ideal automobiles

Because Bethlehem Motor Truck Corporation had at times been confused with Bethlehem Automobile Company, which had produced an automobile called the "Ideal," it would have made absolutely no sense for the company to call its own first foray into automobiles the "Ideal."

But it did. The Ideal was built for export only and cost $3,000 each; perhaps the company did not want to deal with the highly competitive American automobile industry.

The Ideal contained a four-cylinder 40-hp engine built by Bethlehem, (Bethlehem had just bought North American Motors of Pottstown, Pennsylvania, which provided facilities to Bethlehem to build its own engines.)

But it spread itself too thin; later that year, the company moved into receivership, which meant no money for vehicle development. A new management team took over in 1921, and sold the remaining Ideal models at a less-than-ideal price of $1,000 each. Ideals were built only in 1920.

Bethlehem trucks

Bethlehem trucks were built starting in 1917, 1-1/4-ton models using 23 hp Golden, Belknap, and Swartz motors, while the 2-1/4-ton model used a North American engine of 26 hp. The smaller trucks cost $1,245, and the larger $1,775. A cab and box cost an extra $65; 1-1/2-ton chassis Bethlehems sold for $1,775.

The engine governor allowed speeds of 12 to 18 mph, depending on the model. After 1920, it began offering four models (1 to 4 tons) with engines made by Bethlehem. The company indicated it would enter heavily into

After Bethlehem Motors Corporation of Allentown, Pennsylvania, bought out North American Motors in 1920 so it could start making its own engines, one of the trucks it brought out was this 1-1/2-ton model. "The farmer or businessman who needs a truck to deliver truck service at minimum operating costs invests wisely in a 1-1/2-ton Bethlehem." (Roy Bernick Collection)

This advertisement for Bethlehem trucks appeared in *Farm Implements and Tractors* in 1919, when things were still going well for the Allentown, Pennsylvania, company. Prices for the trucks include $1,495 for the 3/4-ton, $2,095 for the 1-1/2-ton, $2,495 for the 2-1/2-ton, and $3,595 for the 3-1/2-ton Bethlehem truck. (Gary Hoonsbeen Collection)

building cars and buses, manufacturing 20,000 vehicles per year. (In 1919, it made 3,500.)

The company's motto was, "Trucks bought today without electric lights will be out of date tomorrow." Thus it was, that in 1920, all Bethlehem trucks came with an electric starter and electric lighting.

But the floorboards fell out from under the company; despite the focus of new trucks by the new management team, only 24 were built in 1924.

Other models were built during the next few years, including the 1-ton Model KN for $1,595, the 2-ton GN for $2,495, the 2-1/2-ton model L for $3,195, and the 3-1/2-ton Model M for $3,795. In 1925, the company merged with Lehigh Company, and in 1927, that company was sold to Hahn and Company. The last Bethlehem trucks were built in 1926.

Bethlehem Motors Corporation built this 1-1/2-ton truck-D model in 1919, and charged $1,965 for it, or $2,075 for the Express model or the Stake model. These trucks were powered by a 3-3/4- x 4-1/2-inch bore and stroke four-cylinder engine, and produced 22.5 horsepower. The price includes an ammeter, horn, tool box, and tool kit with a jack. (Dan Roen Collection)

Chapter 3

Bryan Uses Steam in Building Tractors, Cars and Trucks

George A. Bryan used his past experience with steam locomotives for the Santa Fe Railroad to decide to build steam vehicles, including a steam tractor, steam car, and steam truck.

In his early days, he wiped railroad engines, eventually becoming fireman, engineer, locomotive inspector, then chief inspector. He decided to adapt the super-heated steam system from locomotives to light vehicles. He and his father, Oscar, formed Bryan Harvester Company of Peru, Indiana.

Bryan steam tractors

The Bryan steam tractor was notable for several reasons: a steam tractor built in the 1920s, after most tractor companies had gone to gasoline, kerosene, or oblivion; and its light weight (3,400 pounds), compared to some early steamers that weighed 50,000 pounds or more.

The 1920 model was a Bryan 26-70, with a 2-cylinder 4- x 5-inch bore and stroke and ground speeds varying from 1/8 to 7-1/2 mph. Its wheelbase was 88 inches, length 142 inches, height 64 inches, and width 72 inches. The instru-

This 1927 Bryan was a 20-70 (compared to 1920s 26-70), with a Stephenson two-cylinder 4- x 5-inch bore and stroke engine. The machine weighed 5,500 pounds and used a Bryan tube boiler with 600 pounds of working pressure and 1,200 pounds of tested pressure. The 20-70 configuration was one of the oddest in all of tractordom, because normally the drawbar-brake ratio is closer to 1 to 1.5 or 1 to 2, instead of 1 to 3.5, as in this tractor. (Roy Bernick Collection)

ment board contained a steam gauge, water level indicator, and a lubrication oil sight feed. The boiler worked at 600 pounds of steam pressure, tested to 1,200 pounds.

Motor Age magazine wrote, "One of the new tractors at the show which created much interest was the Bryan light steam tractor...This tractor marks a new step in tractor practice. For the first time in tractor history, this machine uses a high pressure superheated steam boiler, with a steam atomized fuel burner, in a form that makes it entirely possible to use the very lowest grades of fuel.

"In outward form, this tractor resembles many of the inclosed gasoline engine driven tractors. The conventional radiator is fitted on the front end, but in this case the radiator serves as a condenser for exhaust steam."

The later model was rated 20-70, weighing a ton more (5,500 pounds) than earlier models.

Bryan steam tractors were shipped to the California Bryan Steam Utilities Inc. in Los Angeles, and other shipments were made to Ohio and Illinois state distributors.

Farm Implements and Tractors said, "The Bryan Light Steam Tractor has attracted considerable attention for several years, and the demand for the machine has been almost spectacular. We understand this tractor employs a small, compact steam power plant which is said to be decidedly economical. The fact that a steam tractor is a long-life proposition, having an abundance of stored power for emergencies, gives the new tractor an important place in the industry.

"We read with a great deal of interest the report of Ed Friedersdorf, R.R. No. Q, Peru, Indiana, on this wonderful machine, and those of our friends who are interested in a tractor or truck of this nature, can no doubt obtain valuable information upon inquiry to the factory."

While experimenting with this tractor, George Bryan hit on the idea of a steam home heating plant, and after 1925, he turned his attention toward that, abandoning steam vehicles, and changing the name to Bryan Steam Corporation.

Bryan steam automobile

George Bryan built his first steam car in 1913, testing it through the mountains and deserts of New Mexico. The boiler featured 44 7-foot-long tubes using a Bunsen burner to produce maximum working steam pressure of 600 pounds.

Six of the 4,500-pound cars, which looked like Apper-

Bryan Harvester Company of Peru, Indiana, built this Bryan Steamer in 1923 for the sales manager of the company, Roy Slater. It is painted two-tone platinum gray and robin's egg blue, with black fenders. The boiler is a water tube boiler with 44 tubes each nine feet long. Upholstering is genuine leather. It is a very rare car to be seen working today. (Gary Hoonsbeen Collection)

sons, were built in the Peru plant from 1918-23. One was built especially for the sales manager of the company, Roy Slater, in 1923; it was painted two-tone platinum gray and robin's egg blue, with black fenders. Upholstery was genuine leather. Only a touring style was produced.

Bryan steam truck

Little is known about the Bryan steam truck, except that a prototype was built sometime in the 1920s.

Farm Implements and Tractors wrote about 1920, "The expected has happened. The latest thing in the way of modern power farming...is the first time in the history of the world that a threshing machine has been operated by a small steam tractor, accompanied by a steam truck being used to haul the grain to the machine."

The magazine said two new factories had begun operating in Peru, Indiana, manufacturing trucks and tractors (probably fiction.) "The output of the Bryan factories is said to be contracted far in advance for nearly two years, and there has been a steady increase in the number of men employed for some time past. It is therefore planned that normal production will be under way in a comparatively short time."

This rare photo shows both the Bryan steam tractor and Bryan steam truck together in a field about 1920. *Farmer Implements and Tractors* said, "This photo was recently taken near Peru, Indiana, the home of the Bryan Light Steam Tractor, which is known as the world's only light steam machine of this class. The truck and tractor are both products of the Bryan Harvester Co., and we understand that production has started at two factories of the company at Peru." It may take a good eye to discern that the steam truck is in the very center of the photo, facing right toward the front of the steam tractor. (State Historical Society of North Dakota)

Chapter 4

Buckeye Built First Gasoline-powered Car in U.S.

Buckeye Manufacturing Co. of Anderson, Indiana, built cars long before tractors or trucks. Its first Buckeye vehicle, a Buckeye built in 1891 by founder John Lambert, is considered the first gasoline-powered automobile built in the United States.

But instead of claiming–rightfully–that it was the first gasoline-powered automobile ever built, Lambert allowed another automobile maker, Elwood P. Haynes, claim he had built the first. Haynes wanted to market his automobile as "America's first car," even though his was not first, and was only tested on July 4, 1894 in Kokomo, Indiana. Why Lambert agreed to this silence remains a mystery, although in later years he often circumvented his promise by pointing out the known date of manufacture of his automobile– 1891, which people recognized as earlier than all others.

Lambert tractors

It seems likely that the same Lambert who built Buckeye tractors and Lambert cars also built Lambert tractors, manufactured by the Lambert Gas and Gasoline Engine Company of Anderson, Indiana as early as 1894, when a one-cylinder traction engine was built on a Morton traction truck.

Despite John Lambert's having built the first gasoline-powered vehicle in the United States, he promised he wouldn't quibble if another man claimed his was first: Elwood P. Haynes' Hoosier Horseless Carriage, shown here with Haynes aboard his 1894 contraption.

Buckeye Gasolene Buggy. Buckeye Mfg. Co., Anderson, Indiana.

The Buckeye Gasolene (sic) Buggy, manufactured by John Lambert sometime during the 1890s, was probably the first gasoline-powered vehicle built in the United States. Lambert tried marketing it in Ohio several times during the 1890s, but without much success; he had to wait until after the turn of the century before one of his automobiles would be palatable to the general public, the Union, in 1902. (Gary Hoonsbeen Collection)

The 1894 Lambert, built at a time when John Lambert was experimenting with his Buckeye automobile, was a simple one-cylinder horizontal engine fixed on a Morton traction truck.

The Lambert Steel Hoof was built in 1912 as a 20-hp machine using a four-cylinder engine. It looked very modern compared to most tractors of the day. The "steel hooves" were plates on the rear wheels that could be drawn in for road work or extended, by shifting in the center, for field work and self-cleaning. Each rear wheel had an independent brake to make turning easier. (Dan Roen Collection)

The Lambert tractor didn't show up again until 1912, as a 20-hp Lambert "Steel Hoof," which used a four-cylinder vertical engine of three forward speeds and one reverse. The "hoofs" were movable wheel plates that could be drawn in for road work or extended for better traction for field work. Each rear wheel had an independent brake to facilitate turning.

The company was reorganized as Buckeye Manufacturing Company in 1916.

Buckeye tractors

The first Buckeye tractor was built in 1912 and four years later, the company took over Buckeye Manufacturing Company at Anderson, and began building a small and compact half-track-type tractor called the Buckeye, Jr. Because of its closed-over drive wheel, it resembles the Gray tractor, manufactured in Minneapolis about the same time.

The 1917 model was a true tracklayer, the Buckeye Chain Tread tractor, which created less soil compaction in fields than regular tractors. It used an engine that was 4-

Four 14-inch plows were recommended for this tracklayer tractor, the Trundaar 25-40, manufactured by Buckeye Manufacturing Company of Anderson, Indiana, in 1920. The 8,800-pound tractor was 120 inches long, 72 inches wide, and 58 inches high. It was powered by a Waukesha 5- x 6-1/4-inch bore and stroke four-cylinder engine. (Dan Roen Collection)

1/2 x 6-3/4 inches with a 16-32 rating, and was fancily designed and colored.

The next year, Buckeye produced another new tractor, the Trundaar 20-35, weighing 9,500 pounds and using a four-cylinder Waukesha engine. Trundaar crawlers worked well on rough ground because of their unique oscillating linkage at the front end of the track frame. Each track was supported by nine idler rollers.

In 1920, Buckeye upped the size of the Trundaar to a 25-40. It was powered by a heavy duty Waukesha motor with four bore-and-stroke cylinders 5 x 6-1/4 inches. The tracklayer machine weighed only 8,800 pounds, probably in response to farmers demanding lighter tractors. Buckeye went out of existence in the early 1920s.

Buckeye, Union, and Lambert automobiles

Lambert was a well-to-do businessman in Ohio City, Ohio, in the 1890s when he began tinkering with a gasoline-powered three-wheeled auto. He owned a grain elevator, lumber yard, hardware store, opera house, town hall, jail, and other real estate holdings. He had enough wealth, resources and free time to build and test his three-wheeled surrey-top gasoline-powered vehicle. The machine was his own design, and after successfully testing it in about 1891, he printed a sales brochure and offered to sell Buckeye automobiles for $550 each.

But nobody wanted it. Perhaps the price was too high; perhaps the time for the automobile had not yet arrived. So Lambert turned his attention to manufacturing stationary gasoline engines. In 1895, he sent a letter to newspapers announcing he would soon have a gasoline-powered vehicle on the market. He included a drawing of the same three-wheeled Buckeye vehicle he had tried to market earlier.

Again, nobody was interested. So Lambert spent his time devising a friction transmission, a major feature of all the cars he would eventually market. He tried marketing a

In 1910, this advertisement for the Lambert 7 was published, claiming just about everything good for the 34-hp vehicle. "If you want the simplest, most durable, easiest-operated, built-for-service, economical car, examine the Lambert," it crowed. It cost $2,000 and was made by the Buckeye Manufacturing Co. of Anderson, Indiana. (Gary Hoonsbeen Collection)

This car and chassis is the 1903 Union, manufactured by Buckeye Manufacturing Company during its short sojourn into Union City, Indiana. That city had shown interest in the Buckeye venture, and so it was organized there, and Union cars built. The company remained in Union City, as well as Anderson, Indiana, from 1902-1905, when having two companies was no longer workable, and the Union City plant was closed. (Gary Hoonsbeen Collection)

four-wheel car in 1898, still without success.

Three years later, Union City, Indiana, a town 50 miles distant, showed interest in Lambert's company, so Lambert organized the Buckeye Manufacturing Company there in December 1901. The public was now ready for the automobile.

In 1902, the "Union" was manufactured in Union City, and the parts carted to Anderson and set together there. Its originality, along with Lambert's friction transmission ("No gears to grind or strip, and no clutches to slip") was a strong selling point. *The Automobile Review* of March 1, 1903 said, "The disc surface of the flywheel to which the friction wheel is applied, is covered with a composition metal plate, which is stated to be composed of metals characterized by special friction qualities. The friction wheel is applied to the disk by a foot ratchet and moved toward and away from the center or to the opposite side of the wheels–to secure the speed changes and the reverse–by a lever."

The two-seater runabout with fold-down seat in the dash for two more passengers contained a choice of air- or

water-cooled engines, and cost $1,250. In 1904 and 1905, larger five-seater tonneau-model Unions were built as well. Union engines ran on two cylinders and used a double-chain drive.

The Automobile Review added that "The car was a box front touring car, equipped with a double-cylinder motor of 10 hp. The motor is placed across the frame, over the rear axle. The inlet valves are automatic, and a novel feature is an oscillating valve, automatically governed, or controlled, by hand, which cuts off the intaken charge at any length of stroke, controlling the speed of the motor and automatically controlling the spark."

In 1904, the wisdom of manufacturing the parts in one place and assembling them in another became questionable, so the entire plant was moved to Anderson. The motto for the vehicle was, "In Union there is strength."

About 300 Unions were built through late 1905, when the car was renamed the Lambert, since Union City had been abandoned.

The Lambert two-cylinder models were simply renamed Unions. In 1907, the larger Lamberts contained several models with shaft drive, although most remained chain-

This is the rear view of the Union automobile of 1902, produced by John Lambert in Union City, Indiana. This was one of the few early cars that didn't need a crank to start it, instead using an ingenious contrivance actuated by the foot of the operator. The Union sold for $1,250 without any extras; $100 was required in advance, and the balance to be paid on delivery of the vehicle. (Roy Bernick Collection)

Buckeye Manufacturing Company of Anderson, Indiana, built this Lambert Model V-3 truck in the early teens. It no longer had the in-house engine, as the company began buying outside about this time, using Buda, Continental, Davis, and Rutenber, among others.

driven, and the new 4- and 6-cylinder engines were built by Buda, Continental, Rutenber, Trebert, and Davis, instead of in-house. Some Lamberts contained engines in the rear, some in the middle, and some in the front. Lambert automobiles were built until 1917.

Lambert trucks

Buckeye also built trucks or "commercial vehicles." These were light high-wheeler delivery trucks with the typical friction transmissions and chain drives. Trucks were built from 1906-1918.

In 1914, Lambert Manufacturing Company built a tractor plant in El Segundo, California, with an eye to profiting from the farm tractor market in the West. This was one of the tractors built there. John W. Lambert and his son A. R. Lambert were both involved. (Dan Roen Collection)

Chapter 5

J. I. Case Threshing Machine Company Vehicles

Everybody knows about Case tractors. But Case automobiles? (And racing cars?) Or Case trucks?

Case tractors

Like that of many farm machinery companies, the history of the J. I. Case Company is often the history–that is, the biography–of one person: in this case, Jerome Increase Case.

Case was born on Dec. 11, 1819, in Williamstown, New York, and by the time he reached maturity, had been exposed to "Great Ideas," because his mother's family had already produced one President of the United States, Andrew Jackson. But J. I. Case's great ideas were tempered in the hot sun near Lake Ontario as he labored with the Groundhog, the most efficient thresher of the day.

He heard that farm-family labor was no longer adequate to do farm work, so he invented his own thresher after moving to Wisconsin. He built several units in a rented shop in Racine, Wisconsin, and easily sold them. These "separators" were the first Case implements, and from there the business burgeoned.

Case adopted ideas from his competitors, bought out patents, worked hard, and went to steam. In 1863, his 20th year in business, he incorporated J. I. Case & Company, naming his brother-in-law Stephen Bull vice president.

Case portable steam engines won many awards during the Winnipeg contests in both belt and plowing competition. By 1926, it made steam engine number 35,737, far more than any competitor.

J. I. Case hoped to use stationary engines on his products, but he would not live to see that change; he died in 1891.

Case tractors

Stephen Bull succeeded Case. The next year the company's first gas engine was tested.

By 1911, the company had solved problems of fuel spark and mix, and introduced the Case 30-60 tractor. It made a two-cylinder 20-40, a 12-20, and all these tractors won gold medals at the Winnipeg trials for design, construction, performance, and economy.

Case made a three-wheeler 10-20 in 1916, followed by a 9-18; the highly successful 15-27 came on the scene in 1919; and in 1920, the largest Case appeared, a 22-40 hp with a crosswise-mounted four-cylinder engine.

Tractor designations climbed as engine speeds in-

J. I. Case Threshing Machine Company also manufactured steam traction engines, like this 1908 or 1909 25-hp machine pausing for a picture in North Dakota fields. Notice the wheeled water tank behind the steam traction engine for refilling the water supply to the machine. (Richard Birklid Collection)

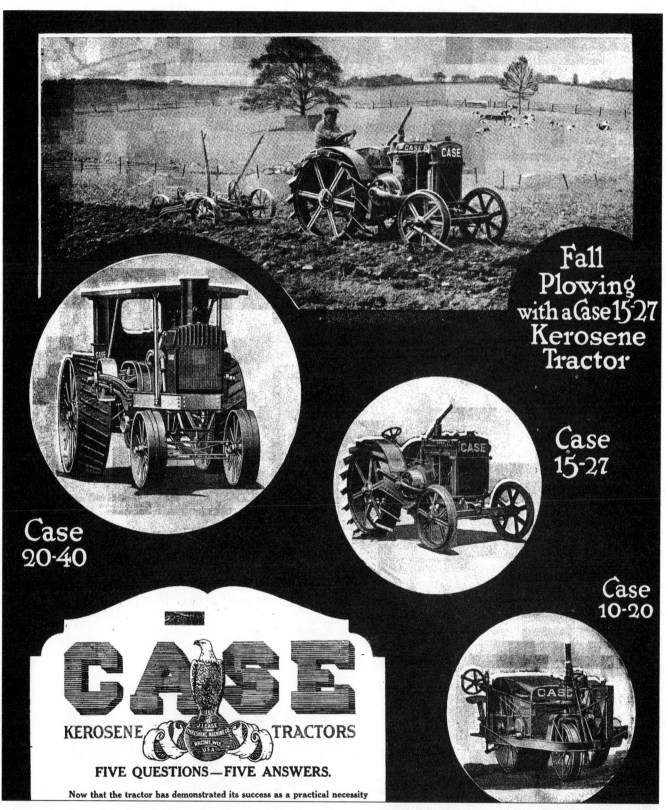

Fall
Plowing
with a Case 15·27
Kerosene
Tractor

Case
15-27

Case
20-40

Case
10-20

CASE
KEROSENE TRACTORS
FIVE QUESTIONS—FIVE ANSWERS.
Now that the tractor has demonstrated its success as a practical necessity

J. I. Case has been best known for its tractors, like these shown in this 1919 advertisement: a 20-40, 15-27, and 10-20. It took Case a few years to solve the fuel spark and mix problem, but it did so in 1916, and shortly thereafter won gold medals at the Winnipeg trials. It is also clear that even at this time, J.I. Case had "Old Abe" as its logo and mascot. (Dan Roen Collection)

After J. I. Case acquired the Wallis moniker, it manufactured this Wallis OKO 15 Orchard tractor at its J. I. Case Plow Works Inc. plant in Racine, Wisconsin. the Wallis OKO 15 used its own 4-1/4- x 5-3/4-inch bore and stroke valve-in-head four-cylinder engine to pull its 3,845 pounds around the orchards it was designed for. (Roy Bernick Collection)

creased and cylinder-head designs improved for better fuel and exhaust flow. The 15-27 grew to 18-32, and the 22-40 increased to 25-45.

As Case purchased other companies–Emerson-Brantingham, which produced tractors and implements; and Rock Island Plow Company; and rights to the Case name from Massey Harris, after Massey Harris purchased Case Plow Works–it continued to bring out new tractors. The CC came out in 1932, advertised as two tractors in one. Tractors were offered on rubber. In 1935, Case produced its motor lift, which allowed farmers to raise implements on the fly with the touch of a button.

The R series came out in 1936. The Model D was the most stunning achievement of the pre-war years, however, as gray paint was replaced with Flambeau Red. The seats were changed, steering wheels adjusted, and tractors were speeded up for road driving.

The V came out; a two-plow-rated S series followed; and the VA replaced the V in 1942, while the VAH, the first high-crop tractor at Case, was introduced in 1942.

In 1953, Case added diesel power and changed colors again. Then came the 400 Series, the 300s, and with the 500s, a combination of Flambeau Red with Desert Sand colors.

Improvements speeded apace: Powr-Torq engines (gas, LPG, distillates, or diesel-powered), 12-speed transmissions, three-point implement hookup, along with six-plow ratings. Case-O-Matic transmissions were introduced in the 700, 800, and 900 Series tractors in 1958.

Today, Case/IH still makes agricultural machines.

Case automobiles

Although Case tried to manufacture its own automobile as early as 1895–it was trying to perfect the Raymond engine, with its rotary valve design–it did not end up with a workable model until 1910, when it purchased a legitimate auto company with an established design, the Pierce-Racine Motor Company of Racine, Wisconsin.

In 1895, Andrew J. Pierce, who worked for the nephew of J. I. Case at the Belle City Hardware Company of Racine, entered the first automobile race ever held in the United States, in Chicago on Thanksgiving Day. Case wanted to enter, but couldn't due to Raymond engine troubles.

About 1908, J. I. Case Threshing Machine Co. financed a major expansion of the Pierce-Racine factory; that year, the factory built 300 cars for the rich, costing $2,500, each. The two largest Case stockholders also sat on the board of directors of the P-C Motor Company, which was variously renamed Pierce Engine Works, and then Pierce Motor Company. But the company owed so much money it could not be salvaged, so in 1910, Case took it over.

The Aug. 11, 1910, edition of *Motor Age* magazine read: IMPORTANT ANNOUNCEMENT, the ad said. "Regarding the Pierce-Racine Automobile. Arrangements have been completed whereby The Case Company have taken over the entire automobile output of the Pierce Motor Company, and the car will hereafter be known as the Case car."

The first Case cars came out in 1911, and were simply renamed Pierce autos. Four body styles of the Case car

Case started manufacturing the Case 12-20 in Racine, Wisconsin, in 1911, when it won a gold medal at the Winnipeg trials for design, construction, and performance. The 12-20 pulled two or three 14-inch plows, used its own 4-1/8- x 5-inch bore and stroke engine with four cylinders, and weighed 4,375 pounds. The 12-20 was just one of the many tractors, both large and small, that J. I. Case manufactured over the years. (Dan Roen Collection)

"Remember the engine when you buy, and you can forget it when you drive."

5 passenger touring car with forward door — $1850.00.

The **CASE** Car

Formerly the Pierce-Racine

The Car with the Famous Engine

Licensed under Selden Patent

FINISHING and furnishings, to which so many car makers call such particular attention, are in no sense the measure of any car. These are simply bought on the open market—can be had by any one willing to pay the price—and are often so over-emphasized simply to call attention away from more vital car characteristics.

The Case Car offers all the finishings and furnishings that can be had in any car and in addition a fundamental car value that few other makers can offer at any price.

The Case is the car with the famous Pierce Engine.

We can allot only 1500 of these desirable cars to dealers. So get in touch with us at once.

J. I. Case Threshing Machine Company

(Incorporated)

RACINE   **WISCONSIN**

U. S. A.

This 1910 *Motor Age* magazine advertisement for the Case car shows clearly that the company had just taken over the Pierce-Racine car business, and took the approach that only a certain number was available: "We can allot only 1,500 of these desirable cars to dealers." This five-passenger touring car model sold for $1,850, and the Selden Patent case had not yet been settled, as noted by the "Licensed under Selden Patent" line. Case also played on the "famous Pierce Engine" to get people to notice this ad. (Dan Roen Collection)

Before J. I. Case finally got its engines to work well enough so it could offer Case automobiles to the public, it worked on the Raymond engine, which was not successful for the company, and entered automobile races with vehicles like this Case shown in a 1904 race. (Gary Hoonsbeen Collection)

were offered: five-passenger touring car; four-passenger suburban and four-passenger torpedo, and two-passenger runabout. The torpedo cost $1,850, while the other three sold for $100 less. Options included a top, windshield, and headlamps for $100 more.

At first, only four-cylinder cars were manufactured, but a Continental six was offered in 1918 in three body styles: touring, sedan, and 'sport,' a close-coupled open four-seater. The engine was 29.4 hp, and increased two horsepower in the next five years. Beginning in 1924, a smaller six-cylinder engine was made. Case cars all carried the eagle emblem, modeled on "Old Abe," the famous mascot of the 8th Wisconsin Regiment beginning in the Civil War. Most Case vehicles were sold by agricultural dealers.

Case also entered into the professional car-racing business, building three cars for the 1911 Indianapolis 500. Three very experienced drivers were chosen: Lewis Strang, Louis Disbrow, and Joe Jagersberger. None of the cars finished; one was struck by another, a steering knuckle broke on a second, and the third suffered a seized piston.

In 1912, Case also raced, with its 290-hp Jay-Eye-See auto, based on a Fiat Red Devil, which was bored out until the cylinders were 9-1/4 inches, and the stroke 8-5/8 inches. That car and another Case didn't finish in 1912; in 1913's Indianapolis event, three were entered, and one finished, in eighth place.

Case cars were originally called the Model K "30" in 1910, the Model L in 1911, Model N in 1913, and in 1915, Model M. Case also built a Model O and a Model T. Case built a Model R "25" for two years beginning in 1915, and a "35" in 1916.

Model U Case cars were made from 1918-19; Model V from 1920-21; Model X from 1922-27; Model W from 1922-24; and Model Y from 1925-27, but a Model Z was

About 1911, J. I. Case Threshing Machine Company advertised its autos for sale in various magazines, four-cylinder machines until 1918. Notice the "Licensed under Selden Patent" line, as the Selden Patent imbroglio, where George Baldwin Selden—who had not built an internal combustion engine at the time—patented it, and his company asked that every automobile produced with an internal combustion engine pay royalties. In 1911, Selden lost the patent court battle. (Gary Hoonsbeen Collection)

never made, as production ceased at Case factories in the fall of 1926, with 1927 models.

Curiously, Case managed to make it through the great agricultural depression of the early 1920s with its cars without any problems, which showed the strength the company had already built up.

Case and the Carhart steam auto

Case actually had a minor connection with one of the first automobiles built in the United States, the Carhart

In 1915, J. I. Case Threshing Machine Company manufactured this Case Touring Car "35," as it was called. This blue-and-gray vehicle was capable of seating five people, had a rated horsepower of 28.9, four cylinders arranged vertically, and sold for $1,600. It used jump-spark ignition, had a multiple-disc clutch, and a wheelbase of 120 inches. The "35" was made in left-side drive, with a selective sliding gear in three forward and one reverse. (Gary Hoonsbeen Collection)

This Pierce-Racine Model D automobile was manufactured by Pierce Engine Company in 1907. Shortly after this automobile was manufactured, J. I. Case Threshing Machine Company sponsored a major expansion of the Pierce-Racine factory; all during this time the two major stockholders in J. I. Case also sat on the board of the Pierce-Racine company. Pierce-Racine modestly said that the Model D Pierce-Racine was the greatest value ever offered in an automobile. "Extreme simplicity." Perhaps that's why J. I. Case took the company over shortly thereafter. (Roy Bernick Collection)

steam auto, which was built and put together in the J. I. Case Threshing Machine Company plant. Perhaps Carhart's steam auto got the Case people interested in automobiles; certainly the Carhart auto got the automobile industry going in Wisconsin. After seeing the Carhart auto, Wisconsin Assemblyman George M. Marshall introduced an act into Wisconsin laws which was, "To encourage the invention and successful use of steam or other mechanical agents on the highways." It was approved in 1875 and laid the foundation for the world's first trackless, self-propelled land vehicle race.

The inventor of the car, Dr. J. W. Carhart, called it "The Spark." A newspaper report said of its forays down Racine, Wisconsin byways, "...when it went down the street, it shot smoke and cinders 15 feet in the air and with the boiler operating under 120 pounds of pressure, it made such a racket as to drive all the teams off the streets and cause the pedes-

trians to fear it might explode. For that reason, no whistle was required although one was provided. Wherever it went, there was no team traffic and the streets were cleared for its passage without the request of the driver..."

Carhart later wrote of the car, saying, "Pneumatic tires were then unknown, and such a thing as ball bearings had not been thought of; nor was oil used as a fuel to produce power. I used hard coal and had a boiler made by the Buttons Fire Engine Company of Waterford, New York. After my buggy was built, the State of Wisconsin offered a prize of $10,000 for the steam road wagon that would accomplish certain conditions."

In a 1914 letter Carhart wrote, "Since then I frequently have heard the cannonading of racing motors lined up for the start (of a race) but frankly, even Disbrow's Jay-Eye-See (a popular race car of the period) could not compare with it for genuine peace-disturbing qualities."

Perhaps it is merely a tenuous hold that Case has on the manufacture of one of the earliest United States automobiles was that it was set together at the J. I. Case Thresher Co. plant in Racine, Wisconsin, in 1872 by its inventor, Dr. J. W. Carhart, who called it "The Spark." A newspaper report of the time said of its forays down Racine, Wisconsin byways, "...when it went down the street, it shot smoke and cinders 15 feet in the air and with the boiler operating under 120 pounds of pressure, it made such a racket as to drive all the teams off the streets and cause the pedestrians to fear it might explode." (Gary Hoonsbeen Collection)

This 1911 advertisement for Pierce-Racine cars had to be one of the last before Case took over the Pierce Motor Company that same year, and began calling this same car the Case automobile. Case had wanted to get into automobiles for many years, but had had little success. The 1911 Pierce-Racine, "The car with a famous engine," as the ad claimed, sold for $1,750 in a four-cylinder, 30-hp model. It weighed 2,600 pounds. (Gary Hoonsbeen Collection)

J. I. Case Threshing Machine Company only made automobiles for about 15 years and this Case "Jay-Eye-See" Brougham built in 1926 was the second-last year of production. This car seated five in touring, brougham, or sedan models. It used a six-cylinder 3-3/8 x 4-1/2-inch bore and stroke engine of 27.34 hp, a 122-inch wheelbase, and sold for $2,500 for the model shown here (as well as the sedan), while the touring car was only $1,885, all in 1926. (Gary Hoonsbeen Collection)

Case trucks

Case entered the truck market after it bought an option in the Stephenson Motor Truck Company of Milwaukee in 1912. Newspapers said Case had bought the company; perhaps the Stephenson company was under the same impression because it disbanded its own dealer network shortly after the option was made, so when Case failed to pick up the option, the company could not market its trucks. It filed bankruptcy in October 1913. In fact, Stephenson also sued Case, but to no avail.

A few Case trucks were made during the 1912-13 period through Stephenson, but Case did not return to the truck business again until the early 1920s.

J. I. Case Motor Trucks Built For Farm Needs

BUILT specially for farm use, the Case Motor Truck combines simplicity, strength and durability. In designing it, J. I. Case Plow Works Company have studied the farmer's every requirement for an efficient farm truck and have selected features that make it unique and beyond competition for the purpose for which it is intended.

To be successful for farm use, a farm truck must possess qualities not found in the average commercial vehicle. These good points are present in full measure in Case farm trucks.

The Case Motor Truck, built by the J. I. Case Plow Works Company, is an important addition to the famous line founded by Jerome I. Case, and perpetuates those principles of honesty and integrity found in all the products of this Company.

J. I. CASE PLOW WORKS COMPANY, RACINE, WIS., U.S.A.

Case trucks were built by J. I. Case Threshing Machine Company in about 1910, but were terminated after a couple of years. The company returned to trucks in 1915. As this advertisement ca. 1915 says, "The Case Motor Truck...is an important addition to the famous line founded by Jerome I. Case, and perpetuates those principles of honesty and integrity found in all the products of this Company." (Gary Hoonsbeen Collection)

Chapter 6

Chase Cars, Trucks, and Tractors

Aurin Chase was an experienced executive when he decided to get into the vehicle-building business for himself. He had been working for the Syracuse (NY) Chilled Plow Company in 1907 as a vice-president when he broke away and formed the Chase Motor Truck Company of Syracuse, New York.

Chase tractors

The first Chase tractor was built in 1908 to take advantage of the road-building craze, and was a gas tractor-roller, which used a small air-cooled engine mounted forward from the operator. It possessed two roller drums side by side on the back, and a single one on the front, all with wood lagging that could be replaced.

In 1913, Chase substituted a three-cylinder two-cycle engine on the machine, which developed 30-brake hp. The wheelbase was eight feet, the drive wheel 30 inches in diameter, and the engine lubrication came from oil mixed with gasoline. The transmission was Brown and Lipe.

Early trucks were often called "Motor Wagons," as was this 1915 model manufactured by Chase Motor Truck Company of Syracuse, New York. Advertising said it could be "adapted to every line of business and to all kinds of roads and weather." It used an air-cooled two-cycle motor without valves, springs, pumps or oiling devices. "Does away with freezing water and lubrication troubles." It averaged 15 miles per gallon of gasoline. The effects of horses could still be felt at this time, as the ad advised, "of vital interest to every man who uses one or more horses for commercial purposes." (Roy Bernick Collection)

This Chase 12-25 tractor was manufactured in 1920 by the Chase Tractors Corporation Ltd., of Milwaukee, Wisconsin, and used "washed air," burned kerosene, and produced "equal power in both wheels," an advertisement for the three-wheeler said. This tractor was made after the original company in Syracuse had gone out of business, and followed another effort to make the Chase tractors in Canada. (Dan Roen Collection)

Chase built a 40-hp tractor in 1915, with the same three-wheeled design as previous models, but its engine was a larger Waukesha four-cylinder. It sold for $1,750.

Chase produced a conventional three-wheeled tractor a year later. This 8-16 (rated a 9-18 after 1918) used the Waukesha four-cylinder engine, Holley carburetor, and Kingston magneto. This Chase tractor might have been the first tractor that could turn in its own length by locking one rear wheel, which became standard on tractors in the next few years to assist in turning. After 1918, a Buda engine was used in this tractor.

Chase went out of business in Syracuse in about 1918, and reappeared in two places shortly thereafter, as Chase Tractors Corporation Ltd. of Toronto, as well as Milwaukee. The 9-18 model was changed, adding a larger Buda engine (4-1/2 x 5-1/2 inches), and boosting horsepower to 12-25.

This Chase 12-25 looked exactly alike in all photos of the tractors made in Syracuse, Toronto, and Milwaukee. They were three-wheelers with a four-cylinder bore-and-stroke engine of 4-1/4 x 5-1/2 inches, with a top rpm of 1,000. The transmission was a sliding gear that offered speeds between 1-3/4 and 2-1/2 mph forward, and 1-3/4 mph in reverse. It weighed 5,200 pounds and cost $1,725, which was evidently too much because after 1921, Chase was not heard of again.

Chase automobiles

The first Chase foray into auto-building was the manufacture of a larger-than-normal one, a $900 highwheeler

Chase Motor Truck Company built this five-passenger Model F Surrey in 1909. The founder of the company, Aurin Chase, had formerly been vice-president of the Syracuse, (NY) Chilled Plow Company belonging to his father. After he left to form his own business, Aurin Chase ended up manufacturing a car, truck, and tractor. (Gary Hoonsbeen Collection)

(large even for that type), probably because the company's main focus was larger vehicles–trucks.

Chase built a "Business Runabout" or Surrey (or Business-man's Runabout), which could be converted from a four-seater, high-wheeled car to a light truck. It was powered by an air-cooled two-stroke three-cylinder engine producing 20 hp with chain drive and solid rubber tires. Cars were built for the last time in 1912, although the company, building trucks and tractors, lasted for almost ten more years.

Chase trucks

The first Chase production was a combination passenger vehicle and light-duty truck, which could be converted to a truck with 700 pounds of carrying capacity and a 100-inch wheelbase. The first engines offered were two-cycle, in two- three-, and four-cylinder models. Continental engines were used in later trucks. Many early trucks used Chase's own three-cylinder 20-hp, 160-cubic-inch, two-

prices started at $750.

The 1912 Chase Model H had a top speed of 12 mph on a 34 x 2 front and 34 x 2-1/2 rear tires of solid rubber. The wheels were wagon-type wood spoke wheels. They had a wheelbase of 106 inches and sold for $1,250.

In 1908, Chase built a 3-ton forward-control truck with a 30-hp engine of the same design as the Chase 160 cubic inch for $3,500. Chase trucks had three-speed sliding gear transmissions, and a few had two-speed planetary units, like the runabouts.

In 1914, Chase switched to four-cylinder Continental engines, and offered 1-, 2-, and 3-ton trucks, adding 3/4- and 3-1/2-ton vehicles three years later, in 1917, the last year the company made trucks. These vehicles had four-speed sliding transmissions and worm drives. Chase trucks were even offered on the British market.

This Chase Motor Company Truck advertisement shows the Chase truck and Chase tractor together, along with the prices for them. The ad is looking for dealer representatives in North and South Dakota, Minnesota, and northwestern Wisconsin. (Gary Hoonsbeen Collection)

stroke air-cooled engines with Bosch ignition. Suspension was leaf springs front and rear. Runabout and light truck

Chapter 7

Corbitt Builds Tractors, Cars, and Trucks

Richard J. Corbitt moved to Henderson, North Carolina, to make his fortune buying and selling tobacco. Unfortunately for him and fortunately for the vehicle industry, big tobacco companies drove him (and other small buyers) out of the business, so he turned to making buggies and formed the Corbitt Company.

Corbitt tractors

Sometime in the late 1940s, the Corbitt Company started manufacturing tractors. It made three 50 series two-plow row crop tractor models, a G-50 (gasoline), K-50 (kerosene) and D-50 (diesel). All three used different engines: a LeRoi D176 3-3/4 x 4-inch four-cylinder in the G; a LeRoi D201 4 x 4 inches in the K; and a Hercules DIX-4D diesel engine with a 3-5/8- x 4-inch bore and stroke in the D. Other features included differential brakes, 1-3/8-inch PTO shaft, and an optional 3-point hydraulic lift. Weight was 3,543 pounds.

The G-50 was tested at Nebraska Aug. 29-Sept. 3, 1949, where under a rated drawbar load of 24.58 hp, it pulled 2,205 pounds at 4.18 mph. A low-gear maximum pull of 3,566 pounds was recorded at 2.65 mph. The machine used a Delco-Remy electrical system and a Zenith carburetor. No repairs or adjustments were made during the 43 hours of engine operating time.

Corbitt automobiles

Richard J. Corbitt was successful building wagons in his Corbitt Buggy Company. Perhaps remembering his experiences with giant tobacco monopolies, he bought into or organized the three other buggy companies in Henderson.

When the horseless carriage arrived, Corbitt decided to manufacture autos, while the other former buggy companies in town turned to hosiery, veneers, and furniture. He organized the Corbitt Automobile Company, and built his first Corbitt in 1907, a very plain highwheeler. Until 1909, he built these Corbitt two-seaters and sold them locally, adding fenders one year and acetylene lights the next.

He went national in 1910, advertising a two-cylinder 18- or 20-hp car with a 90-inch wheelbase. The Model A touring car was a four-passenger, the Model B runabout a two-passenger. The Model A sold for $1,750, and his later Model C five-seater touring car went for $1,800. The 1912-14 Corbitts had 120-inch wheelbases, and were four-cylinder vehicles of 26, 30, or 35 hp. He quit making cars in 1914 because his expanded line, the Corbitt truck, had become so successful.

Perhaps the Corbitt tractor, like this two-plow row crop tractor from the late 1940s, might have made the grade if Corbitt had not been so successful at making trucks. The G-50 model had a LeRoi D176 engine and 3-3/4- x 4-inch bore and stroke in its four-cylinder engine. Other models included the K50 (kerosene) and the D50 (diesel.)

Corbitt trucks

To expand his vehicle line, Corbitt built his first Corbitt truck in 1910. Its success was instantaneous.

His first production truck was a conventional 1-1/2-ton four-cylinder, chain-drive model. In 1916, Corbitt went international, and sold trucks in 23 countries.

The company was nicknamed "The south's largest truck builder," and by the 1920s, Corbitts ranged from 1- to 5-tonners, the smaller ones selling for $1,600. These Model E chassis had 130-inch wheelbases, and Continental N 225 horsepower motors with Stromberg carburetors. The Bimel wheels used 34 x 3-1/2 front and 34 x 4 rear solid rubber tires. The clutch and transmission were Brown-Lipe. An electric generator and starter cost extra.

The 2-ton Model C chassis with 148-inch wheelbase sold for $2,750, and used a 27.2-hp Continental K-4 engine. The 4-ton Model A with 178-inch wheelbase cost $3,800, and was powered by a Continental L-4 32.4 hp engine. The 5-ton Model AA (178-inch wheelbase) was powered by a Continental B7 40-hp motor, and sold for $4,750.

The 7-ton 70 sold for an even $5,000 in 1925. Its smallest and cheapest truck was the three-quarter-ton S Model that sold for $1,300.

Corbitt manufactured this 1-1/2-ton truck in 1926, and sold it for $1,875. Its gross weight was 8,300 pounds, and chassis weight was 4,100. It used a four-cylinder 4-1/4- x 4-1/2-inch bore and stroke 28.9-hp engine. The truck shown here was designated the "25"; others included the two-ton 40, and two-ton C; the 2-1/2-ton B; 2-1/2- to 3-ton R; the 3-1/2-ton A; the 5-ton AA; and the 25-passenger coach bus. Prices ranged from $2,750-$5,000. (Gary Hoonsbeen Collection)

By 1930, Corbitt trucks ranged up to 15 tons. Corbitt trucks served in both world wars, as specially built trucks for the U.S. Army. Some were the 2-1/2-ton 6 x 6 cargo carrier, 8-ton artillery prime movers, and Lycoming-powered armored scout cars.

In 1937, Corbitt listed seven six-cylinder models from 1-1/2-ton ($1,095) through 7-1/2-ton capacity (up to $6,160.) In 1938, sheet metal for the Corbitt 3-ton Model 18BT was stamped from obsolete Auburn dies, giving these trucks a look quite unlike other Corbitts.

Many Corbitt trucks used in World War II remained overseas and continued working in the countries they had served: Austria, Denmark, France, Greece, the Netherlands, and Sweden.

Government contracts ran out for Corbitt in 1950, which hastened the demise of the company; it closed in 1952 when Richard J. Corbitt retired.

In 1957, custom-built Corbitt trucks were manufactured, with "Henderson, N.C." under "Corbitt" to differentiate from earlier ones. The Corbitt plant closed permanently in 1958.

Corbitt buses

Corbitts were the first school buses ever used in North Carolina in 1915. The company also made urban transit buses.

The first Corbitt truck was built in 1910, and it proved to be an instantaneous hit, leading the company to veer off from making automobiles to deal with the success of the truck. This is a 1925 Corbitt 2-1/2-ton B truck, with a chassis weight of 5,235 pounds (11,675 including chassis, body, and load), that ran on a four-cylinder 4-1/8- x 5-1/4-inch 27.23 horsepower rating. The price included tools, jack, tool box, side oil lamps, tail oil lamps, front bumper, radiator guard, front fenders, horn, and driver's seat. It cost $3,000 in 1925. (Dan Roen Collection)

Chapter 8

Deere & Company Try to Build Cars and Trucks, too

Deere & Company of Moline, Illinois, built tractors, two types of cars, and trucks.

Probably the most successful agricultural enterprise ever, Deere got started in 1837 when John Deere built the first steel plow. Through the years, Deere added to its line by developing new machines and absorbing other companies. It eschewed the steam traction engine and thresher business, but by 1912, the company realized it needed to build farm tractors if it was to continue competing in the agricultural field. On March 5, 1912, the executive committee passed a resolution to put the company into the tractor business.

John Deere tractors

Deere experimented with a motor plow, the Dain tractor (100 were built and shipped), but without great success. Then on March 14, 1918, Deere leaped in by buying the Waterloo Gasoline Engine Company and its successful Waterloo Boy tractor.

The Model D John Deere was produced for nearly 30 years beginning in 1924; a two-cylinder tractor rated as a 15-27 GPs, the first tractors with power lifts, were rated 10-20, (later 15-24), and were built from 1928-35; and the Model A from 1934-52, incorporating two industry firsts–adjustable wheel tread, and a one-piece transmission case, with a beginning rating of 16-23, which increased up through 1949. The company built many other tractors, gasoline, diesel, orchard tractors, crawlers, and has been a dominant force in agriculture for many years.

The Blackhawk automobile

W. E. Clark of Moline built his first automobile in 1897, a single-cylinder air-cooled car with a fan mounted on the flywheel. He tinkered with the machine, and his Clark Manufacturing Company announced production of a single-cylinder 4-hp air-cooled runabout, and in 1903 it was ready for market. By this time, he had also developed a two-cylinder model as well. Both of these used the same chassis, with the engine mounted above the frame at the rear with the flywheel horizontal. The single-cylinder cost $750 and the double-cylinder phaeton $850, but was sold for less than a year, perhaps due to financing.

The Deere-Clarke and Deere automobiles

By 1906, W. E. Clark of Clark Manufacturing Company persuaded Deere & Company to bankroll his automobile. Deere bought the defunct Clarkmobile Company of Lansing and moved it to Moline. In 1906, The Deere-Clark Motor Company manufactured the water-cooled Deere-Clark automobile. It was a four-cylinder 30-hp machine with a 100-inch wheelbase. The side entrance touring five-passenger Deere-Clark sold for $2,850, and the limousine for $3,500. These were "cars designed to satisfy."

In 1907, the name was changed to Deere, and the wheelbase lengthened to 106 inches. Prices for the five-passenger, side-entrance touring vehicle dropped to $2,500, same as its new Gentleman's roadster.

In 1907, unsatisfied with the automobile part of its business, the company terminated it. Its dissatisfaction may have been practical, since the next year, 1908, William Lamb Velie, son of Emma Deere and grandson of John Deere, began building his Velie automobiles, selling them through Deere catalogs and dealerships.

Over the years, Deere & Company of Moline, Illinois, has manufactured hundreds of different John Deere tractors, and for the most part, very successfully. This John Deere standard tread model BR (variant BO was for "Grove, Orchard, and Vineyard") was recommended for one 16-inch or two 10-inch plows. It used a John Deere 4-1/4- x 5-1/4-inch bore and stroke two-cylinder engine, a Fairbanks-Morse ignition system, K-W lighting equipment, and weighed a scant 2,889 pounds. (Dan Roen Collection)

In 1929, Deere & Co. built this odd-looking (at least from the top) Model GP 10-20 tractor, capable of pulling two plows or a three-row cultivator. Its Nebraska Tractor Test capabilities showed 24.97 hp at the belt, and 17.24-hp maximum at the drawbar, pulling 2,489 pounds. It used its own two-cylinder engine of 5-3/4- x 6-inch bore and stroke–950 rpm, and came with a goodly number of accessories. It had three speeds forward–2-1/3, 3-1/8, and 4-1/3 mph, and two reverse. Net weight of the tractor was 3,764 pounds, and the Nebraska Tractor Test, with operator, was 4,265 pounds. (Dan Roen Collection)

W.E. Clark, who built the Deere automobiles just a few years later, began with this Blackhawk runabout in 1903. Just three years later, he convinced Deere & Company to bankroll his Clark Manufacturing Company, whose name was then changed to Deere-Clark Motor Company. The Blackhawk lasted but a year. (Gary Hoonsbeen Collection)

This 1907 Deere touring car was the last year the agricultural Deere & Co. made automobiles, since it had been successful in agricultural enterprises for many years, and had little patience for perfecting cars or trucks. This was a four-cylinder 30-hp machine that sold for $2,500. A Deere Gentleman's Roadster of the same year sold for $2,500 as well, while the 1907 Deere Limousine sold for a grand more. (Gary Hoonsbeen Collection)

Farm Implements magazine said, "The assets of the Deere-Clark Motor Car Company have been purchased by C. H. Pope, S. H. Montgomery and other Moline parties, at a price from 35 to 40 cents on the dollar. The property included in the purchase is the plant, consisting of real estate and buildings; personal property, including a considerable amount of parts of automobiles in various states of manufacture; and the accounts receivable. It is the probable intention of the purchasers to continue the manufacture of the Deere automobile. Mr. Pope has been connected with Deere & Co. for many years, and Mr. Montgomery is the head of the Moline Elevator Company."

The Midland automobile

However, the new owners had particular ideas about the auto they would produce. They renamed the company Midland Motor Company, and manufactured Midland cars, "unusual cars at unusual prices," the next couple of years. The cars were 25-, 30-, 35-, 40-and 50-hp and all sold between $1,800 to $2,250, with a few exceptions, like the 1912 Model O six-cylinder, which cost $3,000.

When Pope retired in 1911, Deere took over once again; 200 cars were built in 1912 and 1913. Midland Motor Car Company became the largest bankruptcy case handled in the area courts up to that time. Criminal charges might have been filed for the disappearance of 50 cars,

The car company that succeeded Deere-Clark was the Midland Motor Car Company in 1908. This is a Midland G-9 Roadster made in 1908. (Gary Hoonsbeen Collection)

Deere trucks were only built for two years, 1906 and 1907. This 1907 2-1/2-ton model had a 20-hp engine, three-speed forward gear, and was no longer made after 1907 because Deere & Co. didn't like the vehicle, and withdrew funding. (Dan Roen Collection)

payroll discrepancies, the disappearance of company books, records, and papers, except that Pope was dead. The assets were sold, and the Midland car existed no more.

Deere trucks

At the time Deere decided to pull out its support for the Deere-Clark and Deere automobiles in 1907, the Deere truck appeared, a 20-hp truck with a horizontally opposed engine and three-speed progressive sliding gear transmission and dual chain final drive. The channel steel used for the frame could be changed to suit the length of vehicle wanted by the customer. None were made after 1907.

Chapter 9

Eagle Makes Tractors and Car

Though Eagle Manufacturing Company of Appleton, Wisconsin is best known for tractors, it manufactured car accessories and a prototype car.

Eagle tractors

Eagle tractors were manufactured beginning in 1906 with a 32-hp two-cylinder opposed engine. A German-born creative genius, Richard Miller, began working for the Appleton Manufacturing Company.

He patented a swivel hay carrier, an adjustable land roller, and much more. In 1881, Miller quit and hooked up with John Kanouse and William Polifka to form the Eagle Fork Company, manufacturing a complete line of hay tools–carriers, forks, and so on.

Edward Saiberlich, Miller's cousin, bought Kanouse's interest in the 1880s. A new company was formed in 1888–Eagle Manufacturing Company–and within six years, the Saiberlich brothers, Edward, Frank, and Oscar, owned and operated the entire company. Miller went into business by himself, founding the Appleton Hay Tool Company.

Eagle business doubled yearly, slowed only by a $3,000 fire in 1897. In 1899, Eagle entered the gasoline engine field. By 1911, it was one of the largest business concerns in northern Wisconsin.

The next business step seemed logical, and Eagle entered the tractor business in 1906. Its first, a 32-hp machine, used the only known opposed engine configuration by an Eagle engine. It was not very successful, and little was done with Eagle tractors for the next few years.

In 1910, Eagle offered three different tractors: a 16-30, 25-45, and a 40-60 weighing nearly 10 tons.

In 1911, the Eagle 56-hp model came out. Eagle also designed two new tractors in 1913, the 8-16 and 12-22, small ones designed to meet farmers' clamor for smaller tractors. (The Little Bull tractor was becoming the fastest-selling tractor ever.)

But innovation and change in the tractor designing and building field required big money, and the Saiberlich brothers didn't have it. But they pushed ahead.

New shares of capital stock were offered, and Charles Hagen joined the company, urging more expansion. *Farm Implement and Tractors* wrote, "The Eagle Manufacturing Company...has recently been re-organized, and the capital stock increased from $200,000 to $500,000." In 1917, capital stock was increased to 5,000 shares, a new machine shop was built, and the company was refocused to make its objectives clearer.

Eagle made, in order, series D, F, and H tractors, then series E, and then series A, B, and C. Nobody knows why this "backward" letter configuration was chosen.

With new blood in the company and different people wanting to go different directions, someone had to lose: the Saberlich brothers were tossed out. They went off to build another company that manufactured Fox tractors, which resembled Eagle tractors.

By about 1920, farmers got suspicious of some Eagle advertising. Some suspicion was generated by outright lies in other tractor company advertising ("Pan Tank-Tread Tractor Will Win the War") or ("We know no way to make our tractors better," as Little Giant claimed), along with specific, but erroneous, claims about number of plows different tractors might pull, or what kind of work might be done considering the claimed horsepower. "Many tractors

Eagle Manufacturing Company of Appleton, Wisconsin, manufactured this Eagle 6A in 1936, a time when the company was running into dire financial straits during the Great Depression. This Eagle was recommended to pull three or four 14-inch plows, weighed 5,000 pounds, used a Waukesha 4- x 4-3/4 L-head engine, and had a selective sliding gear of 2-/2 to 4-/2 mph forward and 2-1/2 mph in reverse. Rubber tires were optional on this tractor.

The Eagle Model F 16-30 from 1920 weighed 7,100 pounds and sold for $1,750 after its manufacture by Eagle Manufacturing Company of Appleton, Wisconsin. It used as a final drive a spur gear to both rear wheels, and was powered by its own 8- x 8-inch bore and stroke two-cylinder engine. (Dan Roen Collection)

were over-rated," tractor historian Chuck Wendel writes. "After digging up a large amount of money for a three-plow tractor, it was quite a surprise to find out the machine would handle but two plows. Fuel, oil, and water consumption were other factors that experience alone would reveal. Again, this could deal a heavy financial blow to the farmer if the tractor had been misrepresented."

Eagle made claims that couldn't be substantiated, but were probably mostly harmless: "The Eagle tractor has made such an enviable reputation wherever sold that one of our distributors has aptly termed it, 'The tractor with the troubles left out,'" for example. Eagle also claimed its tractors ran as well on kerosene as on gasoline.

When the Eagle was tested at Nebraska in August and September 1921, Nebraska Test #80 used 16-30, serial #1037; while 12-22, serial #1023, went through test #81. Both units burned kerosene and met their rated power, 20-32 for the 16-30, and 14-1/2-23 for the 12-22.

In the concluding remarks, the testers were concerned that certain Eagle Company claims in its advertising literature were not necessarily borne out in the tests. These included the effectiveness of the air breather, quality of engine governing and claims that the engine burned kerosene as perfectly as gasoline. All in all, they came through the tests reasonably well.

With the H series of tractors already made, Eagle Manufacturing next created the E Series of tractors in 1928, its last two-cylinder tractor, a 20-35. About 100 of the Model E tractors were made.

In the early 1920s, a six-cylinder tractor was developed of the road and cultivator type. Eagle was known as a steady-running tractor, most suitable for threshing work and sawmilling because the pulley was in the operator's sight line. The engine was a sure starter, had that long stroke staying power, good governor control under changing loads, and long life with few repairs.

Two more six-cylinder tractors followed, the 6B in 1936, and two years later, the 6C, one of the most practical designs produced by the company.

In the 1930s, the Great Depression and poor tractor sales began to takes it toll on Eagle; stockholders had not been paid dividends for several years, and it became clear that Eagle could no longer continue. In 1940, the Eagle Company was sold to the Four Wheel Drive Auto Co. of Clintonville, Wisconsin, with shareholders receiving 10 cents to a dollar. The manufacture of tractors was discontinued.

Eagle automobile

Eagle began by making automobile accessories, and in 1910 decided to manufacture cars. It reorganized, increased capital stock, and changed the name to Eagle Automobile Manufacturing Company. Two autos were proposed: a four-cylinder 30-hp car for $2,000, and a 40-hp four-cylinder car at $3,000. A prototype was built, but because the company did not sell enough capital stock, the plan to build an automobile was abandoned.

Z & B, Badger and FWD automobiles

The Four Wheel Drive Auto Company of nearby Clintonville bought out Eagle in 1941. The owners were machinists

The company which eventually bought out Eagle Manufacturing Company of Appleton, Wisconsin, the Four Wheel Drive Automobile Company, or simply FWD, made this 1912 FWD touring automobile, a four-cylinder, 45-hp machine with 128-inch wheelbase. It sold for a surprisingly high price: $4,500. FWD automobiles were only made from 1910-1912. (Gary Hoonsbeen Collection)

who had built an early car called Z & B (Otto Zachow and his brother-in-law, William Besserdich), in 1908, then followed with the FWD Badger, a four-cylinder 55- or 60-hp machine in 1910, and FWD automobiles in 1911 and 1912.

About 1908, the two men designed and patented a double-Y universal joint in a ball-and-socket, which allowed the front wheels of a vehicle to be powered and steered at the same time.

A second automobile, called "The Battleship," weighed 4,500 pounds and had a new engine, a 45-hp gasoline motor. Both were test automobiles and not marketed.

In 1909, with financial backing, the Badger Four Wheel Drive Automobile Company was organized to make autos using the Z & B patents.

The first successful car was the Badger; they were built only in 1910 (Badgers), and 1911-12 (FWD autos.)

FWD trucks

One FWD automobile was converted into a scout truck and tested under difficult situations by the United States Army, and fared so well, that Z & B built a factory in Clintonville in 1913 and began building FWD trucks.

With the outbreak of World War I, the U.S. Government ordered so many FWD trucks that other major truck manufacturers ended up making FWD trucks too.

The Model B was the best-known FWD truck, powered by a four-cylinder Wisconsin engine with a three-speed transmission. It weighed 6,400 pounds and hit 16 mph as its top speed.

So many FWD trucks were returned to state highway departments after the war, that FWD didn't suffer the fate of other companies, which could not sell their vehicles because of the glut on the market, and went under. Instead, since 15,000 FWD trucks had been allocated to state highway departments, spare parts were needed. That kept FWD above water until the demand for trucks grew again.

"By late 1941," Richard Mannen writes in *A History of the Eagle Manufacturing Company*, "with America's entry into the World War imminent, the (FWD) Company...began to plan for plant expansion since it produced an extensive line of military items. Soon after the attack on Pearl Harbor, FWD tendered its entire output to the war effort and initiated a $500,000 upgrading at the Clintonville factory."

FWD then transferred all of its domestic truck and spare parts production and some military work to Appleton. It continued an inventory of parts for Eagle products.

Chapter 10

Fageols Build Expensive Machines, Plus First Iowa Car

The Fageol brothers built expensive machinery: their tractors, cars, trucks, and buses all cost more than other vehicles of the day.

Frank R. Fageol was born near Ankeny, Iowa, in 1882. By the time Frank and his brother, William, were in their teens, 17 and 19 respectively, they built the claimed-as-first automobile in Iowa in 1900, a steam-driven eight-passenger vehicle.

For a fee, they motored passengers ten miles to and from Ankeny, Iowa, to the state fair near Des Moines.

They became automobile dealers until Frank headed to San Francisco in 1904. Eventually William Fageol followed, and he and Frank became the Rambler automobile distributor, operating out of a tent–probably because of the San Francisco earthquake–but in 1906 or 1907 moved into a frame building.

Other Fageol family members followed, and by 1912, all the Fageols listed in directories were associated with Fageol Motor Sales Co., which distributed Garford trucks and Rambler cars; Fageol Motors Co. was formed in 1915.

The 'Fadgl' train

J. H. Fort writes in *The Fageol Success*, "When the Panama-Pacific Exposition was being planned, the problem of transportation within the grounds confronted the directors. Many proposals were submitted and considered, but none seemed as practical as that of R. B. Fageol and F. R. Fageol.

"The Fageols proposed to build a small tractor, using the motor of a popular automobile, to draw the passenger trailers. The idea amused and appealed to the directors; the Fageols were awarded their transportation concession."

These trains actually were the first Fageol (or as the project bankroller, financier Edward P. Brinegar required the brothers to call themselves, "Fadgl," printed plainly in large letters on the vehicles) tractors. The company was called Fadgl Auto Train, Inc.

The tractors used Ford auto motors, pulling open-sided trailers around the Expo at Golden State Park. Each trailer held 20 passengers, and was built in Frank Fageol's auto agency.

The tractors used to pull passengers during the Exposition looked more like a small car, with four small wheels, barrel-shaped hoods and large mesh-filled front bumpers. The wheels of the trailers were shrouded so passengers wouldn't catch clothes or feet in the spokes as they sat in the small cars with their legs dangling off the edges. If they stretched, they could touch the ground with their feet. A sightseeing trip cost 10 cents, and the project was a huge success.

With that success, the Fageol brothers decided in 1917 that they would build their own factory for passenger cars, trucks and tractors. When ground was broken on June 10, 1917, 2,000 were there. One writer said the company would build military tractors, but that proposal was probably never fulfilled, because the war ended a year after groundbreaking.

Fageol tractors

Fageol also built an odd-looking orchard tractor, the purpose of which was to tow wagons.

Unlike either the caterpillar or broad-wheel-type of tractor, or the convertible automobile tractors in common use, this tractor used long, blade-like teeth on the wheels.

This was Fageol's beginning venture into manufacturing vehicles (not counting its Iowa car), the "Fadl" sightseeing train for the Panama-Pacific Exposition at Golden Gate Park in San Francisco in 1915. Notice how low the vehicles were, and how many people fit on each trailer.

Fageol also made other products besides the basics of tractors, trucks, and buses, like this 1918 Fageol gas-electric ore train.

Fageols claimed the blades enabled it to walk over all kinds of ground, and go almost any place the farmer or orchardist wanted it to go.

The first Fageol was a two-wheel power plant with a ride-on dead axle at the rear steered by gearing around a quadrant at the back of its frame. It cost $1,085. It had a pressed steel frame, four-cylinder engine and drive to the wheels by internal gearing, all of which ran immersed in oil.

Despite weighing only 1,730 pounds, it exerted a considerable drawbar pull.

Butler-Veitch Company contracted for all of the Fageol orchard tractors and Fageol became a sales agent for Butler-Veitch in Oakland in 1918.

In 1918, Fageol made a true four-wheeled tractor, rated an 8-12 or 9-12 with the trademark "spudded" drive wheels. In the drum of each driver was an internal expanding clutch which coupled the solid live axle to the drive wheel, and no differential on the axle.

It had a Lycoming four-cylinder bore-and-stroke engine 3-1/2 x 5 inches and only one forward gear. Steering was by tiller, and an enormous replaceable filter air cleaner took care of the California dust. The carburetor was by Tillotson, and magneto ignition by Dixie. The whole transmission was generously provided with ball and roller bearings. Total weight was 3,600 pounds (more than double the orchard tractor) and the price was correspondingly high, ($1,525 in 1922) which resulted in few sales. The vents on the hoods of the Fageol tractors were very distinctive, like other Fageol vehicles of the time.

Delivery of tractors for farm and vineyard purposes began in 1918, but ceased five years later, probably due to a combination of the agricultural recession, the high cost, and the need of the company to turn to other, more secure government contracts for making trucks.

This photo, ca. 1917, in *Farm Implements and Tractors* was accompanied by a story which said, "The tractor manufacturer who seeks permanent market on the Pacific coast should guard against extravagant advertising claims. Often it has been found that a tractor advertised to pull three plows has been unable to pull more than two under the conditions peculiar to this territory. The dealer should remember that the test upon which such ratings are based were made in other sections of the country where the draft per (plow) bottom does not run so high." This photo shows a Fageol tractor working in a California orchard. (Dan Roen Collection)

Fageol automobiles

The company's first undertaking–and the reason the new factory was built–was the design and fabrication of the Fageol automobile, which it wanted to be the finest passenger car ever offered to the motoring public. The first Fageol was exhibited at the Foreign Car Salon in Chicago in January 1917. The phenomenal interest, and international publicity it elicited, promised brilliant prospects of success. These were enhanced by its introductions to New York and San Francisco.

Pacific Service Magazine said in its June 1917 edition, "The company builds the Fageol Car equipped with the famous Hall-Scott 125-hp military hydro-aeroplane engines. This car can be started from dead stop, reach a speed of twenty-five miles and stopped all within forty feet. It is elegantly equipped and sells for $12,000. The Chevrolet factory, near by, sent a floral tribute with the words, 'From the lowest to the highest price car.' "

The cars used 135- to 145-inch wheelbases along with a 125-hp, six-cylinder engine. Fageol patented a hood design of rear-facing fin louvers atop the hood to help with cooling, although the louvers were mostly for looks.

Unfortunately, America's entry into World War I stopped the production of Fageol autos because of their

In 1920, Fageol manufactured this 9-12 Fageol tractor, one of a series of its tractors which had the most unusual wheels ever made, with blades or teeth all around the rim. The Fageol brothers claimed this allowed the tractor to walk or go where other tractors could not. California saw a few different tires on tractors in an attempt to deal with boggy conditions in farmland areas. The 9-12 used a Lycoming four-cylinder vertical L-head engine with 3-1/2-inch x 4-inch bore and stroke to pull a recommended two 14-inch or two 12-inch plows. The 9-12 weighed 3,500 and sold for $1,525. (Dan Roen Collection)

This 8-12 Fageol tractor from 1920 used a Lycoming 4-cylinder engine of 3-1/2- x 5-inch bore and stroke, at 1,250 rpm. It weighed 3,500 pounds and cost $1,525, identical to the 9-12. It had only one speed forward and reverse, 2-1/3 to 3 mph, and used a Dixie H.T. magneto with 1/2-inch spark plugs. (Dan Roen Collection)

Fageol Motors Company of Oakland evidently loved sharp designs on its vehicles; the tractor wheels had knife-like edges, and its 1917 Fageol touring car, shown here, has louvers on the hood that give a teeth-like appearance viewed from the side. This was the only year Fageol made automobiles, unless you count its first experimental car about the turn of the century. (Gary Hoonsbeen Collection)

cost; additionally, the two men instrumental in designing the autos were called up by the military to design vehicles: E. J. Hall, a noted engine designer, and Col. J. G. Wallace, formerly Packard's chief mechanical engineer. They designed the Liberty airplane engine in the service.

Only three Fageol autos were built, probably because they cost an astounding $12,000 each. The third was made after the war in 1921.

Fageol trucks

After World War I, Fageol Motors Co. began building trucks, using four-cylinder engines. They were 2-, 3-, 3-1/2-, and 5-ton models, with the same specifications for all of them: Wheelbase, standard 12 feet; engine, Waukesha 4-1/4 x 5-3/4, four-cylinder; transmission, three-speed constant mesh type; wheels, artillery type; rear axle, Timken worm gear; and tires, front 34 x 4 inches and rear 36 x 7 inches. The first truck built was cause for a 300-auto parade through Oakland.

Fageol trucks were successful for several reasons: first, the development of the compound transmission by William Fageol which suited the higher speeds of trucks due to pneumatic tires (they called it a seven-speed transmission–five forward, compared to the usual four–and two reverse.) The high reduction ratio (7.65 to 1) in low gear provided easier starting under load and fewer gear changes at speed.

Second, the Fageol truck introduced the multiple-speed transmission, the air cleaner, the reservoir oiling system, and many other features which became standard on all American trucks.

Third, it catered to the unique needs of West Coast truckers. "From the outset," says J. H. Fort in *Oakland Outlook*, "the company recognized its position of advantage over Eastern producers because of its Western location. Its birthright was a knowledge of Western conditions, the extremes and adverse trials that trucks in industrial service must undergo: long hauls, consistent over-load, steep grades, and difficult ground. All these emphasized the demand for a truck that was not a mere automobile with an attached commercial body."

Fageol's prospective customers thought in terms of tonnage, not pounds. The objective was to build a truck that could cope with the rugged Western conditions, that could travel from below sea level to mile-high altitudes under tremendous loads in a single day's run, and do it faithfully while meeting the abuse of the desert sands and virgin timber countries equally. When Fageol conquered the dicey problems associated with those terrains, it earned the reputation for being rugged and reliable trucks.

In the early 1920s, Fageol trucks were made of 1-1/2-ton to 5-ton capacity, for $3,000 to $5,700, considerably more than most trucks of that time. But their high quality

In the early days of trucking, all kinds of tests and contests were held to see which vehicles would hold up the best. This Fageol truck set a speed record on an 878-mile run between San Francisco and Los Angeles and back, doing the trip in 32 hours, 40-1/2 minutes, and averaging 26.8 mph with this 3-1/2-ton truck.

Fageol began building its truck bodies of aluminum and said in its literature, "The reduction of weight in trucks does not need to be confined to bodies alone. Just as much, and sometimes more, dead weight can be removed from truck chassis by using light, strong aluminum alloys for both sprung and unsprung parts." This chassis had a load capacity of 10 tons and possessed the same factor of safety as steel chassis, while reducing the weight 2,895 pounds.

and durability proved worthwhile, and the trucks sold.

In 1925, Fageol built 2-, 3-, 4-, and 6-ton trucks, models 234, 340, 445, and 645, for $3,300, $4,000, $5,100, and $5,800, respectively. Waukesha engines from 25.6 to 32.4 hp moved the trucks, using Fageol transmissions, Timken axles, and Ross steering.

Four years later, Fageol made a 10-ton, six-wheel truck with an optional six-cylinder Hall-Scott engine.

Fageol buses

The Fageol Motors Co. began building buses in the early 1920s because a careful survey of the transportation field showed a demand for a flexible, versatile vehicle to operate on city streets and inter-urban highways.

Buses at the time were converted trucks, required to choose between a truck chassis with a resultant ungainly body, or a touring car that had been lengthened and changed to accommodate more passengers than it was intended for. A typical reworking of these vehicles often used second-hand vehicles, the frame of a heavy automobile or a 3/4-ton truck (most often a White), which was lengthened by six feet, allowing 14 passengers. Cars made for 11 passengers were often lengthened to hold more. Also, a new driveshaft was needed, a heavier read end and

Fageol built this 1918 truck with a 7-speed transmission, delineated by the number "7" on the front of the radiator.

axle, and oftentimes dual rear wheels.

But there were more dangerous problems: the brakes often failed because of the added weight and size, the center of gravity was too high and the front track was too narrow. Reports of overturned buses of these types on the narrow unpaved roads were common, yet hundreds of them were in use in California.

So Fageol set about designing a vehicle expressly made for the peculiar needs of this field, discarding all the traditional thinking in the process. It thoughtfully designed a vehicle suited to this new function–fast, safe, and comfortable, for economical mass transportation.

In 1921, the company built its first Safety Coach, a low wide-track design that allowed for comfortable 22-passenger seating and ease of entry and exit. Closed cars had become the rage, so the Fageol bus was fully enclosed with sturdy posts between the individual doors and with glass all around. Inside, too, it was much like an auto, with full-width seats and not much headroom. There were two seats alongside the driver, and luggage was still tied onto the back.

The biggest changes were in chassis design. The floor height, at first 20, then 22 inches, was about a foot lower than the autos and Whites and half a foot lower than in specialized bus chassis just then coming onto the market. The bus business was so brisk the Fageols opened a sales agency in Cleveland in 1924, and a factory was bought in Kent, Ohio, strictly to make buses.

This closeup of Fageol's aluminum truck chassis shows the aluminum frame construction that reduced the standard chassis weight from 12,375 pounds to 9,480 pounds. One Western truck driver said he had a Fageol with an Alcoa Aluminum gasoline tank and completely aluminized tank trailer, which saved him $100 in operating costs per month.

This Fageol Safety Coach is representative of the types of buses that the company made. This was widely sold throughout the Midwest, and was a 29-passenger parlor type with a six-cylinder Hall-Scott engine.

They also made specialized buses, like streetcars (Chicago, North Shore and Milwaukee 1 and 2 are believed to be the earliest streetcar-type Fageols, placed in service in July 1922), and inter-city stages. The San Diego-Tijuana, Mexico Stage Line of Fageols was familiarly known as the "alcohol special" in those prohibition days.

The biggest improvement in these motor stages compared to others on the market involved the chassis design. The final drive was a worm gear beneath the differential gear, which allowed the floor to be lower (making the center of gravity lower, and the vehicle more stable.)

Fageol also made tour buses. The company continued to improve its products, with steel brakes, air brakes, six-cylinder engines, and others, many of them industry firsts that quickly became standards. In 1926, no Fageols were involved with Fageol Motors Co. any longer; Louis H. Bill was calling the shots.

In 1929, Fageol Motors Co. was forced to file bankruptcy; and in 1932, the company went into receivership as the Great Depression deepened.

Waukesha Motor Company and the Central Bank of Oak-

This advertisement discusses the length of service and success of the Fageol Truck & Coach Company in 1933.

land assumed control of the operation. Despite the financial difficulties, new models were introduced for the next six years, and production was continued. But when Sterling Motors acquired the assets in November 1938, it was announced that production would cease at the end of the year.

T. A. Peterman, a lumber magnate from Tacoma, Washington, came to the rescue, and purchased Fageol in April 1939 to build a chain-driven logging truck. Two units were built, but neither proved successful.

However, regular trucks continued and sold well, and were soon renamed Peterbilt, still built today.

The Fageol plant was located on Hollywood Boulevard in Oakland, as shown in this mid-1920s photo. By this time, some 1,800 buses had been built in this plant.

Chapter 11

Fairbanks Morse Makes Tractors, Trucks, and Cars

Fairbanks, Morse & Company of Chicago, Illinois began with a manufacturing business in St. Johnsbury, Vermont, in the 1820s. Erastus and Thaddeus Fairbanks invented the platform scale in 1830, which helped them prosper and go international. Charles H. Morse apprenticed with the company in 1850, and was soon a moving force.

He established Fairbanks, Morse & Company offices in different U.S. cities. In 1893, Morse induced James A. Charter to work on gas engines for the company.

Fairbanks-Morse built a railway inspection car in 1905, a single automobile by the name of Charter prior to 1908, and a single touring car in 1908. This was also the year the company decided to experiment with truck production.

Fairbanks-Morse tractors

Fairbanks-Morse was best known for its line of tractors, which it experimented on for years until it produced a F-B 25-hp gas tractor in 1910.

In 1911, it produced a 15-25, with an engine similar to the 25-hp, a single-cylinder, low-tension ignition, volume-governed machine. Starting required an air pump to build cylinder pressure until at the moment the giant flywheel began to turn, the operator activated a match-starting device that flared a kitchen match outside the cylinder. This tractor was rated 15-30 a year later.

In 1912, Fairbanks-Morse lugged out its 30-60 model, a two-cylinder engine of 10-1/2-inch bore and 12-inch stroke. It weighed 28,000 pounds, had a 5-inch thick

crankshaft, and 78-inch drivewheels. It carried 200 gallons of water and 80 gallons of fuel.

Other Fairbanks-Morse tractors included an improved 15-25, a 10-20, 12-25, and others. The Fair-Mor 10-20 was built in 1920 when Fairbanks-Morse had turned mainly to building gasoline engines, and continued into the 1920s. This 10-20 was probably a stripped-down Reliable tractor from Reliable Tractor & Engine Company of Portsmouth, Ohio.

Fairbanks-Morse was much more aggressive in the Canadian market than the American. The 15-25 and 30-60 models were built in both countries, and a 20-40 was built in Canada from 1912-1914.

The Charter automobile

In 1903, Charter completed his highly unusual automobile which used gasoline and water mixture for fuel. Gasoline vapor and atomized water entered the cylinder at the same time, and heat from the explosion formed superheated steam, which moved the piston.

The car was a four-cylinder, producing 50-hp, and sported a rear-entrance tonneau body. Everything was conventional except the gas/water fuel mixture, which might have prevented it from catching on. At least one prototype was built.

In 1920, Fairbanks-Morse made this Fair-Mor 10-20 tractor recommended for a pair of 14-inch plows. It used a 6- x 7-inch bore-and-stroke motor with two cylinders, and a force feed lubrication system. (State Historical Society of North Dakota)

Fairbanks-Morse & Co. advertised its 25-hp F-M Gasoline Tractor in a Gas Engine Review advertisement in 1910, the first year it produced the vehicle after years of experimenting with them. F-M had been making gasoline engines for many years, and as this advertisement proclaims, "Other engines from 1 HP to 500 HP." The bottom of the ad also says the company made Fairbanks scales, electric light plants, windmills, pumps, and saw rigs. (Dan Roen Collection)

This Fairbanks-Morse ad shows a 15- to 25-hp tractor. Fairbanks, Morse & Co. also made other tractors, including a 30-60 hp. In trying to convince the farmer to buy this tractor, the ad says, "We had learned how to build engines before we tackled the tractor problem. Our task has been merely to apply an engine already known and widely used, to the conditions to be met in tractor practice."

Fairbanks-Morse automobile

Model 1, Number 1, was the only Fairbanks-Morse automobile ever built, a touring car powered by a four-cylinder engine in 1908. The chassis had a 108-inch wheelbase, and double-chain drive, and sold for a whopping $3,850. The idea for this car might have been scrapped because the company realized it would do better in the commercial car or truck field.

by a Sheffield engine and constant-mesh four-speed transmission with double-chain drive. The 25-hp engine was limited by a governor which prevented speeds more than 10 mph. These trucks and delivery wagons were only built in 1908, when F-M decided to stick to production of its tractors.

James A. Charter built this water-gasoline motor car in 1903 while he worked for the Fairbanks-Morse Company. The water was atomized into the combustion chamber, and the gasoline vapors were taken into the cylinder at the same time as the suction stroke of the piston, one part water to two parts gasoline. Super-heated steam forced the piston to move.

Fairbanks-Morse trucks

In 1908, Fairbanks-Morse experimented with truck production, manufacturing delivery wagons of 1,000-, 1,200-, and 3,500-pound capacity, as well as a 3-ton truck powered

Chapter 12

Success of Model T Gets Ford Into Tractor Business

American farmers were convinced that if a cheap and useful car could be manufactured, so could a tractor with the same qualities. Henry Ford heard their cries.

But another Ford tractor came out first, attempting to cash in on the well-known Ford name. The Ford Tractor Company of Minneapolis had nothing to do with Henry Ford or Detroit, but used the Ford name to sell tractors. That became obvious when the "Mr. Ford" in the company knew nothing about tractors, and often didn't even have to report to work.

So rather than muddle with similar names, in 1917 Henry Ford called his first tractor the Fordson.

The Fordson was not a perfect tractor: a tester's unfavorable responses to the tractor were suppressed–though leaked to the press–and the tractor suffered from poor starting and carburetor problems, mostly due to poor maintenance, as farmers were unsophisticated about machines. Fordsons carried a four-cylinder 4- x 5-inch bore and stroke engine and weighed 2,700 pounds. More than 700,000 of them were built until 1928, including many in England.

In the early 1920s, Fordsons were sold below cost to increase cash flow and reduce inventory during the national depression. A variety of Ford tractors followed over the years, including the 9N, Super Major, and in 1968, the first 100-hp tractor, the Model 8000.

Early 'Ford' tractors

Experimental models had been built by Ford Motor Company first in 1907, called the Automobile Plow, using a 1905 Model B car engine, and steering gear from other Ford autos. It was never put into production. Other experimental models followed.

Only seven of these Fordson buses were made, probably none for public sale; instead, Henry Ford used them to shuttle visitors from his private airport to his office in Detroit. This is the only one known to exist.

Ford tractors are still produced today, but they are no longer built by the car company. The tractor division was purchased by Fiat, and the Ford name is being phased out today in favor of New Holland.

Ford automobiles

On Christmas Eve 1892, Henry Ford tested the first Ford gasoline engine in the kitchen sink of his Dearborn, Michigan home, with his wife Clara dribbling gasoline into the intake valve. From those humble beginnings, an empire was built.

In 1896, Henry built his first automobile in a shed behind his home. When he was finished, he had to cut a wall down to get it out. This quadri-cycle performed well, using a leather belt and chain and a two-cylinder four-stroke horizontal engine of four hp, at 20 mph. He hadn't planned on selling it, but did when offered $200; he used the money to build his second vehicle.

By 1899, his work came to the attention of investors, and the Detroit Automobile Company was organized. When Henry Ford decided to build a race car instead of regular automobiles, stockholders were displeased, and pulled out. The Henry Ford Company was organized on Nov. 30, 1901, but after disagreements, Ford left and built

Like the Ford Model T automobile, this Fordson tractor from 1936 was a long-lived machine, first breathing life in 1917. In 1936, the tractor used a two-cylinder Ford engine with 4-1/8- x 5-inch bore and stroke, and was recommended for pulling two 14-inch plows. It weighed 3,310 pounds and was light as many of the tractors of the era were. The Fordson is one of the most successful tractors ever produced by any company, and they were called "Fordson" instead of "Ford" because at the time, Henry Ford wanted to get into tractor production, another Ford tractor from a company in Minneapolis was already on the market. (Dan Roen Collection)

By the time this 1911 advertisement for a Ford Model T Light Delivery Car was published, more than 100,000 Ford cars were in service, and as the ad says, "Demand for Ford Cars Doubles Annually." The Ford name was known nationwide by this time. It's interesting to note what the $700 would buy, as this vehicle came "fully equipped": automatic brass windshield, speedometer, three oil lamps, two gas lamps, generator, horn, and tools. Ford also said in the ad that Bell Telephone Company uses more than 1,000 Ford Model T delivery cars in its business. (Gary Hoonsbeen Collection)

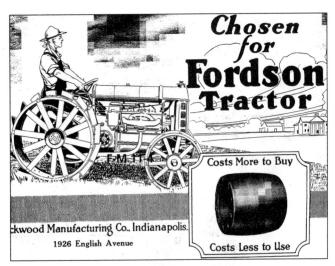

This photo shows an early Fordson tractor equipped with the steel crawler drive designed by Bates Machine & Tractor Co. of Joliet, Illinois. Dynamometer tests showed an increase of 25-30 percent drawbar pull on soft ground. "The tractor is fitted with two crawler turning devices, each having an independent foot lever so that either crawler can be slowed down or stopped entirely for short turning, with the result that an inside turning circle of two feet is obtained." (State Historical Society of North Dakota)

This 1919 ad for the Rockwood Paper Drive Puller used the notoriety of the Fordson to proclaim that Fordson had chosen its pulley especially for Fordson use. "The manufacturers of the Fordson tractor know that belt power is an essential and important feature of tractor service. And yet, until they had tested and approved the Rockwood Paper Drive Pulley, they built and shipped thousands of Fordson Tractors and offered no pulley at all rather than recommend some inferior type of pulley that did not measure up to the Fordson standards of quality, value and service." Though the Fordson was only in its third year, this ad shows the power the tractor company already wielded. (Dan Roen Collection)

gine, two-speed planetary transmission, and a 100-inch wheelbase. It got 25 miles per gallon of gasoline.

Motor Age magazine responded to the Model T in its March 21, 1912 issue, thus: "Ford and other low-priced cars are doing full-capacity business."

Ford has since been a leader in the American automobile market.

Ford trucks

Henry Ford's first foray into trucks, a delivery wagon in 1900, was not successful, and it wasn't until his third attempt, in 1903 at age 40, that the trucks worked. The first commercial vehicles appeared two years later on Ford chassis. A Model A was fitted with a cargo box that year.

The first factory-produced commercial vehicle was the Model C Ford Delivery Car, fitted with a delivery top.

All early Ford vehicles were renegades, as Henry Ford ignored the license required under the Selden patent to build automobiles, and sued to prove his point—and won.

In 1912, Ford's Delivery Car, 250 of which had been tested for two years by Bell Telephone, did not sell well. Sales were spotty until 1917, when Model T trucks hit the market, along with the 1-ton Model TT trucks.

more race cars. In 1903, the Ford Motor Company was organized and the first Ford Model A runabouts were manufactured and sold for $750 each.

Other models were produced, some Ford didn't like, but his financial backers did, like the Model B for the higher priced market (it cost $3,000). Models B and F came out in 1905, Model K later that year, and finally in 1908, the Model T was born, the affordable car that would change American motoring habits. It was sold for nearly two decades. It contained a 20-hp side-valve four-cylinder en-

This was the first tractor Ford ever built, a 1906 test jobbie with a four-cylinder vertical engine with copper water jackets. The rear wheels came from an old grain binder, while the front wheels, axle, steering post, and radiator were appropriated from an early Ford Model K car. It had forward and reverse speeds, and produced 24 hp. (Roy Bernick Collection)

This Fordson chassis and frame were the handiwork of Henry Ford, when he decided the power plant of the Model T was good for a light-pulling truck, but that the Fordson tractor powerplant would be good for a heavy-duty truck. Very few were built, and only one is known to exist.

A quick perusal of this ad by Association of Licensed Automobile Manufacturers will show that Henry Ford's company did not subscribe to the ALAM's belief that "United States Letters Patent No. 549,160, granted to George B. Selden, Nov. 5, 1895, control broadly all gasolene automobiles which are accepted as commercially practical." Ford did not get a license from ALAM to manufacture autos; in fact, Ford contested it, and won in court. (State Historical Society of North Dakota)

In 1920, Ford trucks possessed demountable rims as an option, and the Ford heavy duty truck was designed, a 3-ton cab-over-engine truck which didn't go into production, partly because of the agricultural depression.

However, from 1922 to today, Ford trucks have been a mainstay in American motor vehicle production.

Fordson trucks and buses

Henry Ford saw how powerful the power plant in his Fordson tractor was, and how that tractor had a wide variety of heavy-pulling uses on the farm, like pulling out tree stumps. He also knew his Model-T power plant was good for a light truck, but he wanted something for a heavier

This Model TT Ford truck was produced by Ford Motor Company in 1912.

truck, so he used the Fordson power plant in a Fordson truck, and Fordson bus.

Very few Fordson trucks were built–probably a dozen or so–and all were probably prototypes. Engineering drawings and prototype Fordson trucks appeared a few years after Henry Ford's 1919 buyout of minor shareholders of Ford Motor Co. Photos show dates from 1920-1924, and in 1926, Ford sent a Fordson truck to his friend, Arthur Brisbane, to test on his ranch in California.

But the Fordson truck was never put into production, probably because of the success of the Fordson tractor. There simply wasn't space or tooling available to build Fordson trucks; plus, the power plant's top speed of 6.75 mph would have to be increased, which required considerable re-engineering. The truck was probably also not built because Henry Ford had turned the reins of the company over to his son, Edsel, who was not interested in trucks and tractors.

Seven Fordson buses were built, used mainly to chauffeur visitors from the airport to Henry Ford's Detroit offices. Only one Fordson bus and one Fordson truck are known to exist today.

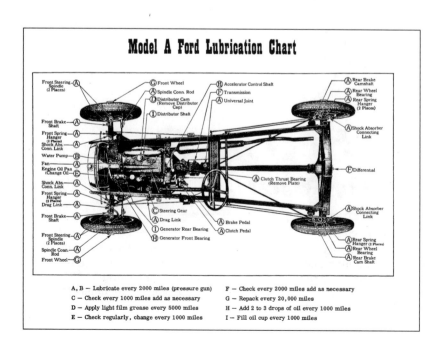

Model A Ford Lubrication Chart

A, B — Lubricate every 2000 miles (pressure gun)
C — Check every 1000 miles add as necessary
D — Apply light film grease every 5000 miles
E — Check regularly, change every 1000 miles
F — Check every 2000 miles add as necessary
G — Repack every 20,000 miles
H — Add 2 to 3 drops of oil every 1000 miles
I — Fill oil cup every 1000 miles

One of the things Americans liked about Ford automobiles was their simplicity. This chart shows how Model As were to be lubricated and when. (Roy Bernick Collection)

THE FORD

is an automobile with a reputation. We have proven our ability to make and sell for $900 a car equal to any machine costing less than $2000.

What is more, **THE FORD** has stood the test of time and hard usage. The double opposed motor is the same type of engine used in the most expensive touring cars.

FOR THE PHYSICIAN and Business Man the reliability of the Ford is its strongest recommendation.

Its simple construction enables any member of the family to easily master the mechanism and to readily learn to operate it.

Write for catalogue and full particulars to

FORD MOTOR CO.
DETROIT, MICH.

One of the peculiarities in early automobile advertisements was in how the companies targeted people with money, like doctors, in this 1904 Physician's advertisement. Doctors also needed automobiles that were reliable. This 1904 Ford sold for $900, although the company said it was the equal of any car costing $2,000. The simplicity of the machine was also touted: "Its simple construction enables any member of the family to easily master the mechanism and to readily learn to operate it." (Gary Hoonsbeen Collection)

Chapter 13

Galloway Builds Tractors, Cars, and Trucks

William Galloway started as territory man for an implement company in Iowa. Tired of the pressure to sell, he moved to Waterloo, Iowa, and turned to automobiles, tractors, and trucks.

A booklet, *Manufacturing Companies of Gasoline Engines in Early Waterloo*, says, "Much of the industrial development of early Waterloo centered around William Galloway."

In 1906, the William Galloway Company produced chiefly a harrow cart. "Later, Mr. Galloway added manure spreaders, cream separators, and gasoline engines to his long list of general merchandise," the booklet says.

Galloway had high praise for one of his competitors: "When we moved to Waterloo (about 1902)," Galloway said in a May 1946 interview in the *Waterloo Daily Courier*, "it was a town of about 12,000 population. Thomas Cascaden was the leading industrialist of the city. He had a factory down on Commercial Street where he manufactured gasoline engines."

Sometime ca. 1910, Galloway bought Cascaden Manufacturing Company, and began manufacturing Cascaden's gasoline engines.

The Farmobile tractor

By the time Galloway produced the Farmobile tractor in Waterloo in 1916, he had been involved in the vehicle business since 1900. The 12-20 Farmobile used a four-cylinder engine with a 4-1/2 x 5-inch bore and stroke. It

weighed 5,450 pounds, had two forward speeds, and would pull 2,000 pounds in high gear.

In 1910, Galloway convinced Fred Maytag to bring his Maytag automobile company to Waterloo, and convinced Maytag to build a tractor, built only one year. After an unsuccessful stint in Waterloo, Maytag returned to Newton, Iowa, and washing machines.

In 1916, Galloway manufactured 1,100 tractors, and sold $1.3 million of them to Great Britain for use during World War I. The "Farmobile" built in Great Britain was called the Garner. Unfortunately, Great Britain never paid $450,000 of the money owed, and thus Galloway couldn't pay his bills.

The company went bankrupt in 1920, resurfaced in 1927, and then slipped into obscurity.

Galloway automobiles

William Galloway bought a carload of one-cylinder Cadillacs in 1902, parked them in front of his office, and began selling them like crazy.

In 1904, he and fellow Waterlooan carriage builder, Henry Greutsmacher, designed their own automobile. They started selling it in 1908. This two-cylinder, solid-tired, chain-driven highwheeler was supposed to take a

"Galloway's Farmobile" tractor was made in 1916, a 12- to 20-hp tractor with a four-cylinder engine of 4-1/2- x 5-inch bore and stroke. It weighed 5,450 pounds and was sold until 1919. William Galloway, owner of William Galloway Company of Waterloo, Iowa, was involved in a wide variety of motor-vehicle pursuits, including cars, trucks, and, of course, tractors. (Dan Roen Collection)

William Galloway Company made a number of different-named automobiles, including this restored Galloway number.

One of the cars that William Galloway got involved with in his William Galloway Company of Waterloo, Iowa, was the Argo, which had originally been named the Ajax when it was being manufactured in France by Benjamin Briscoe. Though Galloway may not have entirely had his hands involved in the production of the Argo, Briscoe did manufacture the Arabian car–one very much like the Argo–for Galloway in 1915 and 1916. This advertisement is from 1912. (Gary Hoonsbeen Collection)

large family to church on Sunday and haul heavy loads during the week. It possessed only a 14-hp engine and an 85-inch wheelbase, so it was doubtful the loads could have been too big. Galloway said feeding horses corn worth 75 cents a bushel, oats worth 35-40 cents, and hay worth $14-$20 a ton, was a waste of hard-earned money better spent on buying Galloway auto transport.

Galloway enticed the Maytag-Mason Motor Car Company of Newton to move to Waterloo in 1910 by offering to buy into the business. After a year in Waterloo, the discovery that the rear axle of the automobile was faulty scuttled the business.

The Galloway was a renamed Maytag, and was made only in 1911. Galloway turned to his new and more profitable business, making Dart trucks.

Ajax/Argo/Arabian automobiles

When Benjamin Briscoe brought the Ajax Cyclecar back

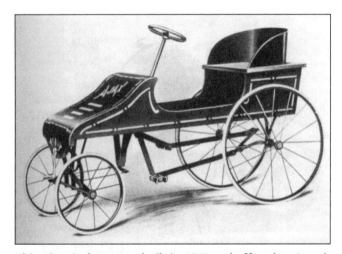

This Ajax Cyclecar was built in 1910 and offered to American drivers as a serious automobile; it had been called Ajax in France, was sometimes called the Ajax Vique in America (to make it sound more Frenchified) and eventually became the Argo. It weighed 750 pounds and cost $295, and came complete with four-cylinder water-cooled engine. The Ajax in this photo was of a model being offered in a catalog. (Gary Hoonsbeen Collection)

This 1910 Galloway truck was made by the Dart Company of Waterloo, Iowa, for the William Galloway Company, and sold through mail order from Galloway. It used a two-cylinder 14.4-hp, with 4-1/4- x 5-inch bore and stroke. It could carry 1,500 pounds.

from France, he renamed it the Argo. He wanted to build the car in New York City, but a plant opened up in Jackson, Michigan–formerly building Standard Electric cars–so he moved there instead in 1914. The Ajax/Argo was a $295 cyclecar with a four-cylinder L-head water-cooled engine using a shaft drive, sliding-gear transmission for its 12-hp engine. It had a 90-inch wheelbase and weighed only 750 pounds.

In the United States, the car was sometimes called the Argo Motor Vique to make it sound more French and exotic. When the cyclecar genre died a quick death, the Argo was redesigned into a larger conventional assembled car in 1916.

During 1915-16, Briscoe built an Arabian automobile for William Galloway in his Jackson plant. Galloway sold it. The 1915 Arabian was a four-cylinder, 12-hp vehicle with a 90-inch wheelbase, exactly like the old Argo cyclecar. The 1916-17 Arabians were four-cylinder, 22-hp cars with either a 96-inch wheelbase in the two-passenger roadster (factory price of $385, same as the 1915 vehicle), or a four-passenger roadster with a 103-inch wheelbase for $435. The last year the Arabian was made was probably 1917.

By 1916, Briscoe sold his company to Mansell Hackett, who reorganized it as the Hackett Motor Car Company in the fall of 1916. At that time, the Hackett cars were built for Hackett in Galloway's plant in Waterloo. Subsequently, the car was renamed the Lorraine, although none of the principal people in this saga had any more interest in it.

Galloway trucks

From 1908-11, Galloway made Galloway trucks. These were highwheelers powered by a 14-hp two-cylinder horizontally opposed engine located under the seat with a planetary transmission and had chain drive to the rear wheels. These right-hand steering trucks had leaf springs front and rear, an open cab, an 85-inch wheelbase with 32- x 1-1/2-inch front and 33- x 3-inch rear carriage-type wood spoke wheels with solid tires. They sold for $570 in 1908. Although Galloway designed these vehicles, the Dart Manufacturing Company, also of Waterloo, manufactured them for Galloway.

Chapter 14

Graham Brothers Build Many Vehicles

Though the Graham-Bradley tractor was built in 1938 by Graham-Paige Motors Corporation of Detroit, Michigan, the principals had been manufacturing cars and trucks for many years, and the history of this company and its vehicles is the history of many companies.

Graham-Bradley tractors

The Graham-Bradley 503.103 model launched the 1938 Nebraska testing season. The 4,955-pound tractor attained speeds in different gears of 2.77, 4.42, 5.67, and 19.8 mph, with their Graham-Paige six-cylinder L-head bore-and-stroke engine of 3-1/4 x 4-3/8 inches. The tractor was tested for 43 hours, and no major repairs or adjustments needed to be made to the Schebler TRX-15 carburetor, Handy governor, Donaldson air cleaner, or any other parts of the tractor. In low gear, the G-B pulled 3,013 pounds.

In 1939, Graham-Paige offered the Graham-Bradley Model 104, which was not tested at Nebraska. Graham-Bradley tractors had an exceptionally wide range of speeds.

To sell more vehicles, GB offered tractor franchises to Graham-Paige auto sellers, or automobile franchises to Graham-Bradley tractor sellers, as an option. G-B tractors disappeared just before World War II, although a 1945 ad announced a new line of Graham tractors for 1946, which never materialized, probably because the company got involved with Kaiser and Fraser automobiles.

This 1938 Graham-Bradley tractor used the same six-cylinder engine to drive the tractor as it did its Graham automobiles. The Graham-Bradley was sold through Sears, Roebuck & Company, among other outlets.

Paige-Detroit, Paige, and Jewett automobiles

After years working for the Dodge Brothers, the Graham brothers, Joseph B., Robert C., and Ray A., returned to the automobile manufacturing field in Dearborn, Michigan, in 1928 when they bought the faltering Paige-De-

This general purpose Graham-Bradley with a six-cylinder engine was produced by Graham-Paige Motors Corporation of Detroit in 1937. Rubber tires were standard, as well as PTO, hydraulic power lift, and electric starting and lighting. Rear wheels were adjustable from 56 to 84 inches, and it wheeled from 3 to 22 mph forward in four gears. The tractor was sold by Sears, Roebuck & Co.

This 1925 Paige Seven-passenger Phaeton sold for $2,165, and was manufactured by Paige-Detroit Motor Car Company of Detroit, Michigan. It used a six-cylinder 3-3/4-inch x 5-inch bore and stroke engine with 33.75 hp, and had three forward and one reverse gears. Curiously enough, even though the man after whom the car was named, Fred Paige, was fired in 1910, the car (which had been called the Paige-Detroit at the time) was renamed the Paige, and so it stayed until 1930. The Paige name was possibly the most hyphenated of all involved in automobile manufacture, having been the Paige-Detroit, and later the Graham-Paige automobile. (Gary Hoonsbeen Collection)

troit Motor Car Company, which had built cars since 1910.

The company has an interesting history: in the summer of 1909, Harry M. Jewett, a coal mining entrepreneur, rode in a car being promoted by Fred O. Paige. Jewett didn't know much about cars, but after the car ran well on the test drive, he organized and invested heavily in the Paige-Detroit Motor Car Company, installing as president Fred Paige, former president of Reliance Motor Car Company.

The first two years (1909-10) the cars were called Paige-Detroits. The Paige-Detroit Model No. 1 was a three-cylinder, 25-hp machine with a 90-inch wheelbase, selling for $800 for a two-passenger roadster. When Jewett was asked about his Paige-Detroit cars, he made an honest assessment. He said, "It's rotten. A piece of junk."

That did not bode well for President Paige, who was ousted, and the car was, curiously, renamed simply "Paige." The 1911 Paige came in Models B and C, four-cylinder, 25-hp cars with 90- and 104-inch wheelbases, respectively, selling for $800 for the Model B two-passenger roadster, and $975 each for the Model C surrey and touring car, while the Model C couple cost $1,250.

Paige autos sold well. In 1915, the company produced its first six-cylinder auto, and from 1916 on, all were sixes. A stripped down 1921 6-66 Paige roadster set a Daytona Beach speed record of 102.83 mph. The next year, the company made a Daytona model for the public.

While involved with these autos, Harry Jewett was involved with manufacturing the Lozier automobile (in another company) for a while, and in 1922 began producing the Jewett, which eased into the Paige line five years later as a Model 6-45 Paige. During the 1920s, the higher-powered Paiges used Continental engines, and the straight-eight model introduced in 1927 used Lycoming engines. All earlier models had used Paige engines.

By 1925, the company was the tenth largest producer of automobiles in the United States, which it celebrated with a brochure titled, "43 Ghosts," the number of car companies that had gone out of business during the previous two years.

But company fortunes took a sudden turn for the worse; after the company lost $2.5 million in 1927, Jewett decided to get out of the business, selling to the Graham Brothers, who continued the Paige as a model.

Graham-Paige and Graham automobiles

First-year sales of their new marquee, Graham-Paige automobiles, totaled 73,195 cars, the most ever for a maiden year to that time. All these four-, six- and one eight-cylinder models used L-head engines with aluminum pistons, hydraulic brakes, and four- speed Warner Gear transmissions.

The good fortune required plant expansion in Wayne, Michigan.

Two years later, it introduced a second line of eight-cylinder Graham-Paiges, and sixes with longer wheelbases. In 1930, "Paige" was dropped and the cars simply became "Grahams." Standard six-cylinder 1930 cars with 115-inch wheelbases sold for $845 (four-door Town Sedan) to $1,065 (cabriolet).

Though millions of Graham-Paige Blue Streak miniature cars were sold by Tootsietoy Company, only 12,967 real

One of the automobiles that Henry Jewett got involved with was the Lozier. Jewett was involved with the Paige-Detroit Motor Company, which he eventually sold to the Graham Brothers. The Lozier in this drawing is a 1912 Lozier that appeared on the cover of *Motor Age* on March 21, 1912. Touring cars sold for $5,000, and limousines for $6,500, both very princely sums at the time. "If you talk with men who are experienced motorists," the front-page ad says, 'the men who know'–they will tell you that the Lozier is the best car built in America, and that Lozier Luxury is always worth the price." (Gary Hoonsbeen Collection)

Grahams–including Blue Streaks–were sold in 1932. That same year, Ray Graham committed suicide.

The company limped on for eight more years, building cars for other companies as well as its own. In 1940, it announced a temporary plant closing, which proved permanent.

Graham Brothers trucks

Graham Brothers produced trucks starting in 1919 in Evansville, Indiana. Its first truck was a do-it-yourself model. The Graham Brothers provided the frame, cab, body, and Torbensen internal gear drives. In 1920, it began building its own trucks, and introduced an 18-passenger speed bus for $3,445.

The president of Dodge, Frederick J. Haynes, bought majority interest in Graham Brothers in 1920, and built

Paige-Detroit Motor Car Company of Detroit made this Jewett five-passenger sedan in 1926, and sold it for $995 standard; $100 more for the Deluxe Sedan; and the same $1,095 for the five-passenger DeLuxe Touring Jewett. This particular sedan had wood wheels, was Killarney gray in color, and used a six-cylinder 2-3/4- x 4-3/4-inch bore and stroke producing 182 hp.

In 1923, Graham-Paige made this Paige Dayton Model 6-70, a car named in honor of the Paige Model 6-66 stock chassis that had established a one-mile straightaway speed record at Daytona Beach, Florida, earlier. (Gary Hoonsbeen Collection)

The year before the Dodge Brothers bought out the Graham Brothers, this 1926 Graham Brothers 1-ton panel truck appeared, weighing 5,690 pounds gross weight, using a four-cylinder 3-7/8- x 4-1/2-inch bore and stroke engine that produced 24.03 hp in its N.A.C.C. rating. It came in five different bodies—a 1-ton chassis for $995, a panel body for $1,295, a canopy body for $1,230, an express body for $1,195, and a stake body for $1,240. This is quite a change from the earliest Graham trucks, which were do-it-yourself models that provided parts of the truck, but not all. (Gary Hoonsbeen Collection)

Graham trucks in Detroit using Dodge four-cylinder engines and transmissions. Dodge also marketed the trucks.

Graham offered five truck models in 1924: 1-ton Model BB for $1,175; and four 1-1/2-ton models—CB ($1,375); FB ($1,425); MB ($1,440); and LB ($1,490). Wheelbases ran from 130 to 158 inches. Front axles, engines, clutches, and transmissions were built by Dodge. The trucks used rear axles and steering made by Graham.

In 1927, Dodge bought out Graham Brothers. As part of the purchase agreement, Graham Brothers could not build trucks, so it turned to automobiles and tractors.

Graham Brothers manufactured this seventeen-passenger sedan bus in 1925, which sold for $3,640 with its four-cylinder 3-7/8- x 4-1/2-inch bore and stroke engine of 24.03 rated hp. (Gary Hoonsbeen Collection)

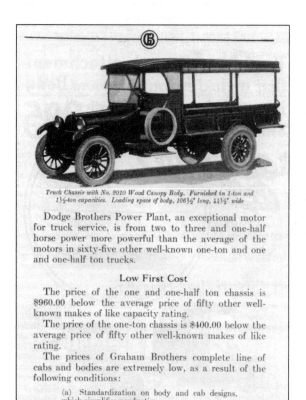

Truck Chassis with No. 2010 Wood Canopy Body. Furnished in 1-ton and 1½-ton capacities. Loading space of body, 106½" long, 44½" wide

Dodge Brothers Power Plant, an exceptional motor for truck service, is from two to three and one-half horse power more powerful than the average of the motors in sixty-five other well-known one-ton and one and one-half ton trucks.

Low First Cost

The price of the one and one-half ton chassis is $960.00 below the average price of fifty other well-known makes of like capacity rating.

The price of the one-ton chassis is $400.00 below the average price of fifty other well-known makes of like rating.

The prices of Graham Brothers complete line of cabs and bodies are extremely low, as a result of the following conditions:

   (a) Standardization on body and cab designs, which simplifies production.

   (b) Low prices on raw material, because of large quantity purchases and the saving in transportation by Graham Brothers Body Plant location, in the heart of the central lumber district.

Graham Brothers advertised this truck chassis with a wood canopy body, which came in 1- and 1-1/2-ton models. It had a loading space of 106-1/2 inches by 44-1/2 inches, and used a Dodge Brothers motor. (Gary Hoonsbeen Collection)

This 1929 Graham-Paige was one of the earliest models made after the Graham Brothers bought the Paige-Detroit Motor Car Company and changed the name to Graham-Paige Motors Corporation. The next year, the car's name was changed to simply Graham.

Chapter 15

Holt History Goes Back Many Years

Holt history began when the Holt father, William Knox Holt, obtained a hardwood lumber mill in the 1850s near Concord, New Hampshire, where brothers Benjamin and Charles learned sawmill and woodworking operations. The business expanded to include the sale of wagon wheels, then the manufacture of wagons, buggies, sleighs, and hardware items.

In 1863, when Charles Holt was 20, he left New Hampshire bound via the Isthmus of Panama for San Francisco. He had been promised a sea-going job, but when he got there, he found that his employer-to-be had gone bankrupt.

He taught college and made extra money keeping books at night for a general store. When he had saved $700, he returned to San Francisco. There in 1869, he established C. H. Holt & Company, importers of hardwood lumber sawed at his father's New Hampshire mill.

Unfortunately, the wood was not properly seasoned for use on the West Coast, so Charles Holt quit that and started manufacturing his own wheels and other wagon articles.

In 1883, Benjamin, the most mechanically gifted of the brothers, migrated West to join Charles in Stockton, California. There the brothers formed their Stockton Wheel Company.

Over the next few years, they made railroad cars, streetcars, and boilers for steamboats, "Fresno scrapers" for road building, mining cars, wagons, drapers, and they sold lumber, leather belting, chains, iron, wrenches, forges, bench planes, mandrels, nails, bolts, harrow teeth, and oil and grease.

Holt Caterpillar tractors

In 1894, Holt was approached by Charles Moreing, a large landowner in the San Joaquin Valley, who had large areas of soft peat that defied conventional steam tractors.

Holt tried to build a tractor with enough flotation to work Moreing's soft peat. The answer was the caterpillar track.

It took ten years to see the possibilities of the track-layer. On Nov. 24, 1904, Holt steam traction engine No. 77 had its wheels removed, and new tracks installed on each side: the first Caterpillar tractor was made. It pulled four gangs of plows two inches deeper with its 40 hp and tracks than a 60 hp did with three gangs of plows.

After much testing, the caterpillar track-layer was perfected. Holt bought out rival Best Manufacturing Company in 1908, made gasoline engines, and expanded across the United States.

Some of its cars included Baby Caterpillar in 1914, one of the first models to dispense with the front-tiller wheel; the Holt-Illinois, a conventional-type tractor made in 1911 with a 45-hp engine; a Caterpillar 25-45 in 1916; and a Caterpillar 70-120, weighing 24,800 pounds and capable of pulling more than half its weight–12,600 pounds, using six cylinders of 7-1/2- x 8-inch bore and stroke. The engine alone weighed nearly 2-1/2 tons, and the crankshaft was 3-3/16 inches. Holt also built the 10-Ton Caterpillar starting in 1919, and the 5-ton in the same year. These last two stayed in production until the company united with Best in 1925.

Holt had many firsts: first to make practical use out of the Caterpillar track; first, in 1910, to use the name, "Caterpillar"; and among the first to harass farmers about using horses instead of tractors.

In fact, its methods took on a harsh, condescending tone, as in its magazine, *Caterpillar Times*: "Possibly some farmers keep their horses for sentimental reasons. If so, well and good. The horse has been a good friend, so keep him, if you wish, as a matter of kindness. It's an expensive proposition, to be sure, but sentiment excuses many luxuries."

This action photo shows a modified Holt 5-ton caterpillar tractor breaking sod in 1919, the first year of production of the machine. It stayed in production until Holt Manufacturing Company of Stockton, California, sold out to C.L. Best Gas Traction Co. of San Leandro, California, in 1925. Holt produced many firsts, including being the first company to make practical use of track-laying machines, and the first to use the name "caterpillar" for the tracks. (Dan Roen Collection)

TRACTORS

PAT. OFF.

10 Ton

HOLT
PEORIA, STOCKTON

"Caterpillar" steadiness and dependability counts at threshing time. Run the 10-Ton Ordnance model (40-60 H. P.) up to the belt of a 60 inch separator, start it going and forget about it. Whether the straw be wet or dry, the feeding regular or uneven, "Caterpillar" power, closely governed, keeps the machine humming steadily.

There is a reserve of power and a surplus of quality in the "Caterpillar" that keeps it working as well after years of service as when it was first bought.

For doing big jobs quickly, easily and thoroughly, there is no tractor better than the "Caterpillar" 10-Ton Ordnance model. The same machine that rebuilt ruined roads in France for the rapid advance of 30-Ton guns—and then brought up the guns—is now ready to do just as heavy work in America.

Run the "Caterpillar" out onto marshy ground that would not support a horse. It takes the plows or scraper, straight through tangled reeds and roots. Over ground only moderately good, the "Caterpillar" moves its load without hitch or halt. The ground pressure of the 10-Ton model is less than seven pounds per square inch, and its drawbar pull at plowing speed is more than 9000 pounds. These things make the "Caterpillar" a most valuable tractor.

Dealers: Whose policy it is to handle only the best, who do most of their business with men who use only the best, should know all about the "Caterpillar" tractor. A letter written in a few minutes returns information leading to years of satisfaction to yourself and your customers.

The HOLT Manufacturing Co., Inc.
There is but one "CATERPILLAR"-HOLT builds it.
Peoria, Illinois
Factories: Peoria, Ill. and Stockton, Cal.

In 1920, Holt Manufacturing Co., Inc., of Peoria, Illinois (it also had a factory in Stockton, California), built this 10-ton Holt. The name "caterpillar" for the tracks had just become more or less standard, introduced by Holt. "For doing big jobs quickly, easily and thoroughly," the ad says, "there is no tractor better than the 'Caterpillar' 10-ton Ordnance model. The same machine that rebuilt ruined roads in France (World War I) for the rapid advance of 30-ton guns–and then brought up the guns–is now ready to do just as heavy work in America." The ad also touted that the ground pressure of the 10-ton is less than seven pounds per square inch, and it could pull more than 9,000 pounds at plowing speed. (Dan Roen Collection)

Holt automobiles

Early in 1899, the Holt brothers engaged an unnamed prominent area mechanic and inventor as their chief engineer. The *Horseless Age* said he had invented a new type of gasoline engine.

But it must not have been good enough, because the prototype auto disappeared without a ripple, and the Holts returned to their successful tracklayers.

Sequoia automobiles

In 1914, Sequoia manufactured electric cars named Sequoia in the same factory where the Best automobiles had been built before 1908, and where Holt had built its Holt truck only a year earlier.

The venture was not very successful. By fall 1914, the new company had begun to manufacture electric trucks and developing an electric car, but by early 1915, the entire project went under, and Holt repossessed the plant.

It is unclear if Sequoia automobiles or trucks were ever made, and if they were, it would only have been very tangential to Holt Manufacturing Company.

Best trucks

The hand of Leo Best can be seen in the manufacture of Best trucks by Holt Manufacturing Company. Holt bought out Best Manufacturing in 1908, and Leo Best went with the company, while Daniel Best retired.

In 1913, Holt began making trucks with the name of Best; it is unclear why they were not called Holts, but perhaps they used patents Leo had applied for while working for Holt, and it was required to credit him.

The company made 1- and 1-1/2-ton trucks, with two- and four-cylinder engines respectively. The 1-ton used a friction transmission and double-chain drive, and the 1-1/2-ton used a selective transmission with shaft drive. In its second and last year of production, the 1-ton cost $1,370. In 1914, Sequoia Motor Car Company absorbed this part of the Holt business and began building Sequoia automobiles.

Leo was interested in gasoline engines, and in 1910, he broke away from Holt and formed C. L. Best Company.

Chapter 16

Independent Harvester Chooses Poor Vehicle Name

Independent Harvester Company of Plano, Illinois, manufactured agricultural equipment, and in 1910 hired Henry K. Holsman to head its newly formed automobile department. The company also made tractors for Parrett Motors Corporation of Chicago.

Parrett tractors

Dent Parrett dabbled in many tractor companies, including the Parrett Tractor Company of Chicago, organized in 1913 with his brother, Henry, and Henry Pollard.

They wanted to build tractors, but had no plant, so they contracted Independent Harvester of Plano, Illinois, to manufacture 25 Parrett tractors.

Results must have been positive, because by 1915, Parrett Motors Corporation opened doors in Chicago to manufacture tractors. C. H. Wendel says in *Encyclopedia of American Farm Tractors*, "At one time, Parrett had one of the largest exclusive tractor factories in the world."

Three different tractors were built: a 10-20; a 12-25 (Model E and H); and the Model K 15-30. The 10-20 Parrett was sold beginning in 1915, a redesigned model similar to the earlier 10-20, but which used a cross-mount engine. Rear wheels were five feet in diameter, front wheels 46 inches, and the 5,000-pound tractor sold for $1,075.

The 12-25 was sold from 1918-1920, a redesign of the 10-20. It used a Buda 4-1/4- x 5-1/2-inch four-cylinder motor. It sold for $1,450 in 1918.

PARRETT MODEL H, 12-25
Parrett Tractor Co., Chicago Heights, Ill.

In 1920, the Parrett Tractor Company of Chicago (or Chicago Heights, Illinois), manufactured this Parrett Model H 12-25 tractor, with a four-cylinder Buda engine with 4-1/4- x 5-1/2-inch bore and stroke. The machine weighed 5,200 pounds, and was recommended for three plows. It sold for $1,450 in 1918. (Gary Hoonsbeen Collection)

PARRETT CULTIVATING 6-12
Parrett Motors Corp., Chicago, Ill.

The Parrett Cultivating 6-12 was another of the tractors made by Parrett Motors Corporation in 1920. This three-wheeler was 160 inches long, and used a LeRoi 3-1/8- x 4-1/2-inch bore and stroke engine. (Dan Roen Collection)

The Model K 15-30 was produced in 1920, but the agricultural depression, tractor wars, and fierce competition spelled doom for Parrett. In 1921, it was called Hicks-Parrett Tractor Company, offering an 18-30 crawler. After 1922, neither company existed any longer.

Holsman autos

Holsman Automobile Company of Chicago was a highly successful producer of highwheeler automobiles, and its success induced many other companies to build them. In 1906, Holsman increased the size of his plant by six times, doubled his capital stock, and started night shifts to keep up with demand.

The two-cylinder carriage auto was originally driven by a 7/8-inch manila rope, which didn't work well during wet weather, so had to be scrapped. Next was a chain braided over with manila and steel wire, and later just a chain. Brakes were hand operated, because, the company's literature said, "in emergencies and under excitement the foot cannot be relied upon to act sub-consciously or automatically, and to do the right thing instantly."

Highwheelers sold for a couple of years. Holsman seemed blind to the changes in the automotive industry, and his company went bankrupt in 1910. He moved to Plano, 50 miles away, and got involved with the Independent Harvester Company, where he could still build his Holsmans but call them a different name.

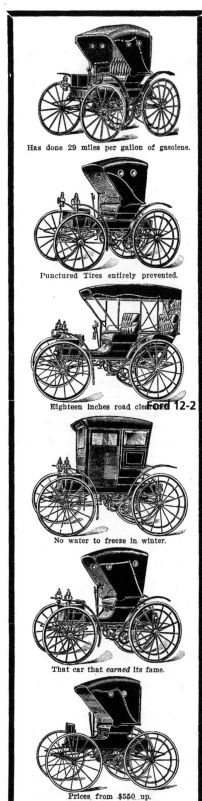
In 1908, Holsman ran this advertisement crowing about the win of the Holsman in the Algonquin Hill Climb race, taking both first and second in the Motor Buggy class event, "against the entire field of 2- and 4-cylinder Motor Buggies, and made better time percentages than 21 higher-powered automobiles of the ordinary type, ranging up to 72 hp. This emphatically demonstrates its supremacy..." Demonstration or not, high-wheelers were on their way out, although Holsman was not ready to admit it, and wouldn't be for another five years. (Dan Roen Collection)

This ad from 1907 shows a pair of Holsman autos, the Model 10 Runabout and the Model M Surrey. The selling point was that these highwheelers had been on the market for five years, longer than many other fledgling car dealers. "The oldest and largest manufacturers of Carriage Automobiles," the ad declares. (Gary Hoonsbeen Collection)

Independent Harvester Company of Plano, Illinois, billed itself as "The Farmers' Company." It sold gas engines, plows, wagons, and other agricultural implements through a web of branch houses across the central United States. Henry Holsman got involved with the company in 1910 when it added an automobile department to its company. It was short-lived; by 1912, the auto department was finished. (Dan Roen Collection)

Independent Harvester autos

Unfortunately, that name was Independent Harvester, abbreviated IHC, same as the well-known International Harvester Company. Perhaps Holsman was trying to confuse buyers; or perhaps he just didn't think of the ramifications.

The experiment only lasted into 1911, when the $750 cars (with only minor detail changes from the Holsman) disappeared forever.

Holsman trucks

During this same time period, 1908-1910, Henry Holsman built some commercial trucks. Little else is known about them.

Independent Harvester trucks

Henry Holsman and Independent Harvester Company of Plano built a light van in 1910 and 1911, using Holsman's design. These commercial vehicles were powered by a water-cooled four-cylinder engine, and sold for $750.

This Holsman Delivery Wagon, advertised in 1908, was one of Holsman's flings into the commercial vehicle—called truck today—market. It was unsuccessful. (Dan Roen Collection)

Chapter 17

International Harvester Result of Giant Unification

Two farm world giants spoke of unification in 1884, but not until 1902 did McCormick Harvesting Machine Co. and the Deering Harvester Co. join to form farm machinery giant International Harvester Company of Chicago, Illinois. Several other smaller companies made the amalgamation complete: the Plano Harvester Company, and Warder, Bushnell & Glessner Company.

Each company brought its unique inventions and expertise to the new company. As IHC, they eventually manufactured tractors, trucks, buses, and cars.

IHC tractors

Before 1906, the companies that united to form IHC mostly made horse-powered farm machinery. In 1905, IHC's patent of its "Famous" gasoline engines changed all that. Production of tractors followed in 1906.

The first IHC tractor was a Morton traction truck–a platform that allowed a farmer to add an engine and make a tractor–with an IHC motor; 14 were built in 1906, and up to a thousand total from 1907-1910.

Canada's massive prairies needed tractors, and IHC turned to meeting those needs in 1908, with its Mogul Type C 20-hp tractor. Farmers still needed large tractors,

In 1936, IHC made this Farmall F-20. It was 140 inches long, recommended to pull a pair of 14-inch plows with its own 3-3/4- x 5-inch bore and stroke four-cylinder engine. The transmission had four forward speeds, 2-1/4, 2-3/4, 3-1/4, and 3-3/4 mph, and one reverse of 2-3/4 mph. Higher speeds were optional. It could ideally handle a 22-inch thresher, and under optimum conditions take on a 28-incher. It weighed 3,950 pounds. (Dan Roen Collection)

so IHC responded with its Mogul 45 hp in 1911; that year, IHC led the farm industry in tractor sales.

The Mogul 8-16 was the most popular of the series, and Mogul 10-20s were also sold. Ten models were eventually made of Moguls, and ten models of the Titan series were also made.

The introduction of the 15-30 Gear-Drive IHC marked a turning point for the company in 1921, marking its entry into the one-piece cast-iron frame, or unit frame, design. The 10-20 followed in 1923.

Through the years, IHC has made a wide variety of tractors under the McCormick-Deering, Farmall, IHC, and Case/IH lines.

Some representative samples include the International 8-16 tractor, introduced in 1917, which contained a four-cylinder 4- x 5-inch bore and stroke engine, three forward speeds (1-3/4 to 4 mph); the Farmall B rounded out the IH farm tractor line during the 1940s. It weighed 3,740 pounds, came in diesel or gasoline, and used a four-cylinder I-head engine rated at 1,400 rpm with a 3- x 4-inch bore and stroke, a Zenith 61AX7 carburetor, and an IHC H-4 magneto.

The merger of the J. I. Case Company and International Harvester Company in the mid-1980s caught the farm world by surprise.

In 1936, International Harvester Company manufactured this McCormick-Deering Farmall F-12 capable of pulling one 16- or 18-inch plow, or two 10- or 12-inchers with its IHC valve-in-head four-cylinder engine. By this time, many farmers were using mostly small tractors because much of the nation's land had been broken, and farms were small. This tractor had three forward speeds of 2-1/4, 3, and 3-1/4 mph, with a reverse of 2-1/4 mph, and highway speed optional. (Dan Roen Collection)

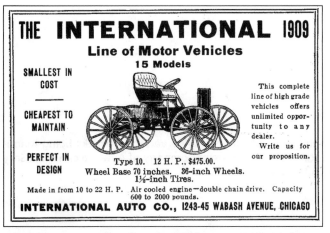

By 1909, International had 15 different models of its automobiles, including the Type 10, 12-hp model depicted here for $475. IHC motors came in horsepowers from 10 to 22. These automobiles had intentionally been made to look like horse buggies, which had served the farm population so well for so many years, and the company figured would convert many people. (Gary Hoonsbeen Collection)

International automobiles

Motor buggy experiments were done in 1899, but automobiles were not approached seriously until 1905 when E. A. Johnston, who had done the original motor buggy work, designed the International Auto-Buggy. It was approved for production a year later, and produced starting in February 1907 in Chicago, and later, Akron, Ohio.

This first car was a two-cylinder, friction-transmission

One of the designations of automobiles built by IHC was called the "Farmer's Automobile," as shown here, with Theodore Roosevelt in the front seat. Roosevelt and Ralph Peters, president of the Long Island Railroad Company (behind the driver), were driven in the afternoon, as the blurb says, "...from Medford to Wading River (no state given), that they might inspect Number 1, and at the same time view the country between the two stations (farms)." (Gary Hoonsbeen Collection)

highwheeler with solid tires; 4,500 units were built. It produced 14 or 16 hp, and sold for $600 as a Model A-passenger runabout or a Model B four-passenger "Farmer's Auto."

In 1910, air- or water-cooled four-cylinder standard models joined the line, and the initials IHC began to appear on the cars. IHC cars were made until 1911, although until 1916, Sunday-go-to-meetin' seats were available for installation in the back of highwheeler truck models, which effectively converted them into cars.

In 1961, IHC entered the automobile market again with the four-wheel-drive Scout cross-country vehicle in a wide range of open or closed bodywork. It also made the Travelall station wagon in 2- or 4-wheel drive and 6- or 8-cylinder V-8. Other options included 3-, 4-, and 5-speed manual gearboxes, or automatic transmissions.

International trucks

International made Auto Wagons in 1909 in the Akron, Ohio plant, and continued through 1912, manufacturing highwheelers using wagon-type wheels up to 44 inches in diameter. In 1912, the name was changed to "Motor Truck," and Models A and M were built. In 1914, "IHC" was changed simply to "International" on the vehicles.

In 1915, a new truck line was introduced, using artillery-type wheels with pressed-on solid rubber tires, or optional pneumatic tires except for the largest 3-1/2-ton model. These models used L-head four-cylinder engines. Five models from 3/4 to 3-1/2 tons were produced in Models H, F, K, G, and L, respectively. These vehicles had rear-mounted radiators for easier servicing.

The Model G engine had the same bore and stroke as the International 8-16 farm tractor. A wide variety of cabs, tops, and bodies for these trucks, along with special attachments, were available through the 1923 production year.

The S truck series followed until 1929. More choices were offered as farmers began to use more and more trucks. The A series with Waukesha or Lycoming engines were produced from 1929-1934. The C trucks begun in

International Harvester Company began making trucks in 1909, and by 1925, when this 3-ton 63 stake truck was built, it was producing seven different models, from the 3/4-ton special delivery, 1-ton speed chassis S, 1-1/2-ton chassis 33, 2-ton chassis 43, 3-ton chassis 63, 4-1/2-ton chassis 94, and 5-ton chassis 103. The Model 63 in this image used a four-cylinder engine of 4-1/4- x 5-inch bore and stroke that produced 28.9 hp, according to the NACC rating. It had four forward gears and one reverse. (Gary Hoonsbeen Collection)

This Farm Implements ad shows a wide variety of trucks being manufactured by International Harvester Company of America ca 1918. (Gary Hoonsbeen Collection)

1934 adapted automotive styling rather than the functional lines of its earlier models.

From 1938-40, the D series trucks were made, then the K trucks which were widely used during World War II, followed by the nearly-identical KB models after the war. The 1950s saw IHC produce L and R model trucks, and the 1960s showed an explosion of truck models, from pickups through semi-tractor models.

In 1986, International's Truck Group adopted the Navistar International Line, and dozens of different models of trucks under both names have been built since then.

International buses

Buses were built by IHC as a body style on the SF-34 and SF-36 models between 1926 and 1929. A 140-inch wheel-

International Harvester Company of Chicago, Illinois, built this Model 54-H-1 Motor Bus in 1925 to hold from 25-33 passengers. It boasted a six-cylinder engine of 4-1/2- x 5-3/4-inch bore and stroke and 48.6 hp. It weighed 8,500 pounds (chassis only), or 16,750 pounds including chassis, body, and load. IHC built buses from 1926-1929. (Gary Hoonsbeen Collection)

base was standard, and a 160-incher could be specially ordered. Disk wheels, hydraulic shock absorbers, and other items were optional equipment.

In 1926, International manufactured motor coaches in four sizes: Model 54-L, 12 to 18 passengers; Model 54-M, 18 to 24 passenger; Model 54-H, 25 to 30 passengers; and Model 54-H, 25- to 33-passenger buses. The 25- to 33-passenger models weighed 16,750 pounds, including motor, body, and "load." The chassis weighed about half that, 8,500 pounds. They were powered by six-cylinder cast-in-pair bore-and-stroke engines 4-1/2 x 5-3/4 inches.

The same 25- to 33-passenger vehicle the next year had a chassis weight of only 8,000 pounds, a carrying weight of a ton less, and a ten-inch-smaller wheelbase, though the engine was exactly the same. IHC quit buses in 1929.

One of International Harvester Company's popular trucks was its "Red Baby," as shown here. An ad for the truck said, "Agriculture smiles her best when Service is at her command. Her millions upon millions of farm machines must be kept at work. Her power equipment must not fail. Her methods must keep pace with the times. ..Thousands of...dealers have equipped themselves with International Speed Trucks like the one pictured on this page–trucks which, because of their flaming red color, speed, and snappy lines, are popularly called Red Babies." (Dan Roen Collection)

Chapter 18

Ransom Eli Olds is the Man Behind Companies

Ransom Eli Olds, founder of Oldsmobile, REO, and other businesses, was the man behind the manufacture of tractors, cars, and trucks.

Oldsmar tractors

In 1915, when a quarter of Lansing, Michigan, was working for Olds' REO Motor Car Company, Ransom Eli Olds tired of his business and turned to land speculation in Florida. He bought 37,541 acres on the north side of Tampa Bay, and formed REO Farms Company, later REOLDS Farm Company. He also built a town called Oldsmar. There in 1917, Olds organized a million-dollar company to manufacture tractors, the Oldsmar Tractor Company.

Oldsmar manufactured small garden tractors.

Kardell tractors

A year later, Olds convinced the owners of Kardell Tractor & Truck Co. of St. Louis to move to Oldsmar. Kardell made the Four-in-One tractor starting in 1917. This 20- to 32-hp machine was a three-wheeled rig designed to do everything on a farm. *Farm Implements* magazine described "4-in-1": "The Kardell motor plow, truck, tractor, and farm power is designed to meet the general requirements of the average diversified farm of from 100 to 500 acres, or over, and with its convertible truck feature will market the farm products just as economically as it will produce them."

The article said the unique tractive design of the wheels, a webbed tread, which loosens rather than packs, yet grips like a horse's hoof, gathers traction on soft ground as well as hard, "and makes it unnecessary to use lugs or cleats to prevent slipping."

The Four-in-One was primarily for plowing, as *FI* magazine said: "The plow unit consists of three 14-inch plows, which are hitched to the front end of the frame by a patented, adjustable spring draw-bar. This 'safety' spring yields enough to release the clutch whenever a rock or stump is encountered, thus stopping the machine automatically and without damage. It also makes it unnecessary to use the extra heavy type of gangs commonly used with tractors, which cause so much excess draft."

The engine was a Waukesha four-cylinder with 4-1/2- x 5-1/4-inch bore and stroke. In 1918, the 5,100-pound tractor sold for $4,600.

Early Oldsmobiles

Ransom Eli Olds worked with his father and brother building small motors, and then steam-powered and later gasoline-powered internal combustion engines for marine and stationary applications. By 1883, Ransom was employed full-time by his father for 50 cents a day, later increased to $2 a day when he invented a successful small steam-powered engine. In 1887, he joined with wagon maker Frank Clark to build a steam-powered auto, followed by a second one in 1892, and his first internal combustion automobile in 1896.

The Oldsmar Tractor Company of Oldsmar, Florida, made its Oldsmar 3-1/2 x 5 tractor with a 99-inch width over handlebars, and a height of 36 inches. It used its own single-cylinder 5-1/8- x 5-inch bore and stroke engine and a Schebler Model D carburetor. Its transmission was through friction belt and pulleys from the engine crankshaft to the drive pinion. It sold for $395 and weighed a mere 1,120 pounds.

This Kardell "4-in-1" tractor was supposed to do pretty much everything on the farm: act as a motor plow, truck, tractor, and farm power for farms mostly under 500 acres, but no smaller than 100 acres. The 4-in-1 was built by Kardell Tractor & Truck Co. in St. Louis, Missouri, before its move to Oldsmar, Florida. (Dan Roen Collection)

A quick perusal of this Kardell ad shows how times have changed for farmers: there is mention of horses ("Replaces five horses on every farm of 200 acres"), then it discusses using the railroad ("The Kardell "Four-in-One" on your farm brings the railroad to your gate"), and the general utility of the tractor as it attempts to be THE tractor that does everything that needs to be done on the farm. (Dan Roen Collection)

In 1887, he built his first crude automobile, powered by a 2-hp Olds steam engine. George S. May wrote in *A Most Unique Machine* that it was "a three-wheeled box with a tiller steering the front wheel in the same way a child's tricycle is steered." It gamboled at 5-10 mph with a rear-mounted engine.

Ten years later, Ransom recalled the event: "I mounted the seat and pulled the lever. She moved slowly, but speed was increased as it went down the platform out of the shop; there was a slight raise, however, before crossing the sidewalk and she refused to ascend the grade, so I at once dismounted, and going behind, gave it a push to be remembered, which did the business, and it reached the sidewalk in safety; I again mounted the seat; there was yet a descent to the street in my favor, so that I had but little trouble reaching the road and running a block without a stop; at this point the efforts of the engine were exhausted, and an assistant was necessary, as it was getting quite light and there was no more time to be lost; I secured two pushers behind, and together with the engine, got it back without an accident, which ended my first trip in a horseless carriage."

That early morning run scared a milk-wagon horse and caused it to bolt, breaking nine quarts of milk and one of buttermilk.

In 1892, he built a four-wheeled cart, powered by two steam engines. He sold this car to a company in London, England, for use in its Bombay, India, offices in 1893.

On Aug. 21, 1897, the Olds Motor Vehicle Company was incorporated with outside investors. R.E. Olds was elected manager. Four to six vehicles were built and tested in 1897, and four were sold.

Olds needed more money, and so reincorporation occurred on May 8, 1899, forming the Olds Motor Works. In 1900, he designed and had built the curved-dash Oldsmobile, and the company was off and running—until March 9, 1901, when fire destroyed the plant.

John A. Heilig says in "Handsome Ransom" in the fall 1993 *Automobile Quarterly* that "James Brady, a timekeeper who discovered the fire and sounded the alarm, pushed the sole surviving car—a Curved Dash runabout—out of the building. Several cars were in the process of construction on the second floor and fell through the floor.

"Legend says that Brady saved not only the car, but the company. The Curved Dash he rescued was allegedly used for measurements to make a new set of drawings to replace those destroyed in the fire," although that is just legend.

The company built 425 cars in 1901, 2,500 in 1902, and 4,000 in 1903, the largest producer of automobiles in the United States at the time.

But the stormy partnership between Olds, and especially Fred Smith, led to Olds' departure from his company.

REO automobiles

On Aug. 4, 1904, Ransom Eli Olds was back in the automobile business with his R. E. Olds Company. By Oct. 15, 1904, REO completed testing on its first of two experimental cars, a five-passenger touring car weighing 1,500 pounds and using a horizontally opposed two-cylinder, 16-hp engine. It was priced at $1,250. Later that fall, a two-passenger runabout for $650 was offered, targeting the Olds company Ransom had just left.

REOs sold well: 2,456 in 1906 (his cross-town Olds company only sold 1,600), and in 1907, gross sales topped

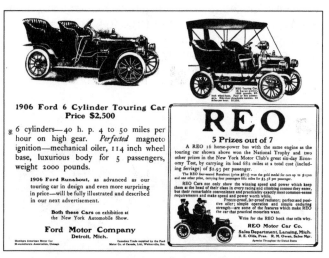

In 1906, REO and Ford automobile ads appeared together, showing the types of cars for sale and their prices. The REO touring car in the upper right hand corner sold for half of the Ford six-cylinder touring car in the upper left hand corner, $1,250 to $2,500. But mostly Ransom Olds wasn't worried about Ford Motor Company; he was more concerned about his former Olds Motor Company, and was at this time starting to sell more cars than Olds. (Gary Hoonsbeen Collection)

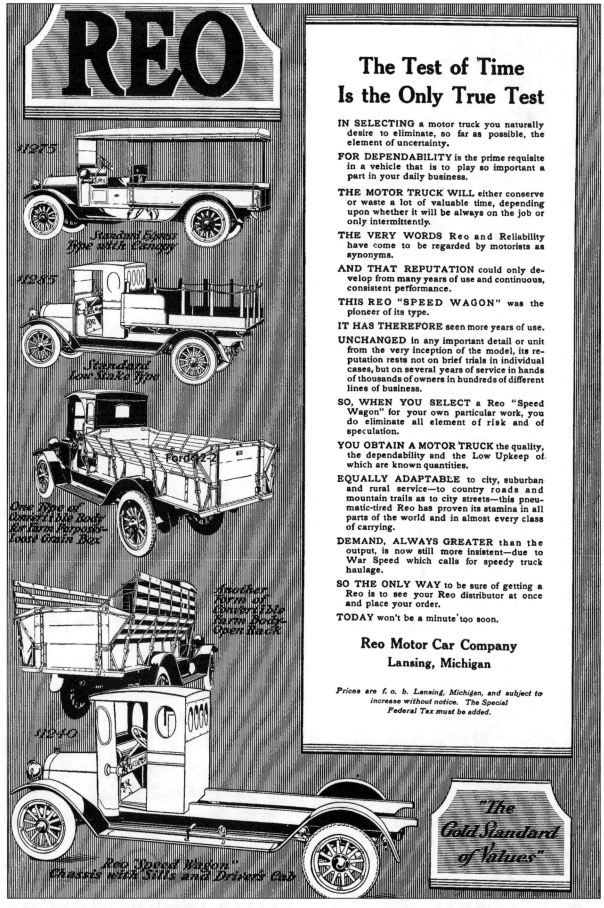

REO

The Test of Time Is the Only True Test

IN SELECTING a motor truck you naturally desire to eliminate, so far as possible, the element of uncertainty.

FOR DEPENDABILITY is the prime requisite in a vehicle that is to play so important a part in your daily business.

THE MOTOR TRUCK WILL either conserve or waste a lot of valuable time, depending upon whether it will be always on the job or only intermittently.

THE VERY WORDS Reo and Reliability have come to be regarded by motorists as synonyms.

AND THAT REPUTATION could only develop from many years of use and continuous, consistent performance.

THIS REO "SPEED WAGON" was the pioneer of its type.

IT HAS THEREFORE seen more years of use.

UNCHANGED in any important detail or unit from the very inception of the model, its reputation rests not on brief trials in individual cases, but on several years of service in hands of thousands of owners in hundreds of different lines of business.

SO, WHEN YOU SELECT a Reo "Speed Wagon" for your own particular work, you do eliminate all element of risk and of speculation.

YOU OBTAIN A MOTOR TRUCK the quality, the dependability and the Low Upkeep of which are known quantities.

EQUALLY ADAPTABLE to city, suburban and rural service—to country roads and mountain trails as to city streets—this pneumatic-tired Reo has proven its stamina in all parts of the world and in almost every class of carrying.

DEMAND, ALWAYS GREATER than the output, is now still more insistent—due to War Speed which calls for speedy truck haulage.

SO THE ONLY WAY to be sure of getting a Reo is to see your Reo distributor at once and place your order.

TODAY won't be a minute too soon.

Reo Motor Car Company
Lansing, Michigan

Prices are f. o. b. Lansing, Michigan, and subject to increase without notice. The Special Federal Tax must be added.

"The Gold Standard of Values"

Under the aegis of Ransom Eli Olds, his new REO company made many vehicles, including this variety of trucks. REO Motor Company of Lansing, Michigan, came into being because Olds and his partners in his original company, Olds Motor Vehicle Company, could not decide which direction the company should go. (Gary Hoonsbeen Collection)

What could be better advertising for REO Motor Car Company of Lansing or better for sales than having the President of the United States go for his first public automobile ride in a REO, in this REO Motor Car Company photo from 1907. Roosevelt is in the rear right of the auto, behind the driver. Ransom Eli Olds is the driver. (Gary Hoonsbeen Collection)

$4 million. In 1911, REO built what it considered its best car, REO the Fifth. "To that," Olds said, "I have added all I have learned in 25 years of continuous striving. So this car, I believe, comes pretty close to finality."

By 1915, Ransom Olds turned control of REO over to Richard H. Scott, and headed to Florida for some land speculating. REO manufactured autos and trucks until 1936.

REO trucks

In 1910, the REO Motor Truck Company was announced in Lansing, with Ransom Olds holding 51-percent interest. The first trucks were the 3/4-ton Model H and the 1/4-ton Model J light delivery truck for $600. Both used a 12-hp engine. The 3/4 had double-chain drive, the 1/4 single. Wheelbases were 86 and 78 inches, respectively. The Model H sold for $750 in 1912.

Other REO models included the Power Wagon, Parcel Delivery model, Speed Wagon, 2-ton Heavy-Duty Speed Wagon, DA and DC model trucks, and many more.

REO made trucks until 1967.

REO buses

In 1935, in agreement with Mack, REO began building buses as a competitive measure. The Mack Junior series consisted of the 1/2-ton 1M, 1-1/2-ton 10M, 2-ton 20M, 3-ton 30M, and a Traffic type 3-ton 30MT, with the engine between the seats.

REO also built school buses, and during World War II, built 300 front-engine buses for the U.S. Navy. It also built a postwar "Victory" bus. REO built buses for a number of years afterward.

Heilig wrote, "Olds never attained the reputation of Henry Ford, partly due to reversals suffered by both the Olds Motor Works and the REO Motor Car Company, primarily because of Olds' inattention to detail and the lack of Ford's driving passion. Where Ford would plow everything back into the company, Olds would use his financial profits for travel or investment."

Nevertheless, "Those labors were also sufficient to ensure his immortality in the world of the automobile."

This REO two-passenger coupe G was a 1926 product of the REO Motor Car Company of Lansing. It used a six-cylinder 3-3/16- x 5-inch bore and stroke engine, with 24.3 rated hp to drive the machine. It sold for $1,495, $100 more than the five-passenger touring E, $100 less than the five-passenger Sedan G, and $200 less than the two-passenger roadster E model Reo for 1926. (Gary Hoonsbeen Collection)

Ransom Olds' REO Motor Car Company built this two-ton heavy-duty speed-wagon in 1926, and sold the 9,230-pound (gross weight) vehicle for $2,310; the chassis alone (3,925 pounds) sold for $1,985. The two-ton used a six-cylinder 3-3/16- x 5-inch bore and stroke engine to produce 24.3 rated hp. (Gary Hoonsbeen Collection)

Chapter 19

Lenox Tractors

Lenox Motor Car Company of Hyde Park, Massachusetts brought out its four-wheel-drive Lenox American Model 20 in 1918. This 20-30 tractor cost $2,500 and ran on a four-cylinder Wisconsin T-head engine with 4-3/4-inch bore and 5-1/2-inch stroke. It weighed 6,500 pounds, but was only produced for one year.

Lenox automobiles

The forerunner to the Lenox Motor Car Company was the Martell Motor Car Company of Jamaica Plain, Massachusetts, which organized in 1908, but never produced an automobile. Lenox took the company over in 1910.

Chester T. Bates designed the first Lenox; he had earlier designed the Morse automobile. The first Lenox was introduced at the Boston Automobile Show in 1911. Five body designs were produced the first two years, including Model A roadster two passenger and four passenger, Model A touring five passenger, Model D speedster, and Model E limousine, which sold for $2,750. The other four sold for $1,800.

While claiming the motto, "The Only Car Made in Boston," the truth was that Lenox looked outside Boston for better plants, and moved to Hyde Park in 1913. It built the Model 4-40 in 1913 in four body styles. This 118-inch wheelbase auto sold from $2,000 to $3,250, depending on style; and the Model 6-60 as a seven-passenger touring car for $2,750, and a seven-passenger limousine for $4,050. These models were sold in 1914, along with different body styles for the Model 6-60: seven-passenger MC touring and NC limousine; five-passenger AC touring; 2-, 3-, or 4-passenger DC roadster; EC torpedo speed car for two people; five-passenger FC limousine; and HC touring for four passengers.

Lenox moved its factory to Lawrence, Massachusetts in 1915 to build trucks and tractors. Lenox serial numbers ran from 100-215 for models CB and DB in 1912; 1000-2000 the next year for models AC and DC, and 15-1525 for model MC; 2000-2015 in 1914 for model A and D; 1525-1550 for model M the same year; 2015 for models A1 and D1 in 1915; 1551-1563 for model M1 the same year; 2500 and 2530 on for model O in 1916 and 1917; and 2554 for series 33 in 1918.

Lenox trucks

A three-ton truck was built in 1916, but little is known about it. Entering the truck and tractor field probably doomed Lenox, as it spread its resources too thin. In January 1917, the assembly line was shut down.

The Lenox Motor Car Company of Jamaica Plain, Massachusetts, manufactured this 1913 Lenox Model 4-40, a four-cylinder, 40-hp touring car for five passengers, costing $2,000. Lenox also made a model 6-60 that year, a six-cylinder, 60-hp machine in two styles for seven passengers.

It is peculiar that companies with particular names–the Lenox Motor Car Company, for instance–decided to go out of its areas of expertise and build, in this case, tractors. The results are often predictable, as with this Model 20 tractor, which weighed 6,500 pounds, and used a four-cylinder Wisconsin T-head engine with a 4-3/4-inch bore and 5-1/2-inch stroke engine, which was built in 1916 and only lasted two more years.

Chapter 20

Moline Plow Company One of the Early Farm Players

The history of the Moline Plow Company of Moline, Illinois stretches back to 1852, when Henry W. Candee, Robert K. Swan, and Andrew Friberg bought a fanning mill factory and began manufacturing hay rakes, chain pumps, and other goods.

Candee, Swan & Company brought in a plowmaker in 1865, and when more capital was needed, George W. Stephens was taken in as a third partner. Other partners joined the firm until in 1870, the six partners renamed it the Moline Plow Company.

Moline tractors

In 1913, Moline Plow Company completed a tractor design, and contracted with International Harvester Corporation to build five experimental models. But tests proved unsatisfactory, so the idea was discontinued until 1915, when Moline Plow Co. bought Universal Tractor Company of Columbus, Ohio, which had just organized the year before and was building motor cultivators with a two-cylinder 4-hp engine, selling for $385.

Moline redesigned the Universal, adding a four-cylinder engine with an electric starter, lighting, and electric governor. In 1917, it used its own engines. The Model D was built from 1918-23, the last year of tractor production at Moline Plow Co. The D weighed 3,380 pounds, used a 3-1/2- x 5-inch bore and stroke four-cylinder motor operating at 1,800 rpm and selling for $1,325 in 1920. Tractors designed like this had a tendency to tip easily, so concrete

On Jan. 31, 1909, the Moline team completed the Glidden Tour race in Kansas City. All of them competed for the same trophy, and all finished the tour, itself a victory. Each of them accumulated a number of penalty points: car No. 100 had 8.3, No. 101 had 1.1, and No. 102 had 49.4. (Gary Hoonsbeen Collection)

ballast was added inside the drive wheels.

In 1929, after a few difficult years, Moline Plow Company merged with Minneapolis Steel Manufacturing Company and Minneapolis Threshing Machine companies to form Minneapolis Moline.

Stephens automobiles

Moline entered the automobile manufacture business for two reasons: it wasn't selling enough farm machinery to stay afloat, and G. A. Stephens headed the company.

E. T. Birdsall, who designed the Selden automobile and many others, was called in to design the prototype Stephens in 1916. The first Stephens Salient Six cars were produced for $1,150 in 1917, for a five-passenger touring

This Moline tractor is discing in North Dakota sometime about 1918. Moline Plow Company combined with two other companies to form Minneapolis-Moline in 1929. (Richard Birklid Collection. Dan Roen Collection)

This illustration shows a Stephens Model 74 sport touring four-passenger car. It was built starting in 1917, and sold for $1,550. It sported a narrow body that was much lower than the standard touring car, and the rear seat was finished in black walnut, along with the instrument door. It also had a drop door in the rear of the seat for steamer rugs and blankets. (Roy Bernick Collection)

The Stephens Model 74 also came in this Special four-passenger Victoria model. (Roy Bernick Collection)

This 1918 Stephens Salient Six made its first appearance in August of that year with its new overhead-valve six, and in a pair of passenger styles, the Model 70, a three-passenger roadster, and the Model 75, a five-passenger touring car. Both of these vehicles had the graceful streamlining and the deep-set seats of their time. They had French-piped Turkish upholstery and ventilating rain vision windshields. Wheelbase on both models was 118 inches. (Roy Bernick Collection)

model or a three-passenger roadster. Continental engines were used that year only.

The 1918 Stephens autos used Root & Vandervoort Engineering Company engines, and in 1919, John North Willys bought a controlling interest in the company, though he kept it separate from his Willys-Overland Company. Moline bought Root & Vandervoort in 1920, and though it made good sense because the company was buying 80 percent of that company's output, it didn't make sense because of the depression that followed.

The Stephens motor department was separated from the Moline Plow Company in 1922, and the Stephens Motor Car Company formed. These were formalities, as the same controllers and board of directors stayed with the company through the Willys change and the Stephens Motor Car Company changes.

Stephens cars were not stylish, but they were dependable, and despite the company's second-best production year ever in 1923, the Stephens autos were phased out in 1924. Models 10 and 20, manufactured in 1923, were six-cylinder engines of 59 and 57 hp, respectively, and 117-

and 124-inch wheelbases. Seven different varieties were manufactured and sold.

Moline trucks

Moline produced the Model 10 Moline truck in 1920, a 1-1/2-ton capacity vehicle powered by a "well-known" Moline four-cylinder engine (similar to the one used in the Universal tractor) with a three-speed transmission, 130-inch wheelbase, and selling for $1,695.

Farm Implements and Tractors magazine hailed the new truck thus: "After many months of experimental and development work, the Moline Plow Company announces that on Oct. 1, it will start production of motor trucks in large quantities. Experimental trucks have completed exhaustive test runs, the majority of which have been throughout the Southwest, where these trucks have been driven under almost every conceivable road condition. Results of these tests show remarkable truck performance."

Electric lights, generator, and starter were extras. "The design also provides for a power take off assembly as an

In 1904, Moline made this Moline touring runabout automobile, a two-cylinder, 12-hp machine with 74-inch wheelbase, selling for $1,000.

This 1-1/2-ton Moline motor truck was first offered in 1920 by the Moline Plow Company of Moline, Illinois. It was powered by virtually the same engine used in the Universal tractor, a Moline four-cylinder valve-in-head type with large-size bearings, force-fed lubrication, and it "possesses," *Farm Implements and Tractors* says, "an unusual amount of power for its size." Additionally, since the truck was going to be marketed through Moline implement and tractor dealers, *FIAT* wrote, "...it is an unusually attractive proposition from (the dealer's) standpoint as they now have stocks of repairs for this motor on hand, as well as service men who are familiar with every detail of its construction." (Gary Hoonsbeen Collection)

extra," *FIAT* says, "which can be put to many uses. It is so arranged that it can be set into operation from the driver's seat and started or stopped at will. A 12-inch pulley is regularly applied, or chain sprocket if desired.

"The Model 10 truck was designed primarily to serve all the purposes of the farmer and fits in admirably with the other power farming implements of this company."

Unfortunately, the Moline truck was discontinued in 1923, probably an after-shock of the early 1920s' agricultural depression.

Moline Plow Company offered this 1-1/2-ton Moline truck in different varieties, including with the stake bed shown here. *Farm Implements and Tractors* wrote of the truck, "There is also evidence in the design of attention to small details such as automatic grease gun connections, with gun; a rugged and durable accelerator assembly; a self-aligning dry plate clutch; rubber bumpers; fan with forced feed lubrication; 2-inch fan belt; strong pressed steel fenders; automatic mechanical-type governor; durable three-piece pressed steel hood; powerful screw-type jack; high-tension magneto with automatic impulse starter; truck odometer driven direct from transmission and mounted to dash; tire carrier assembly applied to runningboard; power driven pump attached to transmission; tool kit containing heavy and practical tools; towing hook attached to frame. All of the above are included as standard equipment." (Gary Hoonsbeen Collection)

This photo shows the rear view of the Moline 1-1/2-ton Moline truck. *Farm Implement and Tractors* said that now that the Moline truck was available, with the Moline tractor and Moline tractor implements, "...practically any farm can now be profitably motorized." (Dan Roen Collection)

Chapter 21

The First Plymouth Company Hailed From Ohio

The first Plymouth vehicle was built by a small Ohio company, not by the giant Chrysler Corporation of Detroit, Michigan, as most people assume. But in the end, the big corporation won out on the name.

In 1909, J. D. Fate joined forces with a group of investors from Toledo, Ohio, and merged with The Commercial Truck Company to form the Plymouth Truck Company to build trucks and sightseeing buses. Production was planned for Toledo, but was shortly moved to Plymouth, Ohio, where it would remain, best-known as the Fate-Root-Heath Company.

The concept for a Plymouth car and Plymouth truck were developed in 1909 in a machine shop of the Plymouth Motor Truck Co.

The Plymouth tractor

In 1933, F-R-H entered the farm tractor business with the Plymouth 10-20, powered by a 20-hp Hercules 1XA four-cylinder motor (3-inch bore x 4-inch stroke.) An unusual feature was the "speed gear" of the four-speed transmission. For field work, the tractor could work as slow as 1 mph, but for "transport," fourth gear provided a top speed of 25 mph. Standard equipment included steel-disc wheels, with rubber tire wheels offered as optional equipment. Also available was a power take off unit in any of the three positions on the tractor (side, draw bar, or splint shaft at the

rear). Following the practice of the 1910 Plymouth (of Ohio) car, the Plymouth tractor combined the hood and gas tank into one unit. Emblazoned prominently on the vee'd radiator shell was the name PLYMOUTH (vertically).

Only 232 Plymouth tractors were made before Walter Chrysler of Chrysler Corporation sued F-R-H over the Plymouth name. Rather than fight a giant company which had deep pockets, Fate-Root-Heath settled the suit for $1, giving rights of the Plymouth name to Chrysler.

Now the Plymouth tractor had to be renamed. An engineer who worked there said, "(The directors) thought (the Plymouth tractor) was the king of all the tractors on the market, and wanted to change the name to king, but there was already a king tractor on the market. They didn't want to give up the king part. One gentleman around the board table had brought a bouquet of silver foliage to put on the boardroom table. Someone said, 'Let's call it Silver King.' "

About 8,600 Silver King tractors were made from 1934-1954; 1937 was F-R-H's best year, when it sold 1,000 tractors because the mower industry was good. F-R-H also made an industrial model tractor. Like its locomotives and many of its trucks, many of the tractors that F-R-H made were custom-made. And because it made a lot of different models—it made ten models alone in one year—all of them are a little bit different from each other.

Silver King tractors were the first to come with a starter, and lights, and rubber tires. Silver Kings were shipped

SILVER KING MODEL R38
Fate-Root Heath Co., Plymouth, O.

This Silver King Model R38 tractor was manufactured by Fate-Root-Heath Company of Plymouth, Ohio, in 1936, and weighed in at only 2,170 pounds. It was recommended to pull one 14-inch plow with its Hercules IXA 3- x 4-inch bore and stroke engine. By rights, this tractor should have remained to be named "Plymouth," if not for some bullying tactics by Chrysler to make sure it owned the Plymouth name. F-R-H had used the name in the early 1900s on several vehicles.

Fate-Root-Heath Company manufactured this Silver King Model R66 in its Plymouth, Ohio, plant in 1936, its third year of production, second as Silver King. The R66 could plow five acres in a 10-hour day with one 14-inch plow. The vehicle was powered by a Hercules four-cylinder 3- x 4-inch bore and stroke engine at 1,400 rpm. It weighed 2,400 pounds.

from the factory they were sent, with both rubber and steel in case the farmer didn't want rubber. But everybody kept the Goodyear Diamond tread rubber tires.

The *Silver King News* said, "We wish every Silver King owner could visit our plant in Plymouth, O. First, you would see the foundry, equipped with all the modern methods for pouring quality castings, then follow them through the machine shops to the assembly line. You'd understand why Silver King tractors are built as nearly perfect as possible.

"The employees of The Fate-Root-Heath Co. pledge themselves to Quality First."

Eventually, Charley Heath wanted to get out of making tractors, so all rights to the tractors were sold. A few more were made before Silver Kings disappeared from the history of tractor-making entirely.

The First Plymouth Car

In 1910, F-R-H came out with a Plymouth car powered by a four-cylinder engine and a double-disc truck transmission with a chain drive to the axle.

It was a seven-passenger touring car body mounted on a 112-inch wheelbase truck chassis, using a 40-hp Wisconsin engine and double friction drive transmission and chain drive (which would also be used on the Plymouth truck.) It carried an unusual feature on the hood: a dome with a gasoline filler cap 8 inches across, designed for the motorist to pour a three-gallon bucket of gasoline into it and down into

the gravity-flow tank. Like many luxury cars of the time, this Plymouth Gasoline Pleasure Vehicle was a massive affair with a water-cooled engine, called a five-passenger torpedo, that traveled 35-40 mph (fast enough considering the state of the roads in 1910) and cost $2,500.

On its maiden voyage, the car suffered a broken cylinder casting, which necessitated the car's being shipped back to Ohio on a train car, and the directors on a passenger train, where they decided to limit the touring car production to one.

Tom Root, of Plymouth, Ohio, son of Percy Root, said, "The car's crude transmission was not suitable for a long life and Henry Ford was building a better automobile."

He says most local historians assume the car that was made was dismantled, "but no one really knows for sure." He says the chassis was the same kind used to build trucks and buses at the Plymouth Motor Truck Co., so it may have been reused for another vehicle. "It just plain disappeared," Root says, "and that's too bad."

Plymouth trucks

The first Plymouth trucks, from 1/2-ton to 3-ton capacity, were built beginning in 1906 using four-cylinder Continental engines, friction transmissions and double-chain drives. Six years later, only two trucks were offered, a 1-ton model powered by a 25.6-hp four-cylinder engine, and a 20-ton truck, powered by a 40-hp four-cylinder en-

This early Plymouth from Ohio automobile was the only one ever built because it did not fare well on its maiden voyage. Its maximum speed was about 40 mph, plenty fast for roads of that day. It disappeared and nobody knows whether the parts of this car were used for Plymouth trucks, or if the vehicle was trashed, or whatever. The Plymouth car was built in 1910. (Tom Root Collection)

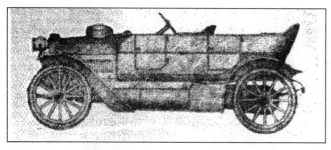

Plymouth Motor Truck Company of Plymouth, Ohio, built one automobile, a huge touring car powered by a four-cylinder 40-hp Wisconsin engine. It had a domed bulge on the hood to house a gravity-feed gasoline tank with a filler cap eight inches in diameter to allow gasoline to be poured in from an ordinary bucket. The car was only built in 1910, for $2,500, because it did not do well on a test drive to New York City.

gine. These trucks sported "cyclops" headlights, a single beam perched on top of the dashboard, with two small lights at the sides.

Some trucks were powered by "square" Rutenber four-cylinder engines (bore and stroke both being 5 inches), with a high tension Splitdorf multi-unit coil ignition and Hancock valve-less automatic force-feed oilers. Later Plymouth trucks utilized Waukesha four-cylinder engines. A unique feature of the trucks was their "gear-less" transmissions which, in actuality, were friction drives. The drive train consisted of a front-drive shaft from the engine which turned a large flywheel near the middle of the chassis. Against this flywheel were two friction discs running at right angles, which transmitted power to still another rotating disc that was parallel to the first flywheel, power being transferred from this flywheel to chains running to each rear wheel.

About 200 trucks were built through 1915, when the line was discontinued because there were better products on the market, and the company could no longer compete.

The Plymouth bus

Plymouth touring buses from three-seaters to those carrying 40 passengers were built by F-R-H. Prices ranged from $1,250 for a delivery wagon to $5,000 for the largest

truck. These trucks were built "to order," as evidenced by a 1911 order contract, dated Aug. 4, 1911, calling for the company to build a "1912 Model H three-ton truck" for the Rose & Johnson Company of nearby Youngstown. Specifications called for a four-cylinder Waukesha motor, 34- x 3-1/2-inch front and dual 36 x 3 rear tires of either Goodyear, Goodrich, or Firestone origin. The truck, priced at $2,475, was to be delivered on or about Aug. 15th–actual delivery took place Sept. 12th, when the truck was shipped to Youngstown by rail.

The Plymouth locomotive

In 1912, a regular customer, the Bigelow Clay Company, asked F-R-H to build a truck.

But a special truck that would run on a rail of 36-inch gauge. That excited the directors, and led to the launching of locomotive serial No. 1, on March 20, 1914, delivered to the National Fire Proofing Company in Haydenville, Ohio, called the Model AL Type 1. These locomotives were serial numbered consecutively with trucks which were being built at the same time.

Each locomotive was built to order, with size and power matched to the customer needs. By October 1920, the company had built a thousand locomotives. By 1974, 7,000.

Today, it is called Plymouth Locomotive International.

Plymouth trucks were made by Fate-Root-Heath Company of Plymouth, Ohio, in its first incarnation as a company in Toledo, where it was called the Commercial Motor Truck Company. The company also built a Plymouth automobile about this time, and in the early 1930s sold the rights to the use of the Plymouth name to General Motors. This 1907 Plymouth was a stake bed truck.

A line drawing of the early Plymouth of Ohio car.

Plymouth made trucks and small buses in its Plymouth, Ohio plant. About 200 of them were manufactured. This is about a 1909 vehicle. (Tom Root Collection)

This 1912 photo shows the first Plymouth locomotive, with one of the Fates. The company got into building locomotives quite by accident, when another company asked it to make a special truck; the end result was a locomotive and became the mainstay of the Plymouth, Ohio, company.

Chapter 22

Renaissance Man Develops Tractors, Cars, Trucks

Milton O. Reeves must have been a fascinating fellow: he studied the lives of musical composers, gave money to the elderly, started a church and was its pastor, played games, received the Edison Award in 1910 for his inventions, and had a prose piece written about his automobile by a well-known writer; yet, in the end, he gave credit to the encouragement, companionship, and inspiration of his wife.

When he started working for his brother's Reeves Pulley Company, he saw the workers could not control the speed of the pulleys used to power the wood-cutting saws. The high speeds caused wood to split and resulted in a great deal of profit-cutting waste. To prevent that, he developed the variable-speed transmission. He also invented the variable-speed transmission for automobiles, and more than a hundred other items.

His newspaper obituary said: "An inventive genius, M.O. Reeves originated and designed the two chief products manufactured by the Reeves Pulley Company, the Reeves variable speed transmission and the Reeves pulley. "After the variable-speed transmission had been brought out, Mr. Reeves' inventive and mechanical ability began to assert itself and much of his time for many years was spent in experimentations and in the perfection of mechanical devices of various kinds..."

Milton Reeves was in one way or another involved in all the Reeves Columbus, Indiana, companies: Reeves Pulley Company, Reeves & Company, Sexto-Octo Company, and others.

Reeves tractors

Reeves began making steam traction engines about eleven years after beginning operations in 1874. Its trac-

Two men using this 40-65 Reeves in 1914 in North Dakota took a break for the camera. Notice that the extension on the rear wheels are not nearly as large as those in the previous photo. The 40-64 Reeves contained the same engine in the Twin City 40-65, since Reeves & Company of Columbus, Indiana, used Minneapolis Steel & Machinery Company to make their engines. MSMC also made Twin City tractors. (Richard Birklid Collection)

tion engines were probably best known for the Clay valve that gave a sharp cutoff and greater economy of steam.

A 1904 yearbook describes the company this way: "From a comparatively small concern, Reeves & Company have grown until it is now one of the largest plants in its line of manufacture, with an annual output of over six hundred complete threshing outfits, and in addition to this has a

It appears the whole family came out to celebrate on this day somewhere in North Dakota, where this picture was taken about 1914. Notice the little girl standing on the hood of the tractor behind the large right wheel; also notice the extensions used on the wheels to get better traction and to pack less of the soil. (Richard Birklid Collection)

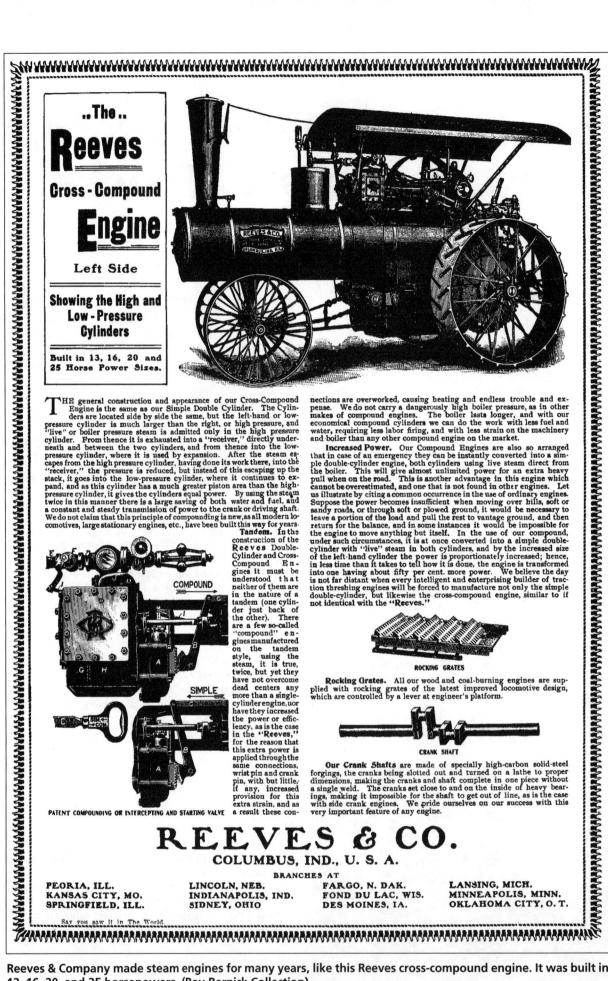

Reeves & Company made steam engines for many years, like this Reeves cross-compound engine. It was built in 13, 16, 20, and 25 horsepowers. (Roy Bernick Collection)

This Motocycle was a 20-passenger bus shipped to Pierre, South Dakota in 1898, but was eventually returned because the roads in that area were too poor and the machine couldn't navigate well.

large trade in clover hullers and their other specialties. They now employ over six hundred men in the home factory... They also have eleven branch houses located in the principal wheat-growing districts of the United States."

In 1910, Reeves & Company built its first tractor, a large four-cylinder machine with an engine built by Minneapolis Steel & Machinery Company (identical to the engine in the Twin City 40-65.) But the tractor never did do well, partly because Reeves & Company was sold to Emerson-Brantingham Company of Rockford, Illinois.

Motorcycle automobiles

In 1888, Milton O. Reeves, his brothers, and uncles, bought the Edinberg Pulley Company and formed the Reeves Pulley Company. There, Milton began work on a variable-speed pulley, and got a bright idea: that it would work in the fledgling automobile industry.

In 1896, he built a pair of variable-speed transmissions, one to install in his Motocycle automobile, and the other in the Reeves Pulley Company plant to vary the speed on a 24- x 10-inch lathe. He bought a gasoline engine from Sintz Gas Engine Company, a two-cylinder, two-cycle, 6-hp marine engine with a reputation of reasonable reliability.

The first successful test was Sept. 26, 1896. This first automobile in Indianapolis, Indiana was noted for gradations of speed up to a top one of 15 mph; automobiles of the time generally ran in one speed.

Milton Reeves was generally satisfied with this vehicle, but figured it was too heavy, plus the engine didn't run as well as he would have liked.

So he built a second Motocycle, which seated seven. This vehicle was known as "Big Seven." Two more Motocycles were built, one a lightweight four-seater built for Claude Sintz; the other was a lightweight vehicle planned to be built for speed.

In January 1898, Milton reported to the Reeves directors: "So far as the devices which I placed on the machine were concerned, they have done their work as well as I had expected, but so many other things have annoyed me at times that I have been discouraged with the machine as a whole.

"Among these I might mention vibration, odor and vapor from exhaust of engine, vapor from cooling water, and others too numerous to mention..."

In 1899, Milton dropped out of the automobile business because better transmissions had been invented for cars; however, in industrial uses, his variable speed transmission was doing very well.

Sears Model "L" Runabout

Price, $495.00

Without Dust Cover

WE FIND that a great many of our customers prefer a car with pneumatic tires, and in order to supply their wants, we manufacture what we call our Model "L." It is similar to all our other runabout models in construction, the difference being in the diameter of the wheels and tires. In order to save our customers all unnecessary tire troubles and expense, we have equipped this car with a 32x3-inch pneumatic tire of the very highest quality. This size tire gives a greater tire capacity than is ordinarily found on runabouts, and the light weight of the car combined with the large size tire means the greatest economy in tire expense. This car is particularly desirable for city use.

No. 21D777   Price, $495.00

Page Six   Sears, Roebuck and Co., Chicago, Ill.

For four years starting in 1908, Reeves components were sold to Sears, Roebuck & Co. to manufacture Sears automobiles. Most of these autos had high buggy wheels fitted with cushion or solid rubber tires. Without a dust cover, the Sears Model L Runabout shown here sold for $495. Tires were a great problem in those days, as the ad says: "In order to save our customers all unnecessary tire troubles and expense, we have equipped this car with a 32- x 3-inch pneumatic tire of the very highest quality." (Roy Bernick Collection)

One of the oddest automobiles ever built was this Reeves Octoauto, immortalized in prose by a famous writer of the time, Elbert Hubbard. The Octoauto had eight wheels, and the goal of the machine was to make a truly smooth ride. None of the machines were ever sold, perhaps due to their $3,200 price–quite a princely sum in 1911 and 1912. (Roy Bernick Collection)

Reeves automobiles

However, Milton did not lose interest in automobiles entirely. After tinkering with a Haynes-Apperson runabout in 1902, by 1904 he had other automobile ideas. Those resulted in two air-cooled, four-cylinder, gasoline engine designs, prototypes that were soon completed and made into running automobiles that could be sold. Ten were made by 1905, four Model D and Six Model E cars.

The D used a bore-and-stroke engine that was 3-1/4 x 3-1/4 inches and 12 hp, while the E had a larger 4- x 4-inch bore and stroke, four-cylinder, 18- to 20-hp engine. Only engines were offered for sale for 1906 as the cars continued to be tests; however, the Ds and Es were sold locally at this time.

Other Reeves automobiles built and sold over the next few years included the Model S, Model N, and others. Eventually stationary gasoline engines were built, and that was the last of the engine effort from Reeves Pulley Company. Production ceased in 1910.

The Octoauto and the Sextoauto

That still didn't stop Milton O. Reeves. In 1911, he formed the Reeves Sexto-Octo Company and turned to the manufacture of some of the oddest-looking cars ever made in autodom, the Sextoauto and the Octoauto, multi-wheeled cars with six and eight tires.

This drawing shows a side view of the driving and very last steering axle of the Sextoauto. Literature said, "The spring A is pivoted at B, which allows perfect freedom of action of these two axles to fit all road conditions, and yet holds them in true alignment with the frame of the car. The end of the spring lying upon the driving axle is clipped to allow for the slight movement which takes place here as the spring acts. The steering mechanism of the rear axle is also shown up to its connection with the bell crank lever..." (Roy Bernick Collection)

The Sextoauto was built by Milton O. Reeves in 1912, after the Octoauto, and was called the Octoauto's "sister." This machine cost $5,000, and was simply too odd-looking and/or too expensive to sell. Reeves formed the Sexto-Octo Company to build the machines outside of his normal business ventures with Reeves Pulley Company, and Reeves & Company, both of Columbus, Indiana. (Roy Bernick Collection)

The Octoauto was eventually converted to the Sextoauto, and is shown in this drawing as a Sextoauto limousine. Specifications included 4 3/4 x 5 1/2 inches bore and stroke, 156-inch wheelbase, and seating room for six. (Roy Bernick Collection)

These were titled the "Easiest Riding Cars in the World," and followed the premise that more tires equals more comfort. Reeves wanted an auto that would "float" over bumps and rough streets. Thus came the Octoauto, which was praised in two pages of prose by well-known writer Elbert Hubbard.

"In the Reeves Octoauto," Hubbard wrote, "the load is distributed over eight wheels, instead of four. In a four-wheeled automobile, a wheel at each corner carries one-fourth of the load. In case of an imperfection in the road, the sudden dropping down into a rut, one wheel may for an instant carry half the load, and it is this sudden jolt and burden that causes the tire trouble."

The Octoauto was a modified Overland automobile of 1910 or 1911. The length of the Octoauto–248 inches–was a huge drawback, along with its price of $3,200. None were ever sold.

In the summer of 1912, Milton bought a brand new Stutz, and converted it into the six-wheeled Sextoauto. Its price was $5,000, and none were ever sold.

By this time, Milton O. Reeves was indeed finished with the automobile; he made patents for other companies, worked for the Pulley Company, but nothing more on automobiles.

Reeves buses

During the late 1890s, Milton O. Reeves built a pair of buses powered by two-cylinder Sintz engines with a variable speed geared transmission of Reeves' design, and double-chain drive. The "Big Seven" bus had three rows of seats in ascending elevation for seven passengers.

The other bus had room for 20 passengers on a single level. It was sold to a Pierre, South Dakota businessman, and though it worked well, it was too wide-tracked, and would not ride in already-established wagon-wheel ruts, so it was returned to Indiana, where Reeves used it on the Big Four Railroad from Columbus to Hope.

Parts of these buses were possibly used to make other Reeves vehicles.

A rear view of the Sextoauto chassis. (Roy Bernick Collection)

Rear view of chassis.

Chapter 23

Samson Purchased to Enhance Company Competition

Samson Tractor Works of Stockton, California, was a prototype vehicle- manufacturing company of the first two decades of the 20th Century. One of its bosses was a big-name (a flamboyant egomaniac, not necessarily common in other companies), the company merged with others, made its products in several cities, and manufactured more than one type of vehicle, including a car and a truck.

Samson Tractor Works started in Stockton, California, in 1902, and prospered under the able tutelage of J. M. Kroyer, successfully manufacturing the Samson Sieve-Grip tractor, with an open pattern of wheels that gripped the spongy soil around Stockton. In 1913, the Samson Sieve-Grip won the state fair against all competition in the 6-8 HP category. They sold for $575.

By 1916, during World War I, Samson advertising said the Model S25 had been, for the previous four years, the most popular tractor on the Pacific Coast. A year later, two models were offered by what had now officially become "The Samson Sieve-Grip Tractor Company." Those models were the 6-12, selling for $775, and the 10-25, which retailed for nearly twice that, $1,350.

About this time, William Crapo Durant, who had taken control of a floundering and fledgling Buick Manufacturing Company of Detroit in 1904, and in three years built it to the second largest and most influential automobile manufacturer in the country, was looking for a tractor company to compete with Henry Ford's Fordsons. Samson

Iron Works came under careful scrutiny before Durant and General Motors purchased it.

Durant was still smarting from losing out on an opportunity to control Ford Motor Company, and was burning to compete with Henry Ford. He bought Samson, and fell in love with the idea of producing a motor cultivator.

One of Samson's tractors was its unusual "Iron Horse" tractor, or Samson Model D, first made in 1919, a mechanically operated, chain-driven tractor guided with a pair of reins, like a horse. The claims made for the machine were myriad and all-encompassing: it would do any job a team of two or three horses would do–cultivate corn, mow, harrow, drill, drag, build roads, haul hay, straw, logs, and stoneboats. In an advertising booklet, Bill Galloway of Waterloo, Iowa, an advertising whiz, wrote: "The long-looked-for, long-waited-for, long-wanted and most-talked-about invention–a two- to three-horse, powerful, efficient, easily controlled, economical, short-turning, four-wheel-drive tractor that enables one man to operate both tractor and implement without any assistance–and at a price below what anybody imagined it could be built for–only $630.00!

"Of all the inventions of modern times, including the electric light, automobile, telephone, and airplane, the "Iron Horse" is the greatest invention up to date for the farmer."

The 1,900-pound tractor (actually a motor-cultivator) sold for $450 in 1920, and was powered by a Chevrolet

The Samson Model D Iron Horse tractor was really a gimmick tractor. GMC President William Crapo Durant fell in love with this type of motor cultivator and tried to sell it to farmers on the strength of the reins that controlled it, like horses. It was perhaps a good ploy in that farmers were waxing nostalgic for horses, but the machine itself was not mechanically sound, and it tended to tip easily (which horses did not), and so it was a sales disaster for GMC. It was manufactured by the Samson Tractor Co., a branch of GMC, in Janesville, Wisconsin, and used a valve-in-head 171 cubic inch four-cylinder engine. (Dan Roen Collection)

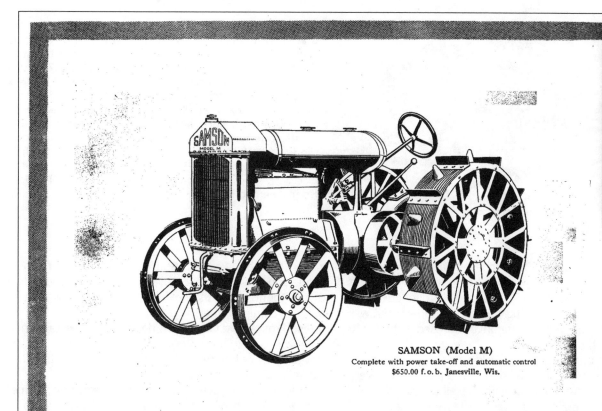

SAMSON (Model M)
Complete with power take-off and automatic control
$650.00 f. o. b. Janesville, Wis.

SAMSON TRACTOR $650

THE above announcement, which appeared in a recent issue of this paper, resulted in receiving thousands of inquiries. Everyone of these we propose to answer in detail. The enormous amount of work involved in classifying these inquiries will, of necessity, delay our replies. On the opposite page, you will find a copy of our letter and the form, which we are asking you to fill out and return to us.

We also invite those who have not answered our first advertisement to fill in blank on opposite page and receive further information.

SAMSON TRACTOR COMPANY,   Janesville, Wisconsin

In 1919, the year after William Crapo Durant and GMC bought the Samson Model M, it sold for $650. Durant's motive in building the Samson Model M was to outdo Henry Ford. Durant had even modeled the M on the Fordson, stripping that tractor down and rebuilding an M by changing some concepts. In the end, it was no contest; the Fordson won hands down. (Dan Roen Collection)

This is the chassis of the Model K-101 A GMC truck manufactured in 1925. Curiously, GMC was one of the only companies that did not advertise the price of its trucks at the time. The chassis weighed 8,975 pounds (21,745 fully loaded), and used a four-cylinder engine with a 4-1/2- x 6-inch bore and stroke, with a 32.4-hp rating. Additional information says that the price includes seat, seat riser, cushion, electric horn, jack, and tool equipment. However, the one-ton chassis was not equipped with a seat. Models for 1925 included the 1-ton K-16, 2-ton K-41, 3-1/2-ton K-71, 5-ton K-101, 5-ton-tractor K-41T, 10-ton tractor K 71-T, and the 15-ton tractor, K-101T. (Gary Hoonsbeen Collection)

engine that was 3-11/16 x 4 inches. It had a four-cylinder vertical motor, high-tension ignition, transmission belt drive, with forward and reverse speeds with independent control for each side of the tractor. No differential was needed. All four wheels were drivers. It used a chain and sprocket final drive.

Under Durant, Samson quickly flooded the market with its new product. Several hundred Iron Horses were sold, but unfortunately for Samson, all but six were returned to the builders. It was riddled with mechanical problems, and could easily tip over.

Next, Durant tried to compete with the Fordson by revamping the Samson M tractor, but with little success (though the Samson M was a better tractor head-to-head; its price was prohibitive).

In 1918, Durant bought Janesville Machine Co. Durant's vision saw Samson provide the farm family with everything it needed, including tractors, cars, and trucks. He was not very successful.

The Samson whole-family car

The lack of success of the Model D tractor perhaps presaged that the Samson automobile might meet a similar fate.

The Samson whole-family car was one of the most unique in the annals of American automotive industry. It was built for multiple uses: the touring car was touted as ideal for taking the farm family to church on Sunday–and livestock or produce to the market the following day.

In *My 25 Years With W. C. Durant*, J. H. Newmark writes, "The body was unusually wide, holding three passengers in the front seat, collapsible seats in the middle of the tonneau for the next three, and the rear seat to take the same number. This unique car aroused much interest. Prospective implement dealers were excited when they were told that they would be appointed distributors. It was a sort of bait held out to them to take on the 'Iron Horse' and the 'Samson' tractor."

The car was attractive, built on a Samson truck frame, with a 118-inch wheelbase and used a Northway four-cylinder engine, with a bore-and-stroke engine 3-11/16 x 5-1/4 inches, a cubic-inch displacement of 224.3 and developing 37 brake hp at 2,000 rpms. The Samson also used Delco ignition, and was equipped with wood artillery wheels like most other cars of its type. Tires were 33 x 4 inches. It had much more room in back than other cars of the time. (Two other cars of the time, the Day Utility and the Dan Patch, were also made for multiple uses, but proved unsuccessful.)

A 1919 Janesville, Wisconsin, newspaper article said all that was needed for the Samson nine-passenger car to be built in that city "was the construction of a plant." But it never happened. The Samson car appeared in the Samson catalog in 1920, the only year the car was made; the total output reached the magnificent figure of one prototype. It was the only car ever advertised by General Motors that it did not build.

Due to its lack of success and its double-use as a cattle carrier with its removable rear seats, the car was sneeringly called the "Nine People and a Bull Calf."

A restored 1921 Samson truck.

General Motors Truck Co., which made the Samson truck in its early years, made this Model 16 truck, one of the GMC truck line which included 3/4- to 5-ton trucks. "Model 16," its literature says, "has the flexibility, economy of operation, and speed required in a 3/4-ton truck, while at the same time it has the power, chassis strength and long-wheel base for all 1-ton requirements."

GMC cars and trucks

Over the years, GMC has built millions of different Chevrolet, Buick, Oldsmobile, and other kinds of automobiles, as one of the "Big Three" United States automakers. It has also built a wide variety of trucks.

Samson trucks

Samson had more luck with its trucks. The first Samson M-15 3/4-ton trucks were built in Flint, Michigan, and in 1920, commenced in Janesville, Wisconsin, building 15 trucks per hour. This truck used 490 engines purchased from the Mason Company. It sold for $655.

Samson also built an M-25 1-1/4-ton truck in 1920, which it sold for $1,095, but which met much less success than the M-15. Both trucks were built for farm use, fitted with extension rims, which had plain cleats in front and shallow cleats in the rear for ease of driving over plowed fields. Both trucks were built from 1920-1923.

Samson trucks continued to be used by the City of Janesville Street Department until the late 1940s, when the last one was retired.

Chapter 24

Velie Automobiles Sold By Deere & Company

The founder of Velie Motors Corporation, Willard Lamb Velie, had a gold-spooned background in vehicles as the grandson of John Deere. His mother was Emma Deere, daughter of John Deere. Velie rose through the ranks of Deere & Company until he decided to branch off on his own, manufacturing automobiles. Eventually Velie built tractors and trucks as well.

Velie tractors

Velie only made one tractor, the 12-24 Velie Biltwel, from 1916-20. The Biltwel engine was protected from the elements, a new concept in tractor manufacture at the time, and the tractor contained a cab, although the model shown in 1920 did not.

The tractor was recommended for two plows, weighed 4,500 pounds, used Kingston dual carburetors, Hyatt and Timken bearings, and its own transmission and bore-and-stroke engine, which was 4-1/8 x 5-1/2 inches.

The Biltwel sold for $1,750 at a time when hundreds of other tractors flooded the market, and the one which it competed with, Henry Ford's Fordson, sold for about a quarter of that amount. The Biltwel was modified in 1917, and production was halted in 1920.

Velie cars and trucks became very well-known, but for some reason, the Velie tractor didn't stick. None exist today.

Velie automobiles

Willard Lamb Velie built carriages at the Velie Carriage Company, established in Moline, Illinois, in 1902. These Velie buggies were of very high quality. The Velie Motor Vehicle Company was formed in 1908 to build automobiles.

Velie's interest in automobiles was piqued when he saw them in a traveling fair in Moline in 1901. Velie knew the area was not yet ready to accept the automobile, so he built buggies until he was sure he could sell cars.

The Velie 30 automobile in 1908 was the first one built. It had a four-cylinder engine of 30 or 35 hp, and was a five-passenger touring car with a 110-inch wheelbase. A thousand of the sturdily built vehicles were sold the first year. A Lycoming engine was used for the Velie 40 the next year, and a year later, 1911, it used its own engine.

Velie autos had many advantages, one of which was inclusion in John Deere Plow Company catalogs and marketing through John Deere dealers.

The company also put cars into races, finishing seventeenth of 46 cars in the 1911 Indy 500.

The company reorganized into the Velie Motors Corporation, and during World War I, filled government vehicle contracts.

Velie cars sold steadily and well through the 1920s, until Will Sr. took ill in 1924. He returned in 1927 and installed his son Will Jr. as vice-president and general manager.

But Will Sr. died of an embolism on Oct. 24, 1928, and his son died of heart disease five months later, dooming the Velie line.

So many happy Velie auto owners lived in a small community near Shreveport, Louisiana, they changed the name of their town to Velie, Louisiana.

Velie trucks

Except for the three years when Will Velie Sr. was ill, 1924-26, Velie trucks were made from 1911-1929 by the Velie Carriage Company in Moline, Illinois.

The first Velie truck venture was in 1911 with a 1-1/2-ton and a 3-ton truck powered by four-cylinder engines. The 1-1/2-ton sold for $2,850, and the 3-ton sold for

Velie made its "Biltwel" tractor for five years, 1916-1920. This is the 12-24 Biltwel, and was not nearly as successful as the Velie automobiles or trucks. This 1920 model was 130 inches long, 66 inches wide, 60 inches high, and weighed 4,500 pounds. No Velie tractors are known to remain extant. (Dan Roen Collection)

This Velie Club Phaeton 60 was manufactured in 1925 by Velie Motors Corporation of Moline, Illinois. The founder of the company, William Lamb Velie, was grandson of the famous John Deere, and had the Velie automobiles included in the Deere & Co. catalogs, as well as sold by dealerships, which gave the Velie a huge advantage over other automobiles of the time. This six-cylinder auto produced 23.44 hp, and came in five different models, selling from $1,250 for the picture Phaeton 60, to $1,925 for a five-passenger Royal Sedan. Others included the Club Phaeton, Coach Sedan, and Sedan, all five-passenger vehicles, like the one pictured. (Gary Hoonsbeen Collection)

$2,350, touted for its ease of engine removal. Both came in 148- or 172-inch wheelbases. The 1-ton Velie took the place of the 1-1/2-ton in 1913.

Biltwel trucks with four-cylinder Continental engines were offered in 1915 in 1-, 1-1/2-, and 3-ton sizes, using governors controlling top speeds to the mid- and upper-teens per hour.

In 1916, Velie introduced its Commercial Car Line, a 1,200-pound capacity truck, and in 1917, two models were offered: 2- and 4-ton capacity trucks.

Various models were offered for the next few years, until Velie took ill; after his 1927 return, trucks were offered once more. The company slogan was "Ask the driver."

The stock market crash of 1929 aided the demise of all the Velie ventures.

In 1926, Velie Motors Corporation of Moline, Illinois, made cars despite the illness of William Lamb Velie. This three-passenger Velie Coupe 60 was painted a two-toned blue lacquer, had a wheelbase of 118 inches, and used a six-cylinder engine with a bore and stroke of 3-3/16 x 4-1/4 inches. The price of $1,425 also included tools, jacks, speedometer, ammeter, voltmeter, electric horn, automatic windshield cleaner, demountable rims, spare tire carrier, rear view mirror, sun visor, cowl ventilator, headlight dimmer, and cowl lights. It even included, for that price, a transmission theft lock. Other models in 1926 included the four-passenger Club Roadster for $1,650; a Club Phaeton for $1,450, Brougham for $1,495, and Royal Sedan for $1,825, the last three being five-passenger models. (Gary Hoonsbeen Collection)

Velie sold this 3-1/2-ton truck 26 for $3,350 in 1916. It sported a four-cylinder 32.4-hp engine with a carrying capacity of 7,000 pounds. The engine had a bore and stroke of 4-1/2 x 5-1/2 inches, and the vehicle's wheelbase measured 172 inches. Velie trucks were made from 1911-29, except for 1924-26, when the senior Velie was ill. (Gary Hoonsbeen Collection)

Chapter 25

Wichita First Vehicle Company Owned By a Woman

From 1911-1932, tractors, trucks, and cars were manufactured by Wichita Falls Motors Company of Wichita Falls, Texas, the first motor-vehicle company operated by a woman, Mrs. Nettie C. McIntyre of Denver, Colorado. She was the chief organizer of the company, and the principal stockholder.

Wichita tractors

The Wichita 20-30 hit the market in 1920 (a bad year, as the agricultural depression was looming on the horizon). The tractor, made only that one year, used a Beaver four-cylinder engine with 4-1/2-inch bore and 6-inch stroke. It cost $2,500 and weighed 5,500 pounds. It was 140 inches long and 74 inches wide, using an Ensign 1-1/2-inch carburetor, high-tension magneto, and a transmission with 2-1/2 mph forward, and 1/7 mph in reverse. It was recommended for three or four plows.

Wichita automobiles

The three-passenger Wichita "oil-field tool pusher," as its four-cylinder, 50 hp, 127-inch wheelbase utility car was announced in late 1920, sold for $2,150. It would carry 1,000 pounds of equipment along with three passengers. The car was built during 1920 and 1921 only.

Wichita trucks

Wichita Falls Motor Company had better luck with its Wichita trucks than it did with tractors or cars. Trucks were built beginning in 1911 with a truck that had a single lever on the steering wheel controlling the spark, throttle, clutch, and transmission. The company built 1- and 2-ton trucks using this

MID-WEST 8-16

Wichita Tractor Co., Wichita, Kan.

Wichita Motors Company made trucks for more than two decades under the tutelage of the female owner of the company. This 1914 Wichita Model A is one of the many Wichita trucks that were sold overseas. They were prized in foreign countries because of the simplicity of their forward-and-backward single-lever control.

"center control." Waukesha engines were used in these trucks, and also when the line was expanded to 5-ton models.

Many Wichita trucks were sold overseas, because the simple forward-and-backward single lever control was prized by people who were mechanically unsophisticated, especially at a time when vehicles needed lots of time and attention.

The company's slogan was aptly, "The Sun Never Sets on the Name of Wichita." The Great Depression ended the company.

It was too bad that Wichita Motors Company of Wichita Falls, Texas, decided to manufacture its 20-30 tractor in 1920. It couldn't know in advance, of course, that the country was about to go into a great agricultural slump, which limited production of the 5,500-pound machine to that single year. It sold for $2,500, and used a four-cylinder, valve-in-head bore-and-stroke engine that was 4-1/2 x 6 inches, and ran in speeds of 2-1/2 to 3-1/2 mph forward, and 1/7 mph in reverse.

SECTION II:

Tractor Companies That Made Cars

Chapter 26

Albaugh Dover Only One of Company's Names

The company that made K-C and Square Turn tractors, and Aldo automobiles, was organized in 1915 as the Kenney-Colwell Company of Norfolk, Nebraska. Partners were Albert Kenney, a farmer, and A. J. Colwell, a machinist.

Square Turn tractors

After capitalizing, the company named its tractor the K-C. In 1916, a mail-order house, Albaugh-Dover Company of Chicago, bought out the company, and probably sold some of the K-C tractors. Evidently it didn't do well enough, so Albaugh-Dover gave up on tractors, reorganized as the Square Turn Tractor Company in 1917, and returned to Norfolk. The "new" Square-Turn tractor was a renamed K-C, an 18-30 front-wheel drive tractor with a single steering wheel in the back.

The Square-Turn used a system of fiber-faced driving cones which allowed the drivewheels to travel different directions when making a sharp turn, thus the name of the machine. It featured a friction clutch pulley, grip transmission (no differential), both power and hand steering, with the ability to turn short and square. It ran in either direction and had a live power hoist for plows.

In 1920, the rating was changed to 18-35. It was recommended to pull three 14-inch plows, weighed 7,400 pounds, and had a turning radius of 8 feet. Its Climax engine was 5- x 6-1/2-inch bore and stroke, and sold for $2,075 in 1920.

The company went bankrupt in 1925. Only three of these tricycle-type tractors are known today, one in the Norfolk, Nebraska Historical Society Museum.

The Star automobile

Gilbert R. Albaugh got involved in the automobile man-ufacture business in 1902 in Cleveland. By this time, he had already worked with Rambler, Olds, and Peerless auto companies, and the other principals of the company had equally impressive automobile resumes–except for H. C. Robinson, the manager, who had been in the chocolate-making business previously, but decided, as *The Automobile* magazine of the time deliciously put it, "the progressive automobile industry was more to his taste."

The prototype Star was completed in 1903, and ten were sold by mid-summer at $1,250 each. The Star was a runabout with a detachable tonneau to add passengers. The one-cylinder 8-1/2-hp machine was a four-stroke engine mounted in the center of the car under the floorboard.

Investors wanted quick returns, and withdrew in 1903 after 20 cars had been built. The assets were sold to Harry S. Moore, who increased the hp of the machine to nine, shortened the wheelbase from 76 to 74 inches, and lowered the price to $950 each. By 1904, the Star was a dead car.

The Wolverine automobile

Autos ran in Gilbert Albaugh's blood. After Star, he moved to Reid Manufacturing Company to produce the Wolverine automobile. Albaugh revised the automobile considerably. It was produced in two- and four-cylinder models with a shaft drive.

But all was not well with Reid; renamed Wolverine Automobile Company in fall 1905, it moved immediately to Dundee and was again renamed as Wolverine Auto & Commercial Vehicle Company. A few Wolverines were produced in Dundee in 1906, but then the factory closed.

In 1904-05, five-passenger touring Wolverines sold for $1,750 (Model C, a four-cylinder) and $1,600 (Model D, a two-cylinder). The 1906 Wolverines sold from $650 to $2,000 in two- and four-cylinder cars.

This Square-Turn 18-35 tractor was manufactured in 1920 with a recommendation of pulling three 14-inch plows with its Climax 5- x 6-1/2-inch bore and stroke four-cylinder engine. The tractor weighed 7,400 pounds, cost $2,075, was 199 inches long, 98 inches wide, and 81 inches high. It used a 1-1/2-inch Stromberg carburetor, and a Giant grip friction transmission, running 2-1/4 to 2-1/2 mph forward or backward. It is difficult to discern if Albaugh-Dover sold any of the Square Turn Tractors. This one was headed "Square Turn Tractor Company, Norfolk, Nebraska." (Dan Roen Collection)

The Aldo automobile

In 1910-11, Gilbert Albaugh was back, building a motor buggy for two passengers called the ALDO (ALbaugh-DOver). It used an opposed 20-cylinder air-cooled engine with planetary transmission and double-chain drive and tiller steering. This highwheeler was one of 20 built in Chicago during this time. They cost $395, but wouldn't sell, so by 1911 the company went out of business.

This Star auto from 1903 was one of the first ones Gilbert Albaugh worked on, arriving to design the new product of the Star Automobile Company of Cleveland in 1902. The prototype was finished in April 1903, and ten Stars were sold by the middle of the summer. The Star cost $1,250 for a single-cylinder, four-stroke 8-1/2 hp runabout with a detachable tonneau for extra passengers.

Gilbert R. Albaugh was brought into the Reid Manufacturing Company of Detroit in 1904, and revised this Wolverine automobile considerably from its original conception. This 1905 Wolverine was a "Hill Climber" with plenty of speed, seating for five people, and a three-speed forward transmission. Later that year, Reid was succeeded by Wolverine Automobile Company, and almost immediately thereafter the name was changed to Wolverine Auto & Commercial Vehicle Company of Dundee, Michigan. Production began in that plant in 1906, but stopped almost immediately.

CHAINLESS WOLVERINE

2 Models—Get New Catalog

20 H. P. A Hill Climber

Plenty speed, simple 3-speed ahead sliding gear, shaft drive, seats 5 people. Full equipment.

New York and Chicago Shows.

REID MFG. CO.
DETROIT, MICH.

CHAINLESS WOLVERINE MODEL "C"

Chapter 27

Best Manufactures Steam Tractors and Cars

Best Manufacturing Company of San Leandro, California, is known for its steam-traction engines, and was the forerunner of the C.L. Best Gas Traction Co. of the same city. Three Best brothers organized the company, and true to the behemoth steam traction engines they made, their automobile was also formidably large.

Best steam tractors

Daniel Best searched for gold in 1859 but had little luck. He tried sawmilling, hunting, and ten years later, ranching with his brother near Marysville, California. One job was to haul grain from the fields to town for cleaning at $3 a ton, and he wondered why the cleaner couldn't be brought to the grain instead.

He built three portable grain cleaners, and began selling them. Eventually the brothers moved to San Leandro, California, built steam harvesters, and one day in March 1888, watched with large enthusiastic crowds while DeLafayette Remington of Woodburn, Oregon, exhibited his steam traction engine, "Rough and Ready."

Daniel Best immediately bought Pacific Coast manufacturing rights for the machine, equipped his factory, and worked at adapting his harvester to it.

In 1890, the Best traction engine won first prize in the California State Fair. By that time, Best was making the 30-hp "Native Son," 40-hp (name unknown), and 50-hp "Pathfinder."

From 1891 on, his next 11 patents were for gas engines. He perfected the Duplex gas engine for street cars which were quiet, safe, and fast, 6-20 mph. Some of these patents would be the basis for his brother's manufacture of gasoline tractors a few years down the road when he formed C. L. Best Gas Traction Company.

In 1908, Daniel Best sold his rights to Holt Manufacturing Company; however, Leo did not sell his rights and started C. L. Best Gas Traction Co., which became a major rival of Holt for the manufacture of Caterpillar tractors.

Best automobiles

In 1898, the three Best brothers built an experimental gasoline carriage, using huge wagon wheels, and a two-cylinder, 7-hp engine that sprayed gasoline into the cylinders. It could hold eight passengers, and when full, reduced speed from a top of 20 mph to 18. Unlike most early automobiles, this Best had left-hand drive, and the vehicle was mostly the work of Daniel Best.

He later wrote, "I remember when automobiles first came into vogue. That was quite a while after I produced my tractor–about 1893, I believe. I was smitten with the automobile fever, and accordingly set about to construct one. I tell you, that machine was a work of art–in my own opinion. Solid rubber tires of a size capable of carrying ten passengers, a lot more in an emergency, and with all the grace of a mud scow. It was a nine days' wonder here. I ran it eleven years."

A year later, Daniel Best made a two-passenger gasoline runabout. "I later gave it to my son," Daniel Best wrote. "He, in turn, traded it for a piano. I think the piano man was

This is one of the Best steam tractors manufactured by the Best Manufacturing Company of San Leandro, California, and forerunner to C. L. Best Manufacturing Company of the same city a couple of decades later.

The Best Manufacturing Company of San Leandro, California, made this 110 Best steam traction engine in 1900. It weighed 20 tons and had huge wood-covered drive wheels.

cheated. I have often thought if I had stayed with automobile manufacturing, I could have out-Forded Ford. Perhaps."

That was to be the last automobile made by Best; when an area minister asked to have a huge carriage made for his touring evangelical church, the Bests turned him down, and went back to their steam traction ways.

Chapter 28

Comet Auto Takes a Shot at Tractor Building

Comet Automobile Company of Decatur, Illinois, was a peculiar outfit, as both the tractor and car it built during its five-year company life (1917-1922) were not manufactured, but assembled from parts purchased from other companies. Also, George W. Jagers, a native of Racine, Wisconsin, began building the cars before he had a factory.

The idea for Jagers to turn to manufacturing occurred when he got control of the Racine Manufacturing Company in 1916. Jagers had worked as a costing clerk for J. I. Case Threshing Machine Co., so he not only knew the basics of manufacturing, but also the parts companies and pricing, all useful in his new venture.

Comet tractor

The Comet tractor was made for two years, 1919-20, using an Erd four-cylinder engine, Foote Brothers two-speed transmission, Dixie magneto, and other OEM parts. Though Comet didn't advertise its tractor as assembled from other company's parts, it could have because the parts-makers were all well-known and established, which meant the tractor would probably be a pretty good one. The Comet tractor was a small one as tractors went at that time, weighing 4,500 pounds and rated a 15-30.

Comet automobile

Without a factory, Jagers set together a dozen Comet cars ("This Comet Has Come To Stay," a play on the 75-year appearing and disappearing act of Halley's Comet of 1913) and presented them at the Chicago Automobile Show in January 1917. Interest was high enough for him to set up a factory eight months later in Decatur, Illinois. Meantime, he worked out of a rented office in Chicago, and loft space in Rockford, as Racine Manufacturing Company, which had formerly made toys and novelties.

First, Jagers used a Lewis six-cylinder engine, but switched to Continental. The 1920 Comet car had a 125-inch wheelbase, a 6-cylinder 303.1 CID engine with a 4.66 gear ratio, and 33- x 4-1/2-inch tires. Models included the C-53 and C-53-2. Open and closed cars were available. Serial numbers began at 701 in 1920, and 5001 in 1921, which indicated modest sales.

But then came opportunity. In 1920, Comet received an order from Antwerp, Belgium, for 40 automobiles. Jagers and company officers decided to go international, and that same year began building a large and expensive factory which would manufacture 200 cars per day.

But the factory and car sales were based on speculation, and when the orders never came, the factory fell through. A bond-sale issue failed, and about the time it went into voluntary receivership, Comet offered a smaller car to go with its Comet Six, this one a four-cylinder for about $1,000.

Jagers wanted to relocate the company at Racine, but nobody bid when the company was offered for sale as a whole late in 1922. When the personal property was sold a year later, stacks of wheels sold at eight cents each; one

The Comet was a tractor built out of tractor parts from other companies, like this 15-30. Comet Automobile Company of Decatur, Illinois, built the tractor. The incentive to buy a put-together tractor like this was that the parts came from well-known OEM companies.

This touring car is a 1921 Comet six, Model C-53-2, and was manufactured during Comet Automobile Company of Decatur's second-to-last year of business. The company got into financial trouble in the early 1920s, perhaps due to the agriculture recession. The model C-53-2 was a six-cylinder, 55-hp car with 125-inch wheelbase, selling for $3,650.

new Comet car sold for only $35.

Eight officers of the company were indicted for mail fraud, but eventually cleared of the charges.

The last model year was 1922.

Comets in top condition today will bring between $28,000-$29,000 in the collector's market.

Chapter 29

Maytag Cars First Ones Designed By Duesenberg

Maytag made more than washing machines during its long history, such as the Maytag automobile and the Maytag tractor.

The company history begins in 1893, when Parsons Band Cutter & Self- Feeder was organized by George W. Parsons and F. L. Maytag, as well as Will Berman and A. H. Bergman. They had great success with their feeder attachment for threshing machines, and also made other farm machinery.

In 1909, Maytag Company was born, and the Newton, Iowa firm started making washing machines at a time when these machines were in their infancy.

Maytag tractors

Maytag Company manufactured a 12-25 Maytag tractor in 1916, weighing 5,000 pounds. It had a peculiar front-wheel design, and was powered by a four-cylinder Waukesha engine. Top speeds were 2.25 and 3 mph and it advertised for $900 for the few months of its existence.

Mason and Maytag autos

The Maytag auto wasn't the first auto this company made; in fact, it wasn't the first chosen name for the vehicle, either. The car designers were Fred S. Duesenberg and his brother, August, who had opened a garage in Des Moines. They decided to build a car and call it the Marvel.

But when Edward R. Mason, a local attorney, offered

money for the company, the car name was quickly changed to Mason. Its motto was, "The fastest two-cylinder car in America." It quickly proved itself adept as a hillclimber, and its advertisements showed it from that view.

As Mason Motor Car Co. (1906-1908), and then the Mason Automobile Co. (1908-1910), it made the Mason auto, a five-seater powered by a two-cylinder opposed engine of 24 hp. It had planetary transmission and single-chain drive. The major change of the Mason vehicle was that two- and four-seat versions were added in 1909. The Mason, along with the car it evolved into, the Maytag, were Fred S. Duesenberg's first car designs.

Duesenberg began making bicycles before he designed his first Mason in 1904. He and his brother, August, made engines with horizontal overhead valves for their 1912 Mason racing cars. A year later, they founded the famous Duesenberg Motors Co. of Indianapolis, Indiana.

Senator Fred Maytag and his son, Elmer H., decided to add automobiles to their agricultural line and so bought controlling interest in the Mason Motor Company, changed the name to Maytag-Mason Motor Car Company and moved it to Waterloo, Iowa in 1910. A new four-cylinder car called Maytag was introduced that year, while

The Maytag Company of Newton, Iowa, experimented with a tractor with its 1916 production of a 12-25 tractor with a Waukesha four-cylinder engine. This tractor sold for $900 and moved at 2.25 and 3 mph. The Maytag Company was often in financial trouble while involved with building cars and tractors, and so this machine was only made for one year.

A great deal of history is evident in this one small advertisement for the Maytag-Mason Motor Co. of Waterloo, Iowa. This ad appeared in 1910, when the change was effected. At that time, Maytag was making six models, costing from $1,250 to $1,750, all four-cylinder engines from 24-35 hp. The company boasted, "For dealers, the 'Maytag' line for 1910 is the only whirlwind on wheels. Write at once for proposition." (Dan Roen Collection)

Maytag manufactured its Maytag Model A (formerly the Mason, and showing in the lower right-hand portion of this advertisement from 1910), in Waterloo, Iowa. The upper left-hand picture shows the Maytag climbing a 50-percent grade, "which no other car of any price or power has ever been able to climb." The models sold from $1,250 to $1,750. (Dan Roen Collection)

the two-cylinder Mason continued. All 1911 cars were called Maytag (although the car never had that name on it), and included three varieties of the two-cylinder 20-hp vehicle, all with 96-inch wheelbases: a Model A Runabout, Model B Toy tonneau, and Model C Touring, selling for $1,250 for the Runabout, and $50 additional each for the other two. The four-cylinder consisted of five models, all 35-hp vehicles with 114-inch wheelbases: a Model D Roadster, Model E Toy Tonneau, Model F Touring, Model G torpedo, and Model H Boattail Roadster, which sold for $1,650, while all the rest sold for $100 more. Galloway offered a Galloway car for sale in 1911, but it was simply a Maytag with a new radiator emblem.

The company was in financial trouble from the start, and in 1912 the Maytags, after overpurchasing automobile parts, couldn't pay bills, and dropped out of the car business. Control reverted to Edward R. Mason.

The Duesenbergs, meanwhile, reclaimed the Mason name and made Mason race cars, almost qualifying for the Indy 500 in 1912. They moved to St. Paul, Minnesota, but promised to build another car for Edward R. Mason, to be called a Mason-Mohler, for 1914. It would be a four-cylinder vehicle with a Duesenberg engine and 65 hp, costing $3,000.

But the company was overextended, and its creditors refused more time, despite E. R. Mason telling *Motor World* in its Oct. 16, 1913 issue that he still had hope of saving the property.

In September 1915, however, the plant and its holdings were sold at auction, with the plant bringing $35,000.

Since this two-cylinder Mason automobile was built in 1906 by Mason Motor Car Company, it could have been built in its first home, Des Moines, Iowa, or even Waterloo, where the company moved that same year. The Mason was originally supposed to be called the Marvel, but when a local attorney named Edward R. Mason provided the money for the company, the name was quickly changed to Mason, one of several names the car would have.

In 1908, this ad for the Mason car was published. In 1910, the name was changed to the "Maytag," although the car essentially remained the same. It was the Mason when Edward R. Mason was the principal backer, but when that backer became Fred R. Maytag, the name of the car was changed. Maytag was only in the automobile business until 1912, and in financial trouble constantly. (Dan Roen Collection)

Chapter 30

Middletown Company Starts Before 1890

The work of Charles W. Shartle is what started the Middletown Machine Company of Middletown, Ohio. In 1886, Shartle started a small shop doing general machine repair work for Middletown manufacturers, says *The Middletown Journal* of Jan. 1, 1901. He also invented a shafting collar of an improved pattern which he manufactured in a small way.

"His work gave such promise," *The Journal* says, "that in 1889 the Middletown Machine Company was incorporated," by Shartle and five other men. Business kept increasing, and a year later, the company was reorganized, taking in one more man. "By this time," *The Journal* says, "their manufacturing business had increased to such an extent that the repair business was given up and their entire attention...centered upon the building of gas and gasoline engines and shafting collars."

Middletown tractors

The Miami and the Woodpecker–those were the two tractors sold by the Middletown Machine Company of Middletown, Ohio, or more accurately, the names of its engines. The company started manufacturing gasoline engines early, and designed its tractor to use its engines of 6, 8, 10, 12, 15, and 25 hp. The Miami used a fuel pump and a remotely located fuel tank; the Woodpeckers used a gravity fuel field. Those were the only differences in the engines. *The Journal* says, "The Miami engine built by them is conceded by experts to be the best engine on the market."

The Miami was most often used for in-building work on the farm, and the Woodpecker was most often used on tractors.

Middletown automobiles

The company got started at the turn of the century in Middletown, Ohio, and five years later was producing six engines a day and employing 60 mechanics. A few of the engines–the Miami and the Woodpecker–were installed in buggies and sold locally as the Middletown automobile. One reference says the company went out of business in 1906, another says the engines were still for sale six years later.

Middletown Machine Company of Middletown, Ohio, made its own engines, and used them on its own tractors. These engines came in horsepowers of 6, 8, 10, 12, 15, and 25. The Miami engine used a fuel pump and remote fuel tank, while the Woodpecker used a gravity fuel feed.

Chapter 31

Companies Unite to Form Powerful Minneapolis-Moline

Three companies merged in 1929 to form Minneapolis-Moline Company in Minneapolis, Minnesota: Minneapolis Steel & Machinery Company of Minneapolis, originally formed in 1902, the strongest company; Moline Implement Company of Moline, Illinois, (formerly Moline Plow Company, organized in 1870); and Minneapolis Threshing Machine Company of Hopkins, Minnesota, formed in 1887.

Machines and implements were selected for production from each old company by the new one: Minneapolis-Moline Power Implement Company, which had increased its assets to $24 million by the merger.

Tractors

Twin City tractors were chosen to keep in production from Minneapolis Steel. Some of these included the Twin City KT, made in 1930. This "Kombination" tractor (its standard tread design would handle a combination of farm implements: the plow, the cultivator, farm wagon; it could do belt work, or operate PTO implements.) It had a dual air cleaner, controlled heat manifold, oil filter, and individual wheel breaks. Implements were driven from the power take-off shaft. This 11-20 was built for four years.

Out of the Minneapolis Threshing line, one tractor kept was the Minneapolis 17-30 Type B tractor. It weighed

6,800 pounds, used a four-cylinder 4-7/8- x 7-inch engine, and was 11 feet 11 inches long. Type A also was built, and was lighter and shorter. Prices on these two tractors were dropped after the stock market crash in 1929, and sold for $900 for Type B in 1931, and $800 for Type A, both of them $200 less than previously.

Though Moline Implement didn't manufacture tractors, its tillage tools were retained.

The tractors were all eventually renamed Minneapolis-Moline. In 1931, the company entered the row-crop tractor field with its first completely original design, an M-M Universal tractor, which could operate an entire line of implements from M-M. It weighed 4,860 pounds and used a four-cylinder bore-and-stroke engine that was 4-1/4 x 5 inches. Its options included electric starter and lights.

The M-M line grew into one of the most extensive in the industry, with a great number of tractor successes. One of the least-successful tractors ever made was its 1938 Model U-DLX (U-deluxe) tractor, which was shown off to 12,000 invited guests. Unfortunately, the guests thought M-M was showing off, and that the "Comfortractor," as it came to be called, simply had too many comforts. Many

Before the three companies merged to form Minneapolis-Moline, Minneapolis Threshing Machine Company of Hopkins, Minnesota, manufactured this all-purpose 12-25 tractor, which weighed 6,400 pounds and was rated to pull three 14-inch plows. The Twin City design of tractors were chosen for the new company over the Minneapolis design like this one.

Immediately after the merger of the three companies, Minneapolis-Moline continued to make this Twin City 21-32 Model FT in 1929, a three-plow tractor that had produced 39.14 belt hp at Nebraska. It used its own four-cylinder vertical 4-1/2 x 6-inch bore and stroke engine, and weighed 6,463 pounds, with operator.

This 1929 Minneapolis 17-30 Type B was still sold after Minneapolis-Moline was formed. Parts that remained were made into new tractors, and after all those were sold, only Twin-City type models were continued, while the other companies involved got their major problems made by the new farm machinery power.

This Minneapolis-Moline catalog page is from the 1930 version, and shows the tractors the company will continue selling; three of the four are Twin City models, the name the company kept until the mid-'30s, when all the tractors were Minneapolis-Moline.

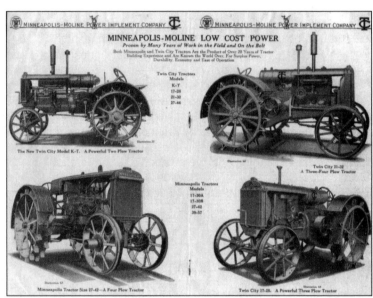

This is a specially made Minneapolis-Moline jeep pulling a mobile anti-aircraft gun during World War II. The jeep could pull that massive load at up to 40 mph. M-M literature claims its jeep was the first one ever manufactured and named, while several other companies claim the same distinction.

farmers felt their peers would look down at them if they bought the machine; only a few more than a hundred were sold of these streamlined, car-looking tractors. M-M had in mind that the farmer would use the tractor in the field, and then hose it off and take it to church on Sunday. These machines also cost almost double of the M-M U tractors–$1,900 vs. $1,000.

M-M engineers continued to make strides with engines; the tractors also took on brighter colors–their Harvest gold–because more colorful tractors was the norm for the industry at this time. M-M was the first tractor manufacturer to take advantage of LPG gas, and it had other firsts as well.

Many other tractors were manufactured by Minneapolis-Moline through the years, until they were bought out by White Motor Company in 1963; M-M tractors met the

same fate as Twin City and Minneapolis tractors: M-M tractors were phased out in 1969.

Minneapolis-Moline Jeep

The Jeep emanated from an all-wheel UTX tractor which was first tested by the Minnesota National Guard at Camp Ripley Minnesota. The vehicle was successful, and a guardsman named it the "Jeep," after a Popeye the Sailor character who could do anything and was named Jeep.

The Comfortractor cab and rear end were used to build the jeep. The jeep had a 425 cubic-inch six-cylinder engine, and added front-wheel drive to make the vehicle a four-wheel-drive machine. Instead of a bumper, a roller was added so the jeep could climb obstacles or push trees down. Eventually the entire front end was rounded.

Other changes were made through the years, including moving the driver more to the middle of the machine. The jeep was 166 inches long, 77 inches wide, and 58 inches high (to the top of the steering wheel.)

The jeep was produced for the Air Force and Army Corps of Engineers as an industrial utility vehicle until 1953.

Though many other companies produced jeeps, it appears the common use of the name came from the Minneapolis-Moline jeep.

This jeep is a four-wheel-drive model manufactured by Minneapolis-Moline for the United States Army. It is hauling a troop carrier during World War II.

The literature about the Minneapolis-Moline jeep declares, "The original jeep is a product of Minneapolis-Moline." This photo was taken during World War II and M-M said, "Current national publicity has obscured the fact that the first war machine named 'JEEP' was born at M-M and christened at Camp Ripley (MN) (with apologies to Ripley–'Believe it or not')."

Chapter 32

Old Company Makes Nichols-Shepard Vehicles

Nichols & Shepard Company of Battle Creek, Michigan, was one of the largest thresher builders in the United States by 1886. It produced Flagg vibrator separators, Red Receiver Special Line threshers, the Steel Winged Beater, and the Beating Shakers, which comprised the famous "Four Threshermen" that Nichols & Shepard advertised for years.

John Nichols started a blacksmith shop in Battle Creek, Michigan, in 1848, and in the early 1850s, with only blacksmith tools, he built a crude thresher acknowledged as the best of its time. David Shepard entered the picture in the 1850s when Nichols wanted to build a foundry and needed a cash infusion. It made agricultural implements, mill irons, and small stationary steam engines.

After its 1886 incorporation, when it was one of the largest builders of threshing machinery in the U.S., the company built its first Flagg vibrator (designed by Eli Flagg, one of its threshing machine experts.)

Nichols-Shepard tractors

The first tractors were steam-traction engines, the most substantial boilers made, with the thickest boiler plate used in traction engine construction. It steamed easily and had ample steam capacity for its engine. It had steel-traction wheels, platform frame, and a draw bar. Hundreds of Nichols-Shepard steam-traction engines were made in horsepowers of 8, 10, 13, 16, 20, 25, 30, and 35, as well as others.

In 1911, Nichols & Shepard began developing gasoline tractors, along with its steam traction engines, which had an enviable reputation and were very solidly built. (As late as 1927, a variety of steam traction models were still available from $2,550 to $3,590.)

A few gas tractors were produced in 1912–the company still believed steam would remain king, but wanted to compete in the other markets–and then came the 25-50 model,

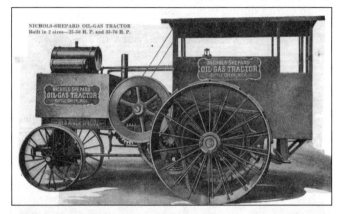

After its initial entrance into the gasoline tractor field in 1912, Nichols & Shepard followed with this Nichols-Shepard 25- to 50-hp engine. It also made 35- to 70-hp tractors at the time. These were both large tractors, as some farmers still needed big ones to break sod in North Dakota and Texas. (Dan Roen Collection)

with a pair of 9- x 12-inch bore-and-stroke cylinders, and sold for about $3,000 in 1927. A larger 35-70, with two cylinders and 10-1/2- x 14-inch bore and stroke was also built.

In 1923, Nichols & Shepard Company made a 20-42 model, redesigned from its smaller 18-36. These machines used a two-cylinder 8- x 10-inch bore-and-stroke engines, ran in two forward speeds, and looked exactly like all the other Nichols & Shepards gasoline tractors, except for size.

Nichols & Shepard automobiles

These automobiles were only built for two years, 1910 and 1911, and very few were made, and even less is known about them.

Long before Nichols & Shepard of Battle Creek, Michigan, began to manufacture gasoline tractors, it made steam traction engines like this 16- to 50-hp engine ca 1912. The boilers on these steam traction engines were generally recognized as the most substantial ones made, which meant fewer dangerous problems. As Jack Norbeck writes in *Encyclopedia of American Steam Traction Engines*, the N&S steam traction engines had "the thickest boiler plate used in traction engine construction. It steamed easily and had ample steam capacity for its engine." (Dan Roen Collection)

This 1910 Nichols-Shepard 30-hp engine is plowing and seeding a North Dakota field at the same time. Nichols-Shepard made a wide variety of steam traction engines. (Richard Birklid Collection)

This Nichols-Shepard 1923 steam engine weighed 16 tons, and was one of the last of its ilk built, since the company stopped making them in early 1924. The company centered out of Battle Creek, Michigan, and had a long history in manufacturing agricultural products. (Richard Birklid Collection)

Chapter 33

Otto Builds World's First Production Four-Cycle

The founder of Otto Gas Engine Works of Philadelphia, Pennsylvania, should be better known: he built the world's first production four-cycle internal combustion engine.

In 1864, Nicolaus August Otto and Egen Langen formed N. A. Otto & Cie, the world's first company to manufacture internal combustion engines. They built many sizes and styles, and produced Otto's four-stroke cycle engine in 1876, setting forth the same principles used in four-stroke engines today. *Antique Automobile* magazine wrote in 1959 that "The Otto engine toured America, receiving acclaim by the public as well as a host of pioneers who believed in the potentials of the horseless carriage. The Otto gasoline engine came early to America, first exhibited at the Philadelphia Centennial in 1876. During the intervening years to 1907, the Otto engine was exhibited and honored with medals and certificates..." in many American cities.

Eugene Langen's nephews, Jakob and Adolph Schleicher, emigrated to the United States about this time, and along with Hermann Schumm, a relative of both, the Schleicher, Schumm & Company was formed, selling Otto engines. The company name was subsequently changed to Otto Gas Engine Works of Philadelphia.

Otto tractors

In 1896-97, the company built a 42-hp, single-cylinder tractor with a 12-inch bore and 18-inch stroke. The engine weighed 14,500 pounds. A later 1897 Otto tractor was much more sleek.

Each Otto engine was unique; each was tested, and whatever horsepower it produced, that was stamped on a plate. By 1904, Otto offered a lighter design than the earlier ones.

This early Otto was built in 1894 and is a 15-hp traction engine. Otto engines were long known for their high quality, so it was no surprise when an Otto traction engine and later, tractor, was built.

Otto and Ottomobile automobiles

The Otto automobile, manufactured by Otto Gas Engine Works in 1910 and 1911, also had a major part in automobile history. In the outcome of the Selden patent case, Judge Noyes' wrote that "had he (Selden) appreciated the superiority of the Otto engine and adapted that type (instead of the Brayton) for his combination, his patent would cover the modern automobile." As it was, Selden lost, and his patent did not cover every automobile (which would have required Selden to receive royalties for every automobile engine ever produced.)

Joseph H. Penrose of Neshaminy, Pennsylvania, said in the June 1959 issue of *Antique Automobile* that his parents had bought a new Otto when he was a kid. "In 1910, there were several cars being manufactured in Philadelphia. The Otto Gas Engine Company...had a very good

By all rights, Nicolas August Otto should be better known, since he built the world's first production four-cycle internal combustion engine. This 1905 ad for Otto engines gives the testimony from St. Anthony & Dakota Elevator Co., in Minneapolis, Minnesota. That company talks about how it compared its Otto engines to "others we had tried," and found the others wanting. "During the season of 1902, we bought 35 more Ottos and now have 127 of them." The ad also says, "A splendid testimonial to the merits of the Otto from people who have tried many others." (Gary Hoonsbeen Collection)

This 1896 Otto was another 15-hp traction engine. By comparing the 1894 and 1896 models, one can see the differences in the two. Both of these were built by the Otto Gas Engine Company of Philadelphia and were gasoline engines.

reputation for its stationary engines...A friend of the family...was a salesman for the company. Although I was not very old at that time, I can remember very well his visits to our home. Mother and father finally bought our first Otto, a five-passenger car. They knew the reputation of the Otto Gas Engine Company, and felt it was well built and would be dependable. It turned out to be just that, and for fifteen years it served us well.

"There was a large folding top, but no windshield or front doors. When the weather became cold, we didn't use it very often, but when we did, we really had to bundle up with buffalo robes, as the wind circulated around under that top. The roads were poor and often muddy, so the car was put away and sometimes jacked up in the winter– horses were still available when the going was tough.

"Well do I remember holding firmly onto the seat while my father drove in second gear for fear it would go too fast; and the time he tried to make a turn and drove up on the trolley tracks, stalling the motor. I sat there with fear that the trolley car would come while he got out to 'Crank it up.'

"A little later in the same year (1910), my brother acquired the second Otto car. This was a roadster, long, low, considered racy for that age. Two bucket seats, side by side,

and a center seat behind them were covered with genuine black leather. The car was painted a cream color with black striping. With the large brass Gray & Davis headlights and two smaller brass lights on each side of the cowl, it made a very striking appearance. About 1920, my brother had abandoned it for a newer car and I acquired it."

Otto automobiles had a long wheelbase of 123 inches, which along with the low profile of the vehicle, made it look long and sleek. The first Otto Four was produced in 30- and 35-hp models in 1911, a two-, three- or four-passenger roadster for $1,950, a four-passenger demi-tonneau for $2,000, and a five-passenger touring model for $2,000.

The 1911 Otto produced only a 35-hp vehicle with a 123-inch wheelbase vehicle from the previous year's selections, dropped the demi-tonneau model, and added six other models, ranging from $1,950 to $3,250 each for the limousine and landaulet.

A remaining catalog said of the Otto car, "When normally loaded, the propeller shaft is practically horizontal, giving a straight-line drive and is carried in a steel alloy torsion tube, free from all strains from the rear axle. The rear axle is a full-floating type, the driving shafts being relieved of all torsional strain except the stress actually required to drive the car, the

This 1910 Otto was a long, low, sleek-looking car that might have become a better seller if Otto Gas Engine Works of Philadelphia had been better marketers. This car came to market about the time the Selden patent case went to court, and in fact the superbness of the Otto engine was one of the major reasons the Selden patent lost. (The patent would have required automobile manufacturers to pay a royalty on each internal combustion engine they made.) The wheelbase on this Otto auto was 123 inches.

The Otto Gas Engine Works of Philadelphia built this 1911 Otto five-passenger Touring car and sold it for $2,000. It used a four-cylinder, 35-hp engine with a 123-inch wheelbase. Seven other styles of Ottos were made in 1911.

When this photo was taken, ca. 1959, this rare Otto was owned by John William Kurtz of Pittsford, New York, and had been made especially for the original owner, so it is a one-of-a-kind. Kurtz rebuilt the car, and had it reupholstered about 1959. Kurtz said in *Antique Automobile* in 1959 that when he took it apart, "The body was in very good shape except for two small holes where rats' uric acid had eaten through. The body and fenders are all aluminum... The engine was in remarkable shape. What a surprise I had when I pulled the pistons out and found thirteen rings on each piston, four small rings in two grooves and five in the other. Fortunately, the grooves were cut of standard size 1/4" x 4-1/2" so there was no problem in getting new rings. The wrist pins were worn a little so new ones were put in."

load being carried entirely on a tubular steel case surrounding the driving mechanism and independent thereof."

In 1912, the name was changed to Ottomobile, and this vehicle design branched out even more, with Model 2, four-cylinder, 38.9-hp engines on the 123-inch wheelbase chassis, and no fewer than 10 types: A, B, D, E, F, G, H, I, J, and L, from $1,850 to $3,250. They also made the Model 3 with a 32.4-hp four-cylinder engine, a Type KK parlor car for five or seven passengers at $2,300.

The company's major problem was marketing; the Otto Motor Car Company of New York went bankrupt in 1911, the Ottomobile Company of Mt. Holly, New Jersey took over and went broke in 1912, and customer confidence was lost. By 1913, no more Ottos or Ottomobiles were made.

In 1912, for unknown reasons, the name of the vehicle was changed to Ottomobile, like this 1912 Type KK parlor car. It was a Model 3 four-cylinder machine of 32.4 horsepower, selling for $2,300.

Chapter 34

Pan Motor Company Builds 'The Tractor That Isn't'

The Pan Motor Company of St. Cloud, Minnesota, has a curious history for its owner and an even more curious one for its tractors and automobiles.

When Samuel Connor Pandolfo sold life insurance to scattered farmers in Texas, Oklahoma, Arizona, and New Mexico during the first decade of the 20th century, he had a lot of time to think. Cars became a passion for him–he owned 37 of them. When the insurance business turned down, he turned to building a better car, and a better tractor.

The 1917 Pan Motor book, "Pictorial Proof of Progress," said, "Mr. Pandolfo had an extraordinary project on foot and was naturally looking for an extraordinary location, one that would supply as nearly as possible all the needs of such an institution."

After a number of months of debating, he finally chose Minnesota, and then St. Cloud.

To get his project rolling, he held a giant free barbecue open to the public in a huge empty lot on the outskirts of St. Cloud on July 4, 1917. More than 70,000 people attended, eating Texas steers shipped into St. Cloud by the railroad carload.

While people waited for food, Pandolfo's salesmen worked the crowd, selling stock. They did much better

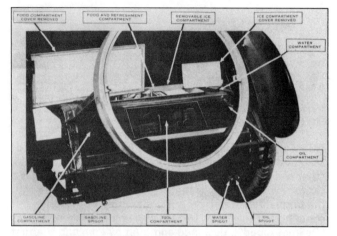

A view of the Pandolfo "commissary" compartment tank, which was standard equipment on the Pan automobile. It was designed with five compartments to hold gasoline, oil, water, food, and tools. The first three mentioned compartments each had their own individual spigot. There was also a compartment for ice next to the water. (Roy Bernick Collection)

than the cooks, who produced raw meat because they had used oak for fire, which did not create enough heat. Restaurants in St. Cloud were swamped with orders, and by

Pan motorcars are lined up inside the Pan Motor Company building just before 1920. The Pan was an interesting automobile, with a wide variety of concepts, like changing the seats into a bed for traveling, and having the Pandolfo Compartment tank. They called this a "commissary department" that provides for needs, like a reserve supply of gasoline, oil, water, all with key-lock faucets. Also compartment for the tools, tire pump, jack, and other supplies, and a well-insulated, rust-proof provision chamber is also provided.

The Tourist Sleeper model was one of Pan's genius ideas, an automobile that allowed the seats to be put down and convert into a bed at night so people could see the U.S.A. and not have to worry about lodging. The Pan literature said that converting the seats into a bed was "simplicity itself." (Roy Bernick Collection)

The 1919 Pan, the Car of the Future, was built by Pan Motor Company of St. Cloud, Minnesota. Though many people speak poorly of the owner of the company, Samuel Pandolfo, many people speak well of him. His automobiles were fresh and innovative at a time when many other automobiles were similar to each other. (Great River Regional Library)

This Model A was manufactured by Pan Motor Company of St. Cloud, Minnesota. "It is a motor car," its literature said, "that will appeal to both the masses and the classes. It is a car for everybody–a car that, we feel sure, will meet with the unqualified approval of a great army of motorists." It contained the DeSmet top (or as the literature says, was "DeSmetopped"), designed and built by Pan, and the first folding top that did not extend out six inches to a foot on each side of the windshield. "The DeSmetop harmonizes with the car," advertising materials said. (Great River Regional Library)

evening, not a pound of meat was left in any restaurant in the city. The remaining live steers were saved for a future barbecue, except they were rustled the next night.

Nevertheless, Pandolfo sold $10,000,000 in stock, and then built a fourteen-building factory, all connected by underground tunnels, 58 houses for the workers, (still called "Pantown" today), and a hotel. He was planning a hospital, community house for entertainment, school, and even a police force. In 1917, Pandolfo cheered, "Hurrah for the Pan Motor Company! Three cheers for the coming giant of the automobile world!"

Pan automobiles

In 1918, the factories started churning out cars, the Pan Model A, "a motor car that will appeal to both the masses

Pan Motor Company manufactured this Tourist Sleeper model Pan for the people who wanted to travel great distances but didn't want to pay for lodging, or couldn't find a place to lodge. It had compartments in the rear of the auto for practically everything the traveler might need: gasoline, oil, water, food, and tools. (Great River Regional Library)

and the classes." It was built by hand, with great detail paid to each process of the assembly. All Pan cars were extremely well built and detailed, using Pan motors built at the St. Cloud factory.

The Model A had a DeSmet Top, which would not stick out on the sides beyond the windshield when it was down. The body was called the Pandolfo Sleeping-Car body. "Converting this body into a comfortable bed is simplicity itself–release the back of the front seat, drop it down on a level with the rear-seat cushion, slide back front-seat cushion and pull out a collapsible foot support, and the 'Tourist-Sleeper' is completed," Pan literature crowed.

Pan cars also had a "Commissary Compartment," with compartments for a reserve supply of gasoline, oil, water, tools, and food. In August 1918, Pandolfo sent ten cars to the Minnesota state fair, then the Iowa state fair. He wanted to expose people to the cars, and get more stock sold so he could build an entirely new 1919 Pan '250' auto.

All ten cars were sold, which meant the drivers and mechanics had to return to St. Cloud by train.

Next, Pandolfo sent three cars on an 11,000-mile trip through the most difficult American terrain he could find. One car, driven by a 480-pound man, did cause a few minor problems. The others, however, did not, making 14 miles per gallon of gasoline, traveling in places without roads, and culminating with a trip up Pike's Peak for a picnic.

Pan tractors

Next, Pandolfo turned to building a tractor. The advertising screamed PAN "WAR TANK" THAT WILL WIN THE WAR. Now is the time when man power must be conserved. The Pan Tank-Tread Tractor saves man power and takes the place of eight horses."

Pandolfo played to patriotism. His ad said, "Thousands of our young men have gone to war, to make the world safe for democracy. It is now up to us to do our part at

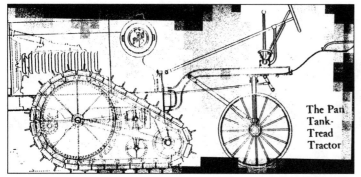

This is the outline of the Pan Tank-Tread Tractor, which was going to help end World War I the company predicted. Only one of these tractors was ever built and for quite a while, it did not have an engine in it. An article in the local newspaper finally made a big deal of how the engine ran.

This "King of the Field" tractor was to be one of Pan's next production models, after its tank-tread tractor, but the end of the company came before the tractor could ever be manufactured. In 1920, the company went out of business, leaving 70,000 investors $10,000,000 total, poorer. (Great River Regional Library)

home. We must raise bigger and better crops. We must do our work with less help and in less time. The Pan Tank-Tread Tractor will do your work better and in less time at a saving of one man and eight horses."

One selling point of the Pan Tank-Tread Tractor was that it could be steered from the seat of a plow, binder, or any other machinery the tractor might be pulling, which made steering the tractor as easy as steering horses.

The St. Cloud Times of Feb. 27, 1918, says, "Without a question, the Pan Tank-Tread Tractor proved the biggest sensation at the National Tractor show from the moment it went in to action until the closing hour of the show." The paper said other tractor men could not conceal their surprise and admiration when they inspected the "Farmer's War Tank." "Hundreds of farmers who had visited the show at Kansas City the first three days–before the Pan tractor arrived–came back to see the Pan. Many showed their disappointment when they found they could not have a 'Tank-Tread' delivered at once." The article said the tractor would revolutionize the tractor industry and farming.

More high praise was found in *Western Magazine*, April 1, 1918; unfortunately, that information and the good news in the St. Cloud paper was untrue, information planted, and some even paid for, by Pandolfo himself.

In 1919, Pan Motor Co. held a parade in St. Cloud for the tractor, followed by a big Pan trailer bus carrying band members, and drawn by the Pan tractor.

But trouble was brewing. An article in the *St. Cloud Times* on Oct. 8, 1919 says, "The famous Tank Tread Tractor, which is so strongly attacked in the suit against the

This is the Pan Tank-Tread tractor, setting in front of Samuel Pandolfo's Pan Motor Company factory in St. Cloud about 1919. Pandolfo had planted stories in the press about how farmers were clamoring for this tractor at the National Tractor Show in Kansas City, Mo. In 1918, and the untruths eventually caught up with him. Only one of these Pan Tank-Treads was ever built.

This is one of the Pan stock certificates given to some 70,000 stockholders before the company went under in 1920. Nearly a million shares of these were sold at $10 each.

Pan Motor Company to be heard in Chicago on the 23 inst. as being impracticable and a physical impossibility, appeared on the streets of St. Cloud this afternoon on its own power. 'In spite of everything that has been said against us because of our claims for the Tank Tread Tractor, it is running and it is a success,' said President Pandolfo. 'It is not only a success, but it is the best caterpillar tractor so far designed and developed.' "

More bad news followed. A pamphlet by the National Vigilance Committee (which monitored advertising) dedicated to the Pan Company said, "Only one model of this much promoted Pan Powered Tank-Tread Tractor has ever been built, so far as can be learned. This model–politeness only could concede it to be a real tractor–was built by the Progressive Machine & Model Works, 119 Southeast 5th St., Minneapolis."

The pamphlet says the information given out at the Kansas City show was certainly optimistic, since the tractor was not in running order at the time, but was there merely for show.

Pan had plans for a second type of tractor as well, the "King of the Field." During hearings, Pandolfo said he had orders for a Pan truck, as well, though little is known about that.

In 1920, the company went bankrupt, leaving 70,000 investors holding $10,000,000 worth of bad certificates. Pandolfo himself went almost non-stop into court, where he was finally indicted and sentenced to ten years in prison for mail fraud. After his release from Leavenworth in 1926, he returned to St. Cloud and attempted to form a new corporation to promote "Pan Health Do-Nuts," which included the manufacture and sale of donut machines, produced in a new plant he built near the site of his old one.

Chapter 35

Southern Perpetuates Major Automobile Fraud

The Southern Motor Manufacturing Association, Ltd., of Houston, Texas, built the Ranger 6-12 and 8-16 motor cultivator tractors, as well as the Ranger automobile, from 1919-1922.

Ranger tractors

In 1919, Southern built the 6-12 Ranger motor cultivator; it used a LeRoi engine to drive all four wheels, which was unusual for the motor cultivator trade. The fad of motor cultivators burst on the scene about this time, and disappeared within five years, part of the different types of machinery that farmers were using, testing, continuing to use, or casting away.

In 1920, the same machine was upped to an 8-16. Recommendation was pulling one 14-inch plow, and the machine weighed 2,600 pounds and cost $1,100. It could cultivate, the company said, twice the average number of acres in a day that many other tractors claimed, that is, two an hour for twenty in a ten-hour day, compared to the ten in ten hours claimed by many larger tractors. The vertical four-cylinder engine was 3-1/8 x 4-1/2 inches.

Ranger automobiles

The first Ranger automobile was announced in *The Houston Post* on Sept. 26, 1920, where the article stated the Southern-built engine was especially designed for Texas' climatic conditions. The first Ranger sported a four-cylinder L-head 31-hp engine built by the Southern Motors Manufacturing Association, Ltd. It had a 116-inch wheelbase, and could be purchased in Ranger maroon or Blevins blue, with black chassis and fenders. The engine had been subjected to a 35,000-mile road test at 50 mph. The roadster was priced at $1,595, and the touring car at $1,850. During the summer of 1921, a six-cylinder model with 123-inch wheelbase and 57 hp was announced. This car's models had names like Commodore, Newport, Blue Bonnet, and Pal o' Mine.

The Horseless Carriage Gazette for September-October 1956 has this to say about the company: "The Southern Motor Manufacturing Association of Houston who came out with The Ranger in 1920 to 1921 was a concern set up to swindle large amounts of money from investors and stockholders.

"Setting up a dummy plant on the Wallisville Road near Houston, and two show rooms in the heart of the city, and with swank offices in the Beatty Building, they proceeded to sell watered stock to the public. The system used by this concern was to show a large production of Ranger cars and thus encourage investors to buy stock. Actually, they produced very few cars. But the investors were led to believe otherwise by rotating the same cars from the show rooms and back to the factory and then back to the showroom again."

Cars were taken from the showroom, taken apart,

RANGER 8-16
Southern Motor Mfg. Assn., Ltd., Houston, Tex.

A single 14-inch plow was recommended for this small four-wheel-drive motor cultivator tractor manufactured as the Ranger 8-16 by Southern Motor Manufacturing Association, Ltd., of Houston, Texas. The Ranger weighed 2,600 pounds and cost $1,100 in 1920. Its engine was a LeRoi 3-1/8 x 4-1/2-inch bore and stroke of four cylinders that could drive the tractor from 1-1/2 to 2-1/2 mph, forward or reverse.

lugged to the factory, reassembled, and brought back to the show room for another selling campaign. Meanwhile, people who saw all this activity–and the company made sure that the stockholders who checked in did–thought a great number of cars were being manufactured. The company certainly was busy.

But being busy does not necessarily mean prosperity or honesty, and in 1922, the company went into receivership, followed by a merger with National Motors Corporation.

Two years later, fourteen members of Southern and National's boards were indicted for fraud, including the shocking realization that one was a woman who had been indicted. The public had been bilked of $6 million, according to the charges. The government claimed that the Ranger Six had not been built at all, and the Ranger Four had been built in small numbers "largely for stock-selling purposes and many times at a loss."

Some Rangers were shipped to New Orleans, some sold in Texas, and some sold to stockholders. Only a couple of Rangers still remain extant.

The Ranger Cultivator 6-12 was recommended for one 14-inch plow. It had a wheelbase of 24 inches and a cultivating clearance of 34 inches. It weighed 2,650 pounds and cost about half a buck a pound, $1,250. Its ignition system was a Dixie Aero-type high-tension magneto, and the cooling system was a Bremer tubular radiator. The transmission was a special geared system running in oil, with the gears always in mesh. Speeds were 1-1/2 to 2-1/2 mph. (Dan Roen Collection)

This is the Ranger 4, Model A-20, and was perhaps one of the model types that was assembled in the factory, taken to a showroom, moved to another showroom across town, and finally disassembled–with the parts being taken back to the factory for reassemblage, to give the impression that a great many more cars were being produced than actually were.

Chapter 36

Waterloo Company Also Claims Invention of Tractors

In the annals of tractor history, at least three companies have claimed they invented the tractor (and at least one said it was invented by someone else who didn't have the money to make a go of it.)

So it was that the Waterloo Gasoline Traction Engine Company of Waterloo, Iowa, also made the claim of having invented the tractor. The company was also, directly or indirectly, involved in the manufacture of at least three different automobiles.

Waterloo tractors

John Froelich of Froelich, Iowa, ran a grain elevator, and sought to make extra money in 1888-92 by custom work–running threshing crews in Iowa and South Dakota. During this time, he invented a knock-apart sleeping and eating car for his workers.

Unfortunately, his J. I. Case steam engine was heavy, clumsy, and difficult to move, and just as likely to set the grain on fire as to thresh.

So he resolved to build a better engine. He and his helper, William Mann, spent hours tinkering with their own machine. When they finally decided they were finished, they fueled it, and cranked it, but nothing happened. It wouldn't start.

So Froelich took a rifle cartridge, removed the bullet,

Most tractor companies of the time advertised their machines as part of the war effort. "Thousands of Waterloo Boy tractors are drafted into service to speed up farm work–standing the most drastic service tests in field and belt work," this ad says. "For war-time speed in all farm work." This 1918 ad shows a Waterloo Model R with a 25-hp engine designed to pull three plows. (State Historical Society of North Dakota)

In 1892, John Froehlich invented what is thought to be the first tractor, a 20-hp gas traction engine like the one shown here. It had 14- x 14-inch bore and stroke with an electric ignition. Today a plaque sets on the site where Froehlich did his work.

and stuck the cartridge into the priming cup. There he smacked it with a hammer. Bam! The flywheel spun and the engine started working. The tractor–or at least a form of it–had been invented! He used it successfully during 1892, threshing more than 72,000 bushels.

Froelich and others joined to start Waterloo Gasoline Traction Engine Company in 1893, the first company organized for the sole purpose of developing a tractor (still called traction engines at the time.) Froelich modified a Van Duzen engine (garnering several patents in the process).

Four were built and two sold, but for various reasons were quickly returned. The disappointment was so great,

Just after the turn of the century, Waterloo Motor Works of Waterloo, Iowa, made its Waterloo gasoline cars. The Phaeton, shown here, went for $1,350, and used a three-cylinder 4-1/2 x 4-1/2-inch bore and stroke engine that produced about 10 hp. The company also made the Waterloo tonneau auto, which sold for $1,750 and had a bit more power, up to 15 hp.

the investors in Waterloo Gasoline Traction Engine Company decided to make only stationary gasoline engines until the tractor could be built and tested properly.

Froelich, impatient, went off to do his own stuff, and the renamed company he left behind was called Waterloo Gasoline Engine Company. In 1896, it produced another gasoline tractor, but only sold one. Another new tractor was designed a year later, with the same results.

Little was done with tractors until Harry W. Leavitt joined the company. He had previously designed a tractor, and in 1912, 1913 or 1914, depending on the reference, the company did as it had promised–it returned to building tractors, and the first successful Waterloo tractors were produced; 20 of the L-A models were sold.

The first Waterloo Boy, the Model R, was brought out in 1914, and 118 were sold. After gathering farmer input and redesigning the tractor, four years later more than 8,000 were sold. Model N Waterloo Boy was introduced, and it became a smashing success. The company payroll rose from 20 to 1,000. A Waterloo Boy tractor was the first one tested in the Nebraska Tests, March 31-April 9, 1920.

John Deere had been keeping an eye on Waterloo Gasoline Engine Company's success. Frank Silloway of John Deere wrote, "I believe that, quality and price considered, it is the best commercial tractor on the market today," says *John Deere's Company*. "The only real competitor it has is the I.H.C. ...The Waterloo tractor is of a type which the average farmer can buy...We should have a satisfactory tractor at a popular price, and not a high-priced tractor built for the few. Here we have an opportunity to, overnight, step into practically first place in the tractor business...I believe that we would be acting wisely if we purchased this plant."

The decision by Deere to buy (after some initial hemming and hawing) was unanimous to buy, which the company did for $2,350,000 on March 18, 1918. Waterloo Boy tractors were produced by John Deere and called Waterloo Boy for the next five years, after which all the tractors manufactured by Deere & Company were John Deere.

Waterloo automobiles

Beverly Rae Kimes and Henry Austin Clark Jr. say in the *Standard Catalog of American Cars 1805-1942*, "In 1902, the Waterloo Gas Engine Company and the Davis engine department of the Cascade Manufacturing Company combined into the Waterloo Motor Works. The reason for the merger of these two stationary engine producers was that Charles E. Duryea had come to town and convinced everyone to get into the automobile field producing cars under his patents."

That, of course, would garner Duryea additional money. But a Waterloo car was built and, "simply a Duryea under another name," Kimes and Clark write. The Waterloo automobile didn't have as many body styles as the Duryea, however. In 1905, a four-passenger folding-seat phaeton was added to the two-passenger Anvil phaeton, which had been the only style built in 1903-04.

The Anvil was a three-cylinder, 12-hp machine with a 72-inch wheelbase, and it sold for $1,350. The folding-seat four-passenger tonneau vehicle sold in 1905 for $1,750.

The Davis automobile

The mists of time often obscure what actually happened, and in the case of the Davis automobile and its involvement with this Waterloo company, information is scant and unclear. Kimes and Clark write, "Although its entry in the *Chicago Times-Herald* contest of 1895 was announced, the Davis Gasoline Engine Company of Waterloo didn't make it to the starting line. The vehicle was subsequently completed, but the Davis firm remained thereafter in the gasoline business exclusively."

In 1902, the Davis Gasoline Engine Company merged with the Waterloo Gasoline Engine Company.

Unnamed Waterloo automobiles

In 1915, Louis W. Witry's stationary Waterloo Gasoline Engine proved such a hit that the company had to build a new factory. "The first automobile ever constructed and used in Black Hawk County," says a pamphlet called *Manufacturing Companies of Gasoline Engines in Early Waterloo*, "was also built in this factory. It, too, was designed by Mr. Witry, but the rapid increase in the demand for gasoline engines caused the company to abandon the manufacture of automobiles in favor of gasoline engines."

These were two-cylinder automobiles and six of them were sold, but stationary engines were selling so fast that all energies and shop space had to be turned toward making and selling them, so the concept of automobiles was abandoned.

SECTION III:

Tractor Companies That Made Trucks

Chapter 37

Allis-Chalmers Struggles Early

In May 1901, the Edward P. Allis Company of Milwaukee; the Fraser and Chalmers Co., of Chicago; the Gates Iron Works of Chicago; and the Dickson Manufacturing Co., of Scranton, Pennsylvania, merged to form The Allis-Chalmers Company. Each brought well-established leadership in certain lines of machinery, together with valuable designs, plant facilities, and personnel. The company billed itself as "The Company of the Four Powers–Steam, Gas, Water, and Electricity."

Perhaps it should have said, "The Company With Four Different Leaders," for it soon became obvious the leadership all wanted to go different directions.

Allis-Chalmers shaped up with 5,000 men working in five plants manufacturing $10,000,000 of agricultural products, with branch offices in ten leading American cities and offices in London, Mexico City, Johannesburg, and Santiago.

Allis-Chalmers manufactured Reynolds-Corliss engines, pumping engines, mining machinery, rock crushing and cement machinery, saw mill, and flour mill machinery. It was indeed well on its way toward its goal of being able to furnish basic machines to practically every major industry.

It diversified into the electrical field, air brakes, air compressors, as well as steam and hydraulic turbines, and gasoline engines.

Nevertheless, Allis-Chalmers found itself in financial trouble almost constantly during its first decade. By April 8, 1912, only a decade after the merger, the company was bankrupt.

These troubles were not without a bright side, as a new and strong leader was brought into the company: Otto Falk, who took over as bankruptcy receiver on April 8, 1912. Falk, a former Wisconsin National Guard brigadier general, realized quickly that Allis-Chalmers had overextended itself.

A new company emerged from the ashes, Allis-Chalmers Manufacturing Company, incorporated on April 16, 1913, with Falk as president.

Prior to reorganization, a strong-minded board of directors had consistently chosen weak presidents who would do their bidding. With General Falk in command, Allis-Chalmers gained a professional executive who believed a board of directors should not dictate policy, but advise on it. Falk believed the president should control the business, and he did.

He consolidated plants and instituted personnel changes that could be summed up this way: Treat others the way you like to be treated.

Falk's first major step in bringing Allis-Chalmers back into competition was to find new products. Three were chosen: the rotary tiller, the farm tractor, and the tractor-truck.

The tractor truck shown in this picture was a dual-purpose machine popular about the time it was built–1915; that is, the machine was popular with manufacturers, but never really caught on with farmers. This tractor-truck was manufactured by Allis-Chalmers to pull loads as well as haul them.

The tractor truck

By 1915, Allis-Chalmers had a prototype tractor-truck built and running. It was a half-track with artillery-style steel wheels in front for steering, powered by a T-head, four-cylinder 68-hp engine. It went 10 mph in fourth gear, and sold for $5,000. It appeared as a long-wheelbase flat-bed truck with crawler treads at the rear beneath the bed.

It was meant to draw plows and carry loads. But because it cost 17 times Henry Ford's Model T truck, and Allis-Chalmers had yet to establish a dealer and service network; it became merely an odd, expensive machine from an unknown company.

Ten were sold to Russia during World War I, and a few more were built until 1918. The last one served as a snowplow and tow vehicle around the Allis factory.

Allis-Chalmers rotary tillers

Another Falk product was the Motoculture Motor-Driven Rotary Plow, which Falk's chief consulting engineer found in Switzerland, and brought to the United States, along with its engineer.

Allis-Chalmers made several major design changes: the wheel design of the Allis-Chalmers rotary tiller No. 1 was entirely different from the European machine. The Swiss version had a transverse engine, while the A-C engine was mounted longitudinally and drove the wheels and tiller through bevel gears.

Ask any one of the 12000 Allis-Chalmers owners

SELLING tractors is merely a matter of giving the buyer what he wants— *the greatest drawbar horsepower per dollar of cost.*

That's the reason why Allis-Chalmers dealers have sold over 12,000 A-C 20-35 tractors to enthusiastic owners everywhere. For who else offers such genuine profit-making features to the farmer? He wants ample power at the lowest possible cost—Allis-Chalmers gives it to him. He wants inherent quality, scientific engineering, and extra features that will make his investment safer and longer-lived—the A-C 20-35 gives him an oil Pur-O-Lator, an air cleaner, a fuel strainer, spark arrester muffler, etc.

All this for only $1295!

During 1929-30, over three million farmers are going to be told of this great tractor value in more convincing terms than ever before. If you're looking for a proposition that has real profit-making merits, and is backed by a world-famous organization, write today for A-C 20-35 facts.

Allis-Chalmers Manufacturing Company
(Tractor Division)
505 - 62nd Avenue, • Milwaukee, Wisconsin
Specialists in Power Machinery Since 1846

What Users Say:

"With this tractor we established what we think is a record for continuous plowing in hard soil. During a 3-week period we averaged 25 acres every day, pulling 4 bottom 14 in. mouldboard plows, stopping only on Sundays. The amount of oil and fuel used was very little, less than 50 gallons of gasoline per day, and never more than a gallon of oil each day."

"Did 100 acres of spring plowing pulling 5 plows. Cut 90 acres of wheat. Pulled 150 rods of hedge. Pulled a 30 in. Separator (plain bearings) 10 days. The A-C had plenty of surplus power at all times. This Engine did $1600 worth of hard work for us with no expense for repairs."

"My choice of the four or five leading tractors is the Allis-Chalmers because of the extra power, its sturdy construction, easy to handle and start."

ALLIS-CHALMERS MFG. CO., (Tractor Division)
505 - 62nd Avenue, Milwaukee, Wis.
Send me complete details about the A-C 20-35 Tractor and the A-C franchise.

Name _____

Address _____

City _____ State _____

$1295
CASH · F.O.B. MILWAUKEE
Convenient Terms Can Be Arranged

Allis-Chalmers 20-35 TRACTORS

Despite the troubles that Allis-Chalmers encountered during the second decade of the 1900s, by 1929 it had become a major tractor producer. This ad shows the Allis-Chalmers 20-35, which was being offered for $1,295. (Dan Roen Collection)

World's greatest drawbar horsepower
-backed by the world's greatest Manufacturer of power machinery

FIFTY
Price $3540
F.O.B. Springfield, Ill.

SEVENTY-FIVE
Price $5350
F.O.B. Springfield, Ill.

THE Allis-Chalmers-Monarch provides the greatest drawbar horsepower, per dollar of cost, of any track-type tractor in its class.

From an engineering standpoint, the Allis-Chalmers-Monarch represents the supreme achievement of engineers whose mechanical accomplishments are famous the world over. Allis-Chalmers believes that performance, based on correct design, quality materials, and scientific manufacturing methods, is the primary factor in determining the value of a tractor to a buyer.

"Well-Engineered" is stamped on every part of the Allis-Chalmers-Monarch. It embodies a wealth of features, such as an Oil Pur-O-Lator, Air Cleaner, pressure lubrication system, modern engine, etc.

Investigate Allis-Chalmers-Monarch today. It is a money-maker for everyone.

ALLIS-CHALMERS MANUFACTURING CO.
Specialists in Power Machinery Since 1846
Monarch Tractors Division   Milwaukee, Wisconsin

Monarch Tractors

PRODUCT OF   ALLIS-CHALMERS

More and more the modern farmer is turning to the Allis-Chalmers-Monarch for efficient and profitable farming. Hauling a 20 foot combine, or pulling 7 plows at one time, is work of equal ease for the lightfooted Monarch.

ALLIS-CHALMERS MFG. CO.,
Monarch Tractors Division,
201 - 62nd Avenue, Milwaukee, Wis.

Send me complete details about the Allis-Chalmers-Monarch, and particulars about the Monarch selling franchise.

Name..

Address.......................................

City.....................State................

To help solidify its tractor line, Allis-Chalmers Manufacturing Company of Milwaukee, Wisconsin, bought out the Monarch Tractor line in 1928. A couple of models are shown here, the Fifty on the left, selling for $3,450 in this 1929 ad, and the Seventy-Five, selling for $5,350 the same year. Allis-Chalmers was also touting the Monarch Tractors from its Monarch Tractors Division for use by farmers on the farm. (Dan Roen Collection)

In 1936, Allis-Chalmers manufactured this Model U tractor, an unusual-looking specimen that came either with steel wheels or with rubber. Nebraska tests listed this tractor as about a 19- to 31-hp tractor. It was equipped with Allis-Chalmers' own four-cylinder I-head engine with a 4-3/8 x 5-inch bore and stroke rated at 1,200 rpm. It weighed 5,030 pounds on steel, and 110 more with rubber. Speeds were 2.33, 3.33, 5, and 10 mph, although the highest speed was recommended only when using rubber tires. (Dan Roen Collection)

The machine had one front steering wheel and two rear drive wheels, 52 inches in diameter and 11 inches wide. With a four-cylinder, 30-hp engine, the tiller weighed 4,500 pounds and ran in three forward gears from speeds of .8 to 3.6 mph.

Unfortunately, like the tractor-truck, the rotary tiller was not a success, and only a few were built.

Allis-Chalmers tractors

The third product Falk decided to hinge the reputation of Allis-Chalmers upon was the farm tractor. At the time, it didn't seem like a better choice than the tractor-truck, or the rotary-tiller.

Falk had two choices: he could collaborate with an existing tractor company–the makers of the Little Bull tractor from Minneapolis offered him a partnership–or he could design and build an Allis-Chalmers tractor.

He decided the company should design its own tractor.

The Model 10-18 was Allis-Chalmers' first tractor. The prototype was finished in 1914, and was green (instead of the later well-known Allis-Chalmers orange.) It used gasoline to start its horizontally opposed two-cylinder engine before it switched over to kerosene. The engine had a 5.25-inch bore, 7-inch stroke, with 10-drawbar and 18-belt hp. It weighed 4,800 pounds.

Despite its advertising–"In its design all superfluous parts have been eliminated–it is a model of effective simplicity and has a remarkable capacity for hard work. Operating costs are low for it is economical of fuel. In plowing it takes the place of six horses and will operate either two or three plows according to the condition of the soil plowed"– it was not a success, except that it introduced Allis-Chalmers to the concept of making tractors.

As early as 1915, while the 10-18 was just beginning production, Allis-Chalmers was hard at work at another tractor, the General Purpose, or 6-12.

The GP was intended to use extant horse-drawn implements, without major modifications. The GP was horse-like: the operator hitched it to the horse-drawn imple-

The Allis-Chalmers 10-18 farm tractor was featured in this *Farm Implements* ad ca. 1918. It says proudly, "In the reputation and achievements of the plant behind it, the Allis-Chalmers Farm Tractor stands pre-eminent. In its development, it has the benefit of the expert engineering corps–the machine building talent and skill–together with the unequalled facilities and resources of the greatest engine building plant in America." (Dan Roen Collection)

ment, sat in the implement's seat and directed the tractor from back there. The GP had great traction because most of its weight was concentrated over the drive wheels.

The Model 6-12 allowed a farmer to use both draft horse and tractor power without the investment in both types of implements, and may have hastened the acceptance of tractors by farmers.

Two versions of the 6-12 were built; the A General Purpose had a high- mounted engine, and pinion gears engaging ring gears mounted around the inner circumference of the drive wheels, as a final drive.

The Model B with a low-mounted engine was adapted to orchards, and used a pinion-internal ring gear final drive, similar the 18-30.

Both versions used the four-cylinder L-head LeRoi engine, with a 3.125-inch bore and 4.5-inch stroke, rated at 1,200 rpm.

In the end, the 6-12 was little better for Allis-Chalmers than the earlier 10-18. But the A-C engineers were determined to find a successful tractor design, and on the third try they did: the 15-30.

The A-C Duplex tractor was a pair of 6-12 tractors hitched together. It did not find acceptance, probably because the operator couldn't get both engines running at the same time, or if he did, he didn't know which way the tractor would go.

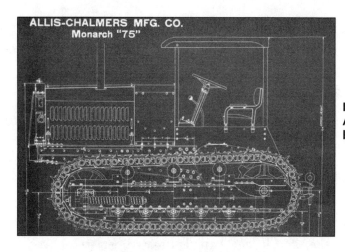

In 1936, *The Tractor Field Book* exhibited this blueprint of an Allis-Chalmers Manufacturing Company Monarch 75 caterpillar tractor. (Dan Roen Collection)

In 1928, Allis-Chalmers took over Monarch Tractor Corporation to bolster its line of construction machinery. However, some A-C Monarch tractors were sold for farm use as well.

Early Monarch models include the Monarch Lightfoot 6-10, probably the earliest model, and the 12-20 Never-slip. The first Monarch to be tested at Nebraska was the 18-30, which was the sole model produced by Monarch for a number of years.

Other earlier Monarch models include the Monarch Model D, 6-60; and the Monarch C, 25-35; the Model F crawler.

Most early Allis-Chalmers tractors were dismal failures. Even the man who had been heading the division, George Gardner, recommended in 1926 that the company get out of the tractor business.

With that attitude, Gardner could do nothing but resign; following long-standing A-C policy, Otto Falk found and hired a man who knew tractors, Harry Merritt, as manager of the tractor department in 1926.

Merritt changed the drab-looking green Allis-Chalmers tractors to its well-known Persian orange, after seeing acres of brilliant orange poppies in bloom.

It was an instant attention-getter, especially in a time when farm tractors were almost always dull. Soon there were bright orange machines operating all over the United States.

One of the most important acquisitions he and A-C made in terms of their tractor division was the 1931 purchase of Advance-Rumely Thresher Company of LaPorte, Indiana. Their OilPull was a tractor with a long history, its first model having come out in 1910. This was the expertise that Otto Falk wanted for his Allis-Chalmers Tractor Division.

With two decades working with farm tractors, and the background and experiences of Advance-Rumely, Allis-Chalmers tractors began to take off.

As Allis-Chalmers came into the modern age, it started making tractors like the Model WD, which had so many new features and improvements that the sales force had to relearn everything except the name Allis-Chalmers. Terms like two-clutch power control, single hitch-point implements, traction-booster, and power-shift wheels gave them plenty to talk about and demonstrate.

For more power, the WD45 followed, and then the CA, after much clamor from farmers wanting a C tractor with all the features of the new WD.

About the same time, the G came along. A number of dealers were frustrated because they had to order the G, whose niche was truck farms, nurseries, and specialty-crop applications. It was a small tractor. Though it was developed by West Allis engineering, it was produced only in the Gadsden, Alabama plant, which also built cotton pickers, mowers, and electrical apparatus.

Next came the D series of tractors, which evolved out of the Cs. The first two models were introduced in 1957–the D14 in the spring and the D17 in the fall. Their new styling was not only aesthetically pleasing, but functional as well, but the most important new feature of these two tractors was doubtless the Power-Director hand clutch with high and low ranges.

D15s followed, then the D15 series II, in 1963, then the D15D grove tractor, and the D10 and D12 tractors, in May 1959. These replaced the earlier Model B and Model CA, and were light one- and two-row tractors. A series III of D10 and D12 was also made.

Toward the late 1950s, it was apparent that a more powerful tractor was needed, and so the Model D18 was first developed, but it wasn't a pleasing-looking tractor, and it just didn't have enough power, so at the last minute, a turbocharger was added, the first tractor with a factory-installed turbocharger, starting December 1961.

The D21 broke the 100 hp barrier for Allis-Chalmers when it came out; the D21 series II tractors were diesels that outperformed the D21s. They came out in 1965. Allis-Chalmers played with hydrostatic front-wheel assist at this time, but discarded it as unworkable for tractors, although the testing provided impetus for use on a combine.

The Hundred Series of tractors followed, then the 220 in 1969, 220, 20, the 7030 and 7050 tractors, then the 7040, 7060, and 7080 tractors. During this time, much more was done than build new tractors of course; other farm machinery was produced, new cabs were designed for Allis-Chalmers machinery, transmissions were redesigned, and much more.

The 7000 series came along, the 6000 series, then the 8000, 8550, 4WD tractors, until Allis-Chalmers became Deutz-Allis in 1985.

Chapter 38

Caterpillar Still Operating Today

Caterpillar Tractor Company resulted first from the union of the Holt Manufacturing Company of Stockton, California, and Best Manufacturing Company of San Leandro, California in 1910, forming Holt; then the merger with C.L. Best Gas Traction Company of San Leandro, in 1925. In 1928, the company purchased the Russell Grader Company of Minneapolis, adding the motor grader to its stable.

Caterpillar tractors

The 1910 merger of Holt and Best brought together the two best tracklaying tractor companies in the United States. Some caterpillars built after the merger included the Caterpillar Thirty, which weighed 9,000 pounds, pulled 7,500 pounds, and produced 30 hp. It was tested three different times at Nebraska, in 1924 and twice in 1936 (one gasoline, one diesel.)

The Caterpillar Sixty weighed 20,000 pounds, pulled 12,360 pounds at Nebraska, and required five gallons of oil to fill the crankcase of the engine, which had a 6-1/2-inch bore and 8-1/2-inch stroke.

After the final merger, three new sizes were produced, the 2-ton, 5-ton, and 10-ton. In 1928, the Caterpillar Fifteen, weighing 7,500 pounds, sold for $1,900.

Through the years, many different models of Caterpillars have been relied upon to dig and fix roads, move dirt, and do every other construction need imaginable.

Caterpillar trucks

The first Caterpillar trucks were manufactured in 1962 by The Caterpillar Tractor Company; they were large, off-highway dump trucks for large road and construction applications. The first trucks included the 35-ton 769B, the 50-ton Model 773, and the 85-ton Model 777. Caterpillar also built bottom dump coal haulers, and truck tractors. By the mid-1990s, Caterpillar was building models 769C, 771C, 773B, 775B, and others. The two lightest were 450-hp diesels. The three largest Caterpillar trucks built were 150-, 195-, and 240-ton capacity.

Of the eleven Caterpillar factories in the United States and Puerto Rico, the Decatur, Illinois, plant has produced all the dump trucks.

Today, Caterpillar manufactures both tractors and trucks.

One of the large types of trucks that Caterpillar builds.

IMPLEMENT AND TRACTOR 31

"CATERPILLAR" FORTY

Caterpillar Tractor Co., Peoria, Ill.

Traction Wheels: Two self-laying tracks, 16x74¾ in.
Tread Width: 74 and 56-in. **Adjustment:** None.
Length: 139⅝ in.; **Width:** 93 and 75 in.; **Height:** 70 in.; **Weight:** 13,910 and 13,310 lbs.; **Price:** $2775 and $2575 f.o.b. factory.
Turning Radius (Outside): 9⅛ and 7 1/12 ft.
Engine: Own, 5⅛x6½, vertical, 4 cylinders, cast in pairs.
Lubrication: Pressure oiling system.
Carburetor: Zenith, 1½-in.
Ignition System: Eisemann high tension magneto.
Lighting Equipment: Bosch generator.
Cooling System: Water, pump circulation, gear driven fan.
Bearings: Largely anti-friction ball and roller.
Transmission: Sliding gear; 1.7, 2.5, 3.2 and 4.6 m.p.h. forward; 1.9 m.p.h reverse.
Final Drive: Spur gears, completely enclosed.
Belt Pulley: 12x10¾; 850 r.p.m. and 2,670 feet per minute at normal engine speed.

"CATERPILLAR" DIESEL RD6

Caterpillar Tractor Co., Peoria, Ill

Traction Wheels: Two self-laying tracks, 16x74¾.
Tread Width: 74 and 56-in.; **Adjustment:** None.
Length: 138⅝ in.; **Width:** 93 and 75 in.; **Height:** 72 1/16 in.; **Weight:** 15,560 and 14,820 lbs.; **Price:** $3575 and $3375 f.o.b. factory.
Turning Radius (Outside): 8⅓ and 7 ft.
Engine: Own, 5¾x8, vertical, 3 cylinders, cast en bloc.
Lubrication: Pressure oiling system.
Starting Equipment: Own two-cylinder gasoline starting engine.
Lighting: Robert Bosch magneto.
Cooling System: Water, pump circulation, gear driven fan.
Bearings: Largely anti-friction ball and roller.
Transmission: Sliding gears, 1.7, 2.5, 3.2 and 4.6 m.p.h. forward; 1.9 m.p.h. reverse.
Final Drive: Spur gear, completely enclosed.
Belt Pulley: 12x10¾; 850 r.p.m. and 2,670 feet per minute at normal engine speed.

"CATERPILLAR" FIFTY

Caterpillar Tractor Co., Peoria, Ill.

Traction Wheels: Two self-laying tracks, 18x81⅝ in.
Tread Width: 74 and 60 in.; **Adjustment:** None.
Length: 146¼ in.; **Width:** 7 ft., 11⅝ in. and 6 ft., 9⅝ in; **Height:** 75¾ in.; **Weight:** 18,890 and 18,080 lbs.; **Price:** $3650 and $3400 f.o.b. factory.
Turning Radius (Outside): 8⅝ and 7⅝ ft.
Engine: Own, 5½x6½, vertical, 4 cylinders, cast singly.
Lubrication: Pressure oiling system.
Carburetor: Zenith, 1½-in.
Ignition System: Eisemann high tension magneto.
Lighting Equipment: Bosch generator.
Cooling System: Water, pump circulation, gear driven fan.
Bearings: Largely anti-friction ball and roller.
Transmission: Sliding gear, 1.6, 2.4, 3.4 and 4.7 m.p.h. forward; 1.9 m.p.h. reverse.
Final Drive: Spur gears, completely enclosed.
Belt Pulley: 13⅝x13; 753 r.p.m. and 2,630 feet per minute at governed engine speed.

This page from the 1936 *Implement and Tractor* shows three of the Caterpillars being built by the Caterpillar Tractor Company of Peoria, Illinois: the Caterpillar Forty, Caterpillar Diesel RD6, and Caterpillar Fifty. The first two had identical forward speeds of 1.7, 2.5, 3.2, and 4.6 mph forward, and 1.9 mph reverse with its own engine, a 5-1/8 x 6-1/2-inch bore and stroke for the Forty, and a 5-3/4 x 8-inch bore and stroke for the diesel, while the Fifty had its own 5-1/2 x 6-1/2-inch bore and stroke engine. The Forty and Fifty each weighed just under 14,000 pounds, while the diesel weighed 15,560 pounds. (Dan Roen Collection)

Chapter 39

TC Tractor Evolves Due to Other Tractor Success

Steam engines were one of the first agricultural products made by the Minneapolis Steel & Machinery Co. in 1903. At the time, the company was also manufacturing bridges, tanks, and other equipment.

For the first few years, MSMC built steam engines, bridges, gas engines, and in 1910, hired Joy-Willson Company of Minneapolis to build a tractor for it. Sales results were so encouraging, the company decided to manufacture its own tractor, the Twin City.

Curiously, while MSMC was building its own Twin City tractors, it also contracted to build tractors for other tractor companies. It built Case 30-60s, and Little Bull tractors. Perhaps the $1 million contract to build Bulls swayed MSMC and blinded it to the fact that it was competing with itself.

In 1914, MSMC contracted with a Canadian Co-op to build the 20th Century tractor. This was the beginning of the end of the association with Bull Tractor Company, as Bull asked MSMC to agree not to sell the 20th-century tractor–which was very much like the Bull–in the United States for a full year. Shortly thereafter, MSMC stopped making Bull tractors, offering that to make Bull tractors, it was forced to neglect its own.

Twin City tractors

In 1910, Joy-Willson Company built five prototype tractors which were tested and redesigned in 1911 and 1912, when MSMC asked Joy-Willson to build about 250 tractors for it. These four-cylinder tractors with 7- x 10-inch bore and stroke were built in 1912, and were called Twin City tractors. Some of the redesigned TC-40 tractors had a 7-1/4-inch bore and 9-inch stroke and were used to break up land in Texas.

Farm Implements discussed "Why a Tractor Should Be Built Narrow" in a Feb. 29, 1916 article about the Twin City tractors: "Side draft has always been an element in the operation of small tractors that manufacturers have found it difficult to eliminate in the construction of the machine. ...When a tractor...is only capable of pulling from four to six plows, if it is built wide, as a machine must be when its motor is placed crosswise on the frame, side draft is bound to develop, especially if the machine is to be kept upon hard ground. In the small sizes of the Twin City tractors, this difficulty has been eliminated by building unusually narrow machines. The Twin City "15" brings out this point in a very clear way. The machine will pull four plows under ordinary conditions, the width of which is practically the same as the width of the machine, which is about five feet. This enables this little machine...to pull its full load of

Minneapolis Steel & Machinery Company of Minneapolis had arguably the nicest-looking drawings of all the companies in the business at the time, as exhibited by these shown on this page. This one is the Twin City 25-45, built in the late teens. By this time the company, which had manufactured Bull tractors and 20th-century tractors for other companies, had given up on that work and was working strictly on its own. The 25-45 was manufactured from 1913-1920. (State Historical Society of North Dakota)

plows without any side draft whatever.

"...The Twin City '15' has a vertical four-cylinder motor and is built almost identically the same design as all the larger sizes of Twin City tractors."

MSMC built a wide variety of tractors: The 25-45 from 1913-20, which weighed 16,000 pounds and sold for $3,850

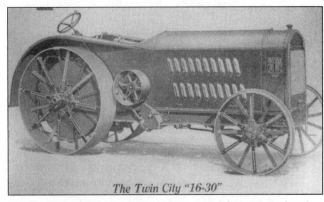

The Twin City "16-30"

The Twin City 16-30 in this image was often touted as being streamlined like an automobile, and indeed it has a very different look, long and low-slung, from most tractors of the day. This machine was built in 1916. (State Historical Society of North Dakota)

119

The 17-28 Twin City tractor shown in this photo had originally been designated a 12-20 model, but was later re-designated a 17-28. None of these Twin City tractors were tested at Nebraska since they were all pre-1920 models. (State Historical Society of North Dakota)

in 1917; and the 40-65, which was tested in Nebraska in 1920 and used a Holley 257 carburetor, K-W Model HK magneto, and 12-inch extension rims. It actually developed 49-66 hp.

The 60-90 was the largest Twin City built, with the same bore and stroke as the 40-65, but six cylinders instead of four. It carried 95 gallons of fuel and needed 116 gallons of water in its radiator. It weighed 28,000 pounds, and sold for $6,000 in 1917.

Smaller Twin City tractors were built, too, like the Twin City 15 with a four-cylinder 4-3/4- x 7-inch bore-and-stroke engine that operated at 650 rpm. The Twin City 16-30 used a four-cylinder 5- x 7-1/2-inch engine; it trotted

along at 2 and 2-3/4 mph.

The 12-20 was a unique Twin City tractor with its four-cylinder, sixteen-valve engine. Two intake and two exhaust valves were provided for each cylinder, and two camshafts were used. It was redesignated a 17-28 in 1927.

In 1929, Minneapolis Steel & Machinery Company united with Minneapolis Threshing Machine and Moline Plow companies to form the Minneapolis-Moline Power Implement Company.

Twin City trucks

From 1918 until the demise of the company, MSMC built Twin City trucks in 2- and 3-1/2-ton capacities. The Dec. 31, 1918 issue of *Farm Implements and Tractors* magazine said, "The Automotive Engineering Department has been established by the Minneapolis Steel & Machinery Company. This department is where automotive apparatus, such as tractors, motors, and trucks, are designed." An issue of the company newsletter talked about experimental models of trucks, two 3-1/2-ton trucks having been built and were running; and two of the 2-ton variety were being built in July 1919.

Twin City buses

In the 1920s, MSMC began building Twin City buses, including a 25-passenger Model DW low parlor coach, which was built in 1925. It used a 60-hp engine and had front-mounted air springs.

In 1919, Twin City Company advertised the Twin City tractor, thresher, and truck in one ad. "Why play with pennies when dollars are waiting for you?" the ad read. The tractor advertised was the 12-20, while the truck was the two-ton Twin City. (Dan Roen Collection)

This photo shows two views of a Twin City truck that made a trip from Minneapolis to Peoria, Illinois, a normal practice of trucks during the first two decades of the century to test the machines and see what they had. This two-ton truck carried a load of 4,700 pounds over 500 miles. The upper photo is in front of the Twin City factory in Minneapolis, the lower in front of the branch office in Peoria. The truck left Minneapolis at 3 p.m. Saturday, June 5, and arrived in Peoria five days later, on June 10, but the lateness was due to "unavoidable weather conditions and bad roads" encountered on the trip. (Dan Roen Collection)

Chapter 40

Morton Could Have Started Tractor Industry

S.S. Morton could easily be credited with launching the American tractor industry, since he invented the Morton traction truck, which allowed companies–and individual farmers–to fit an engine on it and use it as a tractor.

But he was not alone in his love of vehicles and his inventiveness: his three sons and their cousins were all involved in making Morton tractors and trucks.

Morton tractors

Though S. S. Morton built his first tractor at York, Pennsylvania, just before the turn of the century and received patents, the company did not produce tractors until its four-wheel-drive four-cylinder tractor appeared at an automobile show in Harrisburg in February 1912. Somehow, the Morton Tractor, with its 5-1/4- x 6-inch bore-and-stroke engine, was located in the most prominent position in the building (despite the huge advertising budgets used by other major vehicle builders who came to the show). The tractor was the first vehicle anyone saw immediately upon stepping inside the arena.

The location gained the tractor much attention. The engine could be inspected through a glass cab, and the wheels had an open tread design that attracted mechanics and agricultural workers. Morton claimed the tractor replaced 25-50 horses when used for plowing on a large farm. The tractor was also suitable for heavy hauling, and a lengthy newspaper article told everyone so.

The tractor had three forward speeds and one reverse. Steering was applied to both axles. This 40-hp machine was powered by a Buda motor, and was an expensive item, costing $3,000 in 1920. A later Morton four-wheel drive sold for $2,000 more.

Morton trucks

All Morton trucks, manufactured from 1912-16 by the Morton Truck and Tractor Company of Harrisburg, Pennsylvania, were powered by a 30-hp four-cylinder engine with a four-speed transmission and chain drive. The company offered trucks from 1-1/2 to 6 tons during its tenure, and had four-wheel-drive and four-wheel-steering versions.

The first Morton truck was finished shortly after the automobile show referred to above ended in February 1912. A newspaper article from the *Harrisburg Telegraph* in 1913 said, "Two trailer trucks are being built of eight-ton capacity. These trucks differ from the regular type by having a chassis with a wheelbase as short as possible. A fifth-wheel attachment connects the trailer that carries the load."

In March 1913, at a special truck show in Harrisburg, Walter Morton pointed out the special worm drive featured in the new Morton trucks, as well as electric starters and electric lights, uncommon at the time. Curiously, the Morton Company did not advertise for either this show or the earlier one, while all the other large truck concerns did–obviously they had some kind of "in."

Morton also made fire engines during its truck tenure. Many Morton trucks were sold to Russia from 1914-1916, although news stories of the time were unclear as to whether they were actually cars (which it is quite clear

S.S. Morton invented this single-cylinder horizontal hopper-cooled engine and mounted it on a light, short wheelbase chassis in 1899. It was gear driven, except for the friction drive from engine to countershaft. In some respects, Morton could be credited with the invention of the tractor because he invented the Morton traction truck, which was widely used by farmers to "invent" their own tractor by adding an engine. Tractors in those days were still called "traction trucks."

Morton Motor Plow Company made its combination tractor in 1914, a time when these types of machines were popular, as farmers were figuring out not only the type of machinery they needed on the farm, but which kinds of machines would work best. The Morton had a pair of mounted plows.

Morton never made), or trucks or tractors. The area newspaper said the company had received orders from Russia for "300 War Autos…of the four-wheel drive type and of 120 hp capacity. They are to be used for the transfer of ammunition and provisions."

Another newspaper said they were trucks being ordered. Two days later, another newspaper had a photo of a Morton tractor this time and a caption that said, "One of the 300 tractors Russia will use against the Kaiser."

But the company was growing too big too fast. Samuel Morton, the father, spent considerable time supervising construction and testing of the vehicles, and not enough trucks or tractors were being manufactured to fulfill war orders from Russia and Great Britain. On Dec. 12, 1916, the Morton Truck and Tractor Company filed for involuntary bankruptcy.

One of the trucks manufactured by Morton Truck and Tractor Company.

The logo of the Morton Truck and Motor Company, which manufactured trucks in Harrisburg, Pa., from 1911-1916.

Chapter 41

Power Tractors

In 1919, Power Truck & Tractor Co. of Detroit, Michigan, brought out a three-plow tractor that looked suspiciously like the 10-20 Mogul tractor made by International Harvester Company of Chicago. Perhaps there is nothing wrong with co-opting a tractor design when the engine and power is so different, a single-cylinder engine made by Power, with a 9-inch bore and 12-inch stroke for a 15-32 rating, compared to the Mogul's 8-1/2- x 12-inch bore and stroke, a 10-20 rating, two speed-transmission and high-tension magneto.

The Power tractor cost $1,485 in 1919, which was probably the only year it was offered. It could pull 2,500 pounds, and was identical to the Pontiac tractor offered in 1919 by Pontiac Tractor Company.

Power trucks

Power trucks were manufactured from 1917-23, first in Detroit, and later in St. Louis. The 1917 model was a 2-ton, and the next year, 3-1/2- and 5-ton models were offered, all powered by Continental four-cylinder engines and using worm drives. The 5-ton had a wheelbase of 180 inches.

In 1922, Power moved to St. Louis, and manufactured 2- and 3-1/2-ton trucks with Hinkley engines, four-speed transmissions, and worm-drive rear axles.

In 1919, Power Truck & Tractor Company of Detroit offered this three-plow 15-32 tractor that looked a lot like IHC's 10-20 Mogul tractor. It had a huge bore and stroke of 9 x 12 inches, and sold for about $1,500. Its maximum forward speeds were 1-1/2 and 3 mph.

Chapter 42

Germany's Loss is America's Gain: Advance Rumely

A minor mistake on a military drill field created powerful Advance-Rumely Thresher Company of LaPorte, Indiana, so says William N. Rumely, son of Meinrad Rumely, in his *Personal History of Meinrad Rumely*.

"It was the cruel treatment at the hands of a German officer that eventually led Meinrad Rumely, founder of the M. Rumely Co., to come to America," Rumely says.

Meinrad Rumely was born on Feb. 9, 1823, in Germany. After schooling, he journeyed from German village to village, "wherever there was a waterfall or stream suitable for power to operate a grist or saw mill," William Rumely writes.

At the required age, he entered the military service. Two of his brothers, Jacob and John, had already emigrated to the United States and escaped compulsory military duty because they were too short. But not Meinrad. While in the service, he was required to take a three-day examination.

"During the last day of drilling," William writes, "the incident occurred that eventually led him to America: he made the mistake of stepping forward a few inches beyond the line of the (rest of the men in the) company. The Captain, observing the mistake, rushed toward him and struck him a severe blow with his pistol."

Rumely fainted and fell, and was carted off to a military hospital, where he lay in great pain for a number of days. After Rumely told his parents of the brutal treatment, they provided him with sufficient money to come to America. "He embarked from Havre, France," William writes, "and was 64 days on a sailing vessel in coming to this country,

landing in New York."

In New York, the 26-year-old Meinrad received a rude welcome. His trunk was robbed and all of his money stolen. Luckily, he had machine-shop skills, and found a job quickly, earning enough money in a few months to travel westward to Cleveland. From there, he walked the 50 miles to Canton, Ohio, where his brother Jacob worked making wooden pumps.

In 1851, Meinrad learned that a railroad was to be built from Toledo to Chicago, and that shops would be located in LaPorte, Indiana. So he came to LaPorte to seek his fortune, "in a stage that ran over a plank road," William writes.

His arrival would change LaPorte forever.

After looking LaPorte over, and seeing all the newly built railroad-related shops, Meinrad decided LaPorte had a great future and he could be part of it. He sent for John, and together they built a foundry. That little foundry became M. Rumely Company, and later, Advance-Rumely Thresher Company. They built threshers, stationary engines, and a wide variety of other products.

Early agricultural companies constantly had to deal with the dangers of explosions and fires, and the M. & J. Rumely was no different; a new boiler had been installed in 1871, and on Good Friday eight months later, it exploded. "Meinrad Rumely had just left the boiler room to go to the bank," William writes, "when he heard the terrific noise. As he looked back toward the factory, he saw the long smoke-stack blown high in the air and clouds of smoke

The 14-28 was one of many Rumely OilPulls built. This 1917 model weighed 8,700 pounds–many of the Rumely tractors were heavier–and used a two-cylinder motor with "enclosed transmission" (farmers had begun recognizing the value of not having farm field dirt mixing in with the oil in opening in tractors), and ran at forward speeds of 2.1 and 3 mph. "Guaranteed to pull up to five 14-inch moldboard plows–will operate a 24- to 28-inch separator," advertising for this tractor claimed. (Dan Roen Collection)

BRINGS FORTH ANOTHER

PREDICTS A FAR GREATER SUCCESS FOR THE

TYPE "E"---30 TRACTIVE, 60 BRAKE H.P.

which we are now ready to announce for early spring delivery. The *OilPull* type "E" is a four-cycle, internal combustion engine with two cylinders of 10" diameter and 12" stroke. It is equipped with an automatic governor that regulates every explosion to suit the new need; it is oil cooled, has both splash and forced feed lubrication.

We build *OilPull* "E" strong and rigid. The tractor frame is built of 12" x 31½ pound I-beams riveted together in one solid block. Rear wheels are 80" high, 30" face, ⅜" steel tire with 16 flat steel upset spokes. Wheels are reinforced with 4" channel iron on the outer rim and a steel band on the inner rim. All parts solidly riveted together. All gearing is large and massive, composed of steel and semi-steel. All shafts superior to United States Naval specifications.

> *OilPull* "E" compared with animal power for plowing will save a dollar an acre. Turning 20 acres a day, during 1000 days' use, *OilPull* means $20,000.00 profit to its owner.

25121 MAIN STREET
LA PORTE, INDIANA

Though the Rumely OilPull was still in the testing phase when this 1910 advertisement was published, the M. Rumely Company of LaPorte, Indiana, was beginning to narrow down to one of the finest tractors that would ever come onto the market, the OilPull. This Type E 30-60 had a four-cylinder engine with bore-and-stroke engines of 10 x 12 inches. "All gearing is large and massive," the ad says, "composed of steel and semi-steel. All shafts superior to United States Naval specifications." The ad said if a farmer could turn 20 acres a day, in 1,000 days he would be $20,000 richer. (Dan Roen Collection)

Advance-Rumely decided to buy Aultman-Taylor Machinery Company of Mansfield, Ohio, partly because of its long illustrious history in the agricultural field (in operation since 1867) but also because Aultman-Taylor held certain manufacturing and patent rights of John Nichols (of Nichols & Shepard Company) pertaining to the vibrator thresher. This 15-30 Aultman-Taylor tractor was not as good, perhaps, as the exceptional Aultman-Taylor 30-60, but then the 30-60 was one of the best tractors of its time. One item many people forget is that farmers were often building roads in those days, and the 15-30 was a good one for that. "It pulls an 8-foot blade grade in hard going, draws drags, planers, etc.; runs a crusher; hauls road material. In fact, it's a super tractor for road work," the advertising crowed. (Dan Roen Collection)

and dust. Realizing instantly that the boiler had gone, he rushed back to see if any were injured. He began looking for Mr. Pallien, the engineer, but couldn't find him. Carefully searching around the engine, he discovered the man buried under brick and mortar. The engineer was extricated and doctors found his legs broken, all the high ribs on the right side were broken, and his jaw was broken."

John Rumely had been on the second floor, and had just started down the stairs with Mr. Lans when the boiler blew; both were thrown sky-high, and received serious injuries. Another factory worker was struck by the falling smokestack, and suffered a broken collar bone, and a hole in his skull, which took a year to heal.

The engineer Pallien returned three months later to work, and stayed with Rumely for another twenty years. John Rumely and Mr. Lans both recovered in a few months and returned to work.

Tenacity became the company's trademark.

In 1881, The New Rumely thresher was introduced, a huge success which remained essentially unchanged until 1904, when the Rumely Ideal Thresher hit the market.

After Meinrad died in 1904, his nephew, Edward, took over. He had enrolled at Oxford University in England, then at Heidelberg University in Germany, where he struck up friendships with bright men who loved machines: Rudolf Diesel and Prof. Hugo Junkers. Edward Rumely actually graduated as a medical doctor, but returned to LaPorte in 1907 and got involved in the family business, immediately applying many of the economic and business ideals he had absorbed in Europe.

Rumely tractors

Edward Rumely saw the need for a reliable farm tractor with an internal combustion engine. John Secor's work came to his attention; Secor had been experimenting with the internal combustion engine since 1885, subjecting it to intensive scientific tests to extract maximum power using the least fuel. Edward persuaded him to move to LaPorte in 1908, and along with Rumely factory superintendent William H. Higgins, begin working on a farm tractor for Rumely.

Prototypes were built in 1908, and tested very successfully in 1909, when the area newspaper wrote on March 23, 1909, "A test was made this morning of the new tractor. Smooth as a whistle she ran, carting along as dead weight, a ten-ton steam engine. The tractor, in which kerosene is used as the motive power, weighs only eight thousand pounds. From every standpoint, it was the unanimous opinion of the practical men who witnessed the test that the engine was thoroughly practical. Its main value lies in its almost complete independence of labor and material conditions. One man handles the machine with ease. As Mr. Secor commented this morning, 'I've made her as human as possible.'

"Kerosene Annie" was the first Rumely tractor, and after a few refinements, emerged as the Rumely OilPull in 1911, and became the company's mainstay throughout its tractor-producing years. The first OilPull was a Type B 25-45 with two cylinders of 9-1/2- x 12-inch bore and stroke, a 48-inch flywheel with a 6-1/2-inch face. The crankshaft was 4-7/6 inches in diameter, rear axles 5-7/16 inches in diameter, and master gears had a 6-inch face. It shipped at 23,800 pounds, was produced through 1914, and represented the type of huge, powerful, and massive tractors that was being produced during this time.

A wide variety of Rumely OilPull tractors were produced over the next years, with many different alphabetical designations, but they were all the very large, strong, and dependable OilPull.

The GasPull was another Rumely tractor, added after gaining control of the American-Abell Engine & Threshing Company in 1912. It was first rated 20-40, but was lowered to 15-30. It had a two-cylinder opposed engine with a 7-1/2- x 8-inch bore and stroke. It had originally been designed by A. O. Espe, who designed various other tractors. The GasPull was discontinued in 1915.

Rumely also built the ToeHold, an orchard-type tractor.

On Oct. 24, 1911, M. Rumely Company purchased the Gaar-Scott Company of Richmond, Indiana for $4 million. It finished building the Gaar-Scott TigerPulls that parts allowed, and then closed down the line.

In December 1911, M. Rumely Company bought Advance Thresher Company of Battle Creek, Michigan, for $5 million, solidifying its hold on the thresher market.

With the purchase of Advance, Rumely knew it now also owned half of the American-Abell Engine & Thresher Company of Toronto, Ontario, Canada. It would be forced to buy the other half from MTMC to gain full control of the company.

American-Abell also made the Universal Farm Motor tractor in 1911, the same one being built by Universal Tractor Company at Stillwater, Minnesota, and also being sold by Minneapolis Threshing Machine Company. Rumely

Rumely entered the truck market in 1919 with this Model A 1-1/2-ton Rumely truck, capable of carrying a normal load of 3,000 pounds, and a maximum (including weight of chassis), 4,000 pounds. The motor was a heavy-duty truck-type motor with four cylinders of 3-3/4-inch bore and 5-1/8-inch stroke producing 22-1/2 hp. Four of these new trucks left LaPorte, Indiana, on a demonstration run on Aug. 12, 1919, each with 3,500 pounds of repair parts. The route was the central plains, from Texas to North Dakota. "Daily reports," *Farm Implements and Tractors* **wrote, "from drivers are extremely gratifying."**

took advantage of its new acquisition to use the design of this tractor for its GasPull line.

Things looked grand. OilPulls continued to be sold, a great number to Canada in 1914.

But in 1914, Canada suffered a massive crop failure. Most OilPull machines and threshers and other machines had been sold on time, and farmers couldn't make their payments. Suddenly Rumely was staggering under the

One of Advance-Rumely's best and most popular pieces of equipment was its Ideal thresher, which was introduced in 1904, when Dr. Edward Rumely took over the company. One of the problems with early separators was that they didn't get all the grain. An ad for the Ideal says, "The Ideal is noted for the series of lifting fingers that thoroughly shake the straw. By this method—often copied but never equaled—the grain is entirely separated." (Dan Roen Collection)

One of the trucks Rumely manufactured was this Model A Rumely with a brown 20-passenger bus body. It was used in connection with Advance-Rumely Tractor schools ca. 1918. *Farmer Implements and Tractors* magazine says, "In order to give the students of their tractor schools an opportunity to see all points of interest in the ten cities where the schools will be held this winter, the Advance-Rumely Company had had three of their truck chassis equipped with bus bodies to make sight-seeing trips for an hour and a half after school period each day. These buses are strictly up-to-date, and carry twenty passengers on well-upholstered cross seats. They are well lighted and ventilated, and are finished in OilPull red and green. After each school, the buses will be driven to the point of the next school." (Gary Hoonsbeen Collection)

weight of these bad debts.

Rumely pleaded with its bankers to hold off, but to no avail. On Jan. 21, 1915, the company went into receivership, and a new Advance-Rumely Thresher Company was formed.

The company had grown too fast, spent too much money acquiring other companies, and had little wiggle room money-wise; nor did the Rumely family, which was unceremoniously booted from the company it had run for some 60 years.

For the next few years, sales and profits were flat for the reorganized company. The agricultural depression came on in the early 1920s, and kept profits down.

In 1923, Advance-Rumely introduced a new all-steel thresher and a silo filler. It also decided to buy Aultman-Taylor Machinery Company of Mansfield, Ohio.

This company also had a long illustrious history, having been formed as the Aultman, Taylor & Company in 1867 by Cornelius Aultman and Henry H. Taylor. The company had been formed after certain manufacturing and patent rights had been obtained from John Nichols (of Nichols & Shepard Company) pertaining to the vibrator thresher.

The 30-60 Aultman-Taylor was probably one of the best tractors of its time, tractor historian C. H. Wendel says in *Encyclopedia of American Farm Tractors*. First built in 1910 or early 1911, it was 11-1/2 feet high, 18 feet long, weighed 24,450 pounds, and had a square radiator for the first couple of years of its existence, and afterward a tubular one.

Rumors flew hot and heavy starting in 1928 that Advance-Rumely was talking with another company about merging. Indeed, discussions were going on with Otto Falk, president of Allis-Chalmers Manufacturing Company of Milwaukee. That was finally accomplished on June 1, 1931.

Rumely trucks

For ten years (1919-28) Rumely built Rumely trucks. They were all 1-1/2-ton trucks powered by four-cylinder Buda en-

gines and with Fuller transmissions and Sheldon worm-drive rear axles. The wheelbase was 144 inches and the chassis weight was 4,050 pounds. The steering gear was a Gemer. The Model A Rumely sold for $2,150 in 1925.

Farm Implements and Tractors wrote in 1919 that, "The entire truck is especially designed for farm service. It has a unit power plant with a heavy duty motor, three-speed transmission and dry disc clutch. Other features are the large cooling capacity of the radiator, worm drive rear axle, the extra heavy springs, and the extra heavy type express body, suitable for hauling heavy grains, such as wheat, shelled corn, etc. Suitable extensions will give it larger capacity for hauling oats, barley, or other light grains, livestock, baled hay and other farm products. It will be distributed through the large Advance-Rumely dealer organization."

The October 1924 issue of *The OilPull Magazine* had this short article: "Fay C. Hollenbeck of Albion, New York, gives some interesting side lights on the hauling strength of the Rumely truck in his recent letter: I have been running one of your trucks for the past three months and am well-pleased with it. While it is only rated as a 1-1/2 to 2-ton truck, I find that it hauls three or four tons with ease. I haul three tons all the time, and have hauled four, and could not see but what the motor still had reserve power.

"If you ever need a demonstration near here I would be glad to prove to anyone that this truck is the equal of the three-ton trucks on the market, both in construction and power."

Rumely Buses

Rumely built buses to shuttle students in its Advance-Rumely tractor schools, from one place of note to another in the cities holding the schools, about 1918. After classes were over, the buses, painted Oil Pull red and green, were driven to the next city holding A-R tractor school.

Chapter 43

Shelby Enters Manufacturing at the Wrong Time

The Shelby Tractor & Truck Company could not have picked worse years for entry into the vehicle-manufacture field, making tractors and trucks in Shelby, Ohio, from 1917-1921.

Shelby tractors

The agricultural depression and intense competition among hundreds of different tractor builders provided the backdrop in 1919-21 when the Shelby Tractor & Truck Company made its first tractors. Though it only made tractors for three years, it manufactured three different models, the 9-18 with a Waukesha 3-1/4- x 5-1/4-inch bore-and-stroke engine in 1919, a 5,000-pound 15-30 with an Erd four-cylinder 4-3/8- x 6-inch bore-and-stroke engine in 1920, and a 9-18 rerated to a 10-20 a year later.

The 9-18, or Model C, operated at 1,000 rpm in speeds of 1-3/4 to 4-3/4 mph (plowing was accomplished at 2.6 mph), and 1 mph in reverse. The fuel tank had two com-

SHELBY, 9-18
The Shelby Tractor & Truck Company
Shelby, Ohio

The Shelby Tractor & Truck Company of Shelby, Ohio, built this second tractor, a 9-18, weighing 3,500 pounds. It used a Dixie H.T. magneto with 7/8-inch spark plugs, and a four-cylinder engine. (Dan Roen Collection)

The Model D 15-30 Shelby tractor was built by Shelby Truck & Tractor Company of Shelby, Ohio, in 1920, one of three years it built tractors (and it couldn't have been done at a worse time, considering the farm depression that struck during these years, as well as competition from hundreds of other tractor companies.) The tractor weighed 4,600 pounds, pulled three 14-inch plows, and used an Erd 4-1/2 x 6 4-cylinder engine. In 1921, Shelby quit making tractors and trucks and went out of business. (Dan Roen Collection)

partments: one of five, the other of twelve, gallons. Rear wheels were 42 inches in diameter with a 12-inch face, small for the time. It weighed 3,500 pounds with fuel tanks filled, and had a 72-inch wheelbase, and was 117 inches long and 60 inches high. It could pull a pair of 14-inch plows.

The 1920 15-30, or Shelby Model D, as it was called, was recommended for three 14-inch plows, used a Kingston 1-1/2-inch carburetor, a Splitdorf high-tension magneto, and a Modine radiator and fan. It used a special kerosene motor, and ran at speeds of 2.7 and 4 mph forward in low and high, respectively, and one reverse speed. The fuel tank contained 14 gallons of kerosene and four of gasoline located under the hood and equipped with a sediment trap. Drive wheels were 48 inches in diameter, with a 12-inch face. It used angle-iron cleats or spuds for traction. Weight was variously listed at 4,600 or 5,000 pounds. It could pull three 14-inch plows.

The Shelby tractor literature was very general: "The Shelby is built to fulfill the requirements of the practical farmer in all his tractor and belt power needs." Or, "The

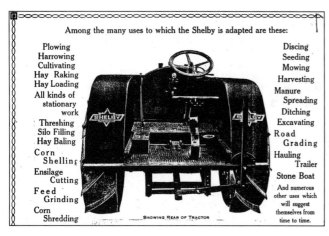

Among the many uses to which the Shelby is adapted are these:

Plowing
Harrowing
Cultivating
Hay Raking
Hay Loading
All kinds of
    stationary
    work
Threshing
Silo Filling
Hay Baling
Corn
    Shelling
Ensilage
    Cutting
Feed
    Grinding
Corn
Shredding

Discing
Seeding
Mowing
Harvesting
Manure
    Spreading
Ditching
Excavating
Road
    Grading
Hauling
    Trailer
Stone Boat
And numerous
other uses which
will suggest
themselves from
time to time.

SHOWING REAR OF TRACTOR

This Shelby advertisement gives a list of the "many uses to which the Shelby is adapted…and numerous other uses which will suggest themselves from time to time." The company said its tractors had great strength and light weight, and that by eliminating side-draft it was self-steering when plowing. "This greatly reduces the work of the operator and he can give almost his entire attention to the plows." (Marvin Memorial Library)

Shelby does more than plow." Or, "The Shelby tractor is one of the best investments on the farm…"

Foreign sales were handled by the Automotive Products Corporation in the Woolworth Building in New York City.

Shelby trucks

Shelby made trucks in 1917-18, but very little is known about them, except that they sold for $900, like the tractors. There is some speculation that the same 9-hp engine was used in both trucks and tractors.

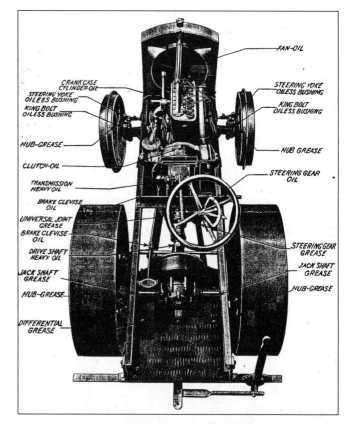

A topside view of the Shelby tractor showing and naming various parts. (Marvin Memorial Library)

The Shelby Model S35 had a maximum capacity of 1,500 pounds and used a Shelby Special Truck four-cylinder motor of 29 hp with a bore and stroke of 3-1/2 x 4-1/2 inches. It weighed 2,400 pounds, and was painted red for the chassis, and the body was black. A Shelby ad for this vehicle had this qualification: "Inasmuch as it is the policy of the Shelby Tractor and Truck Co. to make such changes in specifications from time to time as in their opinion may be beneficial, all specifications and prices are subject to change without notice." It was advertised at $895. (Marvin Memorial Library)

The "SHELBY"

Chapter 44

Traylor Tractors

The Traylor 6-12 was a small tractor using the LeRoi 3-1/8- x 4-1/2-inch bore and stroke, four-cylinder engine and came with plows already in place like other motor cultivators of the time; however, the Traylor had a major advantage: you could take the plows off to use the tractor for other farm work year round, unlike the average motor cultivator, which was a yearly one-season wonder.

Curiously, the price of the tractor kept dropping, from $750 in its maiden year of 1920, to almost half that–$400–in 1928, perhaps due to the farm recession of the early 20s, which stopped the upward spiral of tractor prices, and probably also due to the loss of popularity of the motor cultivator tractors themselves.

When the Traylor 6-12 came out in 1920, *Motor Age* magazine wrote of it, "The Traylor, a newcomer at Kansas City this year, is a 6-12 hp machine for universal purposes on the farm. It is easily adjusted from its normal clearance of 16 inches to 26 inches for cultivating. This is an exclusive feature. The drawbar pull of this job is 650 pounds, and it weighs about 1,700 pounds."

The Traylor 6-12 was the only tractor the Traylor Engineering Company of Cornwells Heights, Pennsylvania, made, and it was marketed all over the United States. Specifications for the 6-12 in the 1920 and 1927 *Implement and Tractor Trade Journal* and *Cooperative Tractor Catalog*, respectively, were exactly the same.

The Traylor Tractor like this 6-12 lasted for at least eight years, with the price for this small tractor rated for pulling only one 14-inch plow dropping from $750 its first year of production, like this one from 1920, until 1928, when it was only $400. (Dan Roen Collection)

Traylor advertised its Traylor Farm Tractors in this 1920 promo, touting the machine's virtues: "The Traylor is driven by the same power plant used in many of the heavier tractors. The Traylor weighs only 1,700 pounds complete with full equipment. Because of its lightness, the Traylor will not pack even the heavy, moist soils of New York State farms. And still it is powerful enough to plow those soils successfully–all day long!" (Dan Roen Collection)

Traylor Engineering & Manufacturing Co. of Allentown, Pennsylvania, built this Traylor 3-ton truck Model D in 1925, along with a 1-1/2-ton B ($2,390), 2-ton C ($2,850), and a 5-ton F ($4,700). The pictured truck weighed 15,000 pounds gross (5,850 chassis only), and used a four-cylinder 4-1/4 x 5-1/2-inch bore and stroke engine that produced 28.9 hp. It sold for $3,300. (Gary Hoonsbeen Collection)

Traylor trucks

Traylor trucks also came out in 1920 in four different models: 1-1/4-, 2-, 3-, and 4-ton trucks containing four-cylinder Buda engines with three- and four-speed Brown-Lipe transmissions.

In 1925, the 1-1/2-ton Model B used a Buda WTU engine, a 22.5-hp four-cylinder motor, Ross steering, Covert

transmission, Sheldon axles and standard pneumatic tires, at a cost of $2,390. The 2-ton Model C used a four-cylinder, 25.6 Buda ITU engine and the same components as the Model B, for $2,850. The third model introduced that year was the largest, a 3-ton Model D, with a four-cylinder 28.9-hp Buda HTU and a Traylor-built transmission, for $3,300.

In 1928, the company disappeared from the market.

The Shelby Truck & Tractor Company of Shelby, Ohio, advertised its trucks as "The truck that delivers." "This chassis, combining frame, motor, transmission, propelling and carrying mechanism, with the ultimate object of obtaining strength, durability and efficiency, is an engineering triumph, affording the Shelby an opportunity of offering the highest quality, and the public of practicing common-sense economy." The company touted the truck's simplicity of design, standardization of parts, economy of operation and efficiency of service. (Marvin Memorial Library)

Another view of the Traylor 6-12.

Chapter 45

Waterous Tractors

After a Feb. 2, 1904 patent, the Waterous Engine Company of St. Paul, Minnesota, made its only tractor in 1905, an unusual tractor with a huge cooling tank above the motor and directly in the view of the tractor rider. It's not difficult to understand why the machine was not a great hit; it was apparently made through 1911.

Waterous had experimented with tractors starting in 1900, and exhibited a gasoline engine at the Minnesota State Fair, while simultaneously selling steam traction engines in a Canadian plant.

A close study of the tractor shows a clutch pulley lever ahead of the flywheel, which allowed the operator to engage the belt from the ground.

Waterous trucks, like this fire engine from the 1920s, were much more popular than the Waterous tractor. They were built by the Waterous Engine Works of St. Paul, Minnesota, from 1906-1923.

Waterous trucks

Waterous began building horse-drawn steam fire engines prior to 1906, and in that year, built the first gasoline-powered fire engine in the United States. It possessed two engines, one for driving the machine, the second for the water pump. A year later, Waterous began using a four-cylinder engine under a large hood, and stayed with it until the demise of the company in terms of vehicles, in 1923. Thereafter, it built pumps and added fire apparatus to commercial chassis until the 1930s. Since then it has built pumps for fire engines.

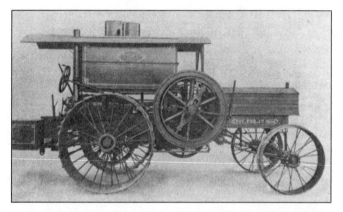

Waterous Engine Company of St. Paul, Minnesota, made only one tractor in one year, this 1906 eight-plow tractor.

Waterous Engine Works Company of St. Paul, Minn., manufactured this gasoline fire engine with a piston pump around the turn of the century.

This Waterous gasoline fire engine is shown in operation near the Mississippi River in St. Paul. The caption on the turn-of-the-century photo says it can throw 200 to 300 gallons of water, but does not say how long. "One or two good fire streams," it says. "Guaranteed to start and throw water in from one and one-half to three minutes from the time the torch is lighted."

SECTION IV:

Tractor Companies That Made Tanks

Chapter 46

Pioneer Tractor Co. Vice President Invents War Tank

The history of the Pioneer Tractor Manufacturing Company of Minneapolis and Winona, Minnesota, is an enigma. Despite having operated in several thousand square feet of buildings, and possessing a workforce of 500 manufacturing huge tractors, not a single word is mentioned about the company in Winona's 100-year history book, county histories or city histories. Even the founder's grandson, Jay Youmans of Rochester, Minnesota, said, "He did something like that, too? I knew about a few of his other businesses, mostly the lumber yard, but not this one. He was quite an entrepreneur."

Early reports were gushing and flowery. GAS TRACTION ENGINES screamed a headline in the *Winona Daily Republican-Herald* of Saturday, Feb. 19, 1910. "*The Republican-Herald* is able to announce today the securing of a big new manufacturing industry for Winona. This industry to be brought here is the manufacture of gas traction engines, the coming machine which is already being used to quite an extent in farm work and in time will very largely take the place of horses."

The company started in Minneapolis, although it appears no Pioneer tractors were manufactured there; on March 30, 1910, the Independent reported, "One engine a week was being made at present, but after July one a day will be turned out–work for five hundred employees next summer." The first models were the Pioneer 15 and Pioneer 30, with a four-cylinder horizontal opposed engine with a 7-inch bore and 8-inch stroke. One of the sales gimmicks for the tractor included balancing a silver dollar on the frame of the tractor, which was running, and taking a one-minute timed photo to exhibit how vibrationless the tractor was.

Some information says experimental models of Pioneer tractors were made in 1913; others say 1916. Perhaps both. The experimental tractors built by Pioneer used a six-cylinder horizontal-opposed engine of the same bore and

stroke as the 30-60. These tractors were rated 45-90, and had rear wheels nine feet tall.

On Dec. 17, 1918, the *Winona Independent* wrote that Pioneer was sending two dozen large machines to Russia for farm use. "Francis J. Lowe, manager for the A. S. Lasalles Company, exclusive foreign agents for the local product, is in Winona and has placed an order for twenty-four large engines to be shipped into Russia and other countries abroad."

Edson Rice of Winona, the article says, "piloted the Pioneer '30' through three different foreign government contests, winning first prize in two and second in the third. In the Hungarian contest, thirty-two tractors were entered and the decision rendered by the government, being a most rigid test."

In Romania, the Pioneer tractors won a gold prize over eleven other engines. In Russia, at the 'Kief trials,' the Pioneer '30' won second prize and nine of a possible ten points of merit. The operator won a prize of five figures in cash.

Pioneer also manufactured the Pioneer Pony, a 15-30 with a four-cylinder engine but a single drive wheel; the Special 15-30 that weighed 8,500 pounds, and the Pioneer 18-36 in 1919. *Farm Implements* said of Pioneer tractors that, "Gearing is completely encased, and runs in an oil bath so constructed as to be dust and sand proof. The motor is cooled by means of a radiator similar to those used on automobiles, which is constructed almost entirely of copper and brass, making it rust proof. The cooling space in the motor cylinder is so arranged that oil may be successfully used in the radiator during cold weather. High-tension magneto supplies the ignition current."

No matter the words of high praise, the 18-36 seemed to be the company's last tractor. Perhaps the changing times bruised the company, or perhaps its ironclad tractor guarantee, which allowed farmers to bring the tractor back in the event of the smallest troubles, or perhaps the

This stylish Pioneer 30-60 tractor had a glassed-in cab and a rear curtain, and was Pioneer Tractor Manufacturing Company's most popular machine, made from 1910-1923. Its steel rear wheels were 8-1/4 feet in diameter, and this machine could pull ten 14-inch plows, or cut a 32-foot swath of grain at one time. It weighed nearly 12 tons–23,000 pounds. In this case, the Setran Brothers of Douglas, North Dakota, were on their way to Douglas elevators, pulling five wagons of wheat. (Richard Birklid Collection)

This ca. 1917 ad advises dealers to see the Pioneer 30 before doing anything else, "Then decide which tractor you want to sell. We challenge any comparison." Prospective sellers are advised to see it at the (Minnesota) State Fair, or "visit our factory and see it in the making." (Dan Roen Collection)

farm recession of 1920–or a combination of all, killed the company. By 1924, the business name had been changed to Pioneer Tractors, Inc., an implement business, and no more Pioneer tractors were being manufactured.

The Pioneer war tank

That the Pioneer Tractor Manufacturing Company of Winona claimed to have invented the tank used in war comes as little surprise considering the huge size of the company's most popular tractor made from 1910-1923, the 30-60, which rode on steel rear wheels 8-1/4 feet in diameter and could pull ten 14-inch plows or cut a 32-foot swath of grain at one time. It weighed nearly 12 tons–23,000 pounds. The experimental Pioneer 45-90, which never made it into full production, was even larger, with 9-foot-high steel rear wheels.

So it seems logical that the company could have invented the first-ever tank used in war. In 1914, E. M. Wheelock, then vice-president of Pioneer Tractor Manufacturing Company, came up with the idea of "a bullet-proof, self-propelled conveyance," says the *Winona Republican-Herald* of

July 31, 1942, "for effective use in attack against entrenched defenders...shortly after the outbreak in Europe of World War I." No commonly used tank existed at this time.

The basic outline that Wheelock proposed remains unchanged in modern tanks. Wheelock's machine was given trial runs on the sand flats and in the shallow areas of the Mississippi River in the east end below the Burlington railroad bridge in Winona.

Though the shape was the same, the details differed. Wheelock made his tank out of three-inch-diameter iron pipes screwed together. He figured it could be transported abroad more easily if the basic parts simply had to be unscrewed, packed, shipped, and then screwed together near the battlefield. He also believed that the pipes that were shattered could be unscrewed, and new ones screwed into place after battle.

The frame was unprotected by armor, making a smaller target for enemy shells and bullets. Only the turret, the box-like structure between the caterpillar drives, was to be armored. The turret was designed to contain the engine, a small cannon, and space for the crew.

George E. West, an officer of the Pioneer Tractor Com-

This "Skeleton Tank" was built for the U. S. Army by the Pioneer Tractor Company of Winona, Minnesota, in 1918, and is similar to the prototype made by the company's vice president, E. M. Wheelock, in 1915. According to records, the plans for the tank were given to the British Army and two years later, a similarly designed war tank was crashing through enemy lines in Europe. Pioneer, however, never was given credit for the invention. This model is now in the tank museum of the Aberdeen Proving Grounds, Aberdeen, Maryland. (Winona County Historical Society Photo)

pany at the time, said in the *Winona Republican-Herald* that many details of the invention are fresh in his memory. "The first tank was operated by a powerful gasoline engine, and its top speed was between 10 and 15 mph.

"The caterpillar-driven endless chain construction was built on an open work frame of three-inch pipe and this is the most noticeable difference between the modern tanks and the original model. There is armor plate covering the caterpillar drive on the modern vehicles.

Wheelock tried to sell his idea to Canada for use by the British, but the U.S. War Department gave him $15,000 for one of his tanks. Nothing further came of it from the War Department, however.

Wheelock got in touch with Francis S. Lowe, an exporter "and a mystery man who signed his name 'Ewol' on export papers," the *Winona Republican-Herald* said.

In 1915, Lowe went to England and showed authorities Wheelock's blueprints, including Chief Nolden of the division of transportation in the London war office. The officials promised to study them carefully.

The Minneapolis Journal of Nov. 29, 1926, wrote that Lowe said, "When Colonel Nolden learned that the armored tractor plans called for a machine weighing more than 25 tons, he said 'Come! Come! This is another Yankee invention to win the war. (Many tractors invented during World War I claimed that they would 'win the war'). It will break down any bridge in Belgium, and besides, you Yanks don't know that we drive to the left of the road instead of to the right, so it will block traffic as well."

That was the last anybody saw of the blueprints; two years later, the British used the tank successfully in battle. "After the battle of the Somme," the Minneapolis newspaper reported, "it was reported that funny-looking cheeseboxes were going over the top and chasing the Germans."

A study revealed that the equipment used in France "during those early drives was exact in design with the plans and blueprints submitted by the Winona inventor," *The Winona Republican-Herald* wrote.

Years of correspondence and trips to England by Lowe failed to reveal any record connecting Wheelock with the invention. "He never received credit for his work or any financial return other than the money paid him for the sample which the United States War department never used," *The Winona Republican-Herald* said.

The Pioneer Tractor Manufacturing Company existed until 1923, when it changed its name and quit producing tractors. Besides the 30-60 ($2,700 in 1911, $4,500 in 1916), the company built a number of other models. The company also promoted a warranty on its tractors that was probably the first of its kind, and a suit over that warranty may have been the final blow that killed the company that perhaps invented the first war tank ever.

SECTION V:

Tractor Companies That Made Cars and/or Trucks: Yes, Maybe, No

Chapter 47

Abenaque Machine Works

One day in 1893, Frederick M. Gilbert backed his horse and wagon up to a bank in Keene, New Hampshire, and rolled out barrels of money, gold, and jewelry. That's how his family had packed their belongings, including their valuables, when they moved to Walpole, Vermont.

In April 1893, that money came to good use when work was started on the Abenaque Machine Works in Westminster Station, Vermont. The corporation was established (in New Hampshire) in 1895. It now had a place to live, a shop, money in the bank, and best of all, an inventor, John A. Ostenberg, who agreed to work for Abenaque for five years for a $1,000 a year.

Ostenberg invented the Abenaque gasoline engine, which was the mainstay of the company for many years. The company manufactured "explosion engines"–portable and stationary gasoline engines in horsepowers of 2 and 25. Abenaque made portable circular and drag-saw units, as well as portable air compressors, concrete mixers, and tractors.

It also made one automobile.

Abenaque tractors

If a person was to choose one place where a company might not manufacture a tractor, that area might be Vermont, because of its great distance from the large farming areas of the central plains. Nevertheless, Abenaque did build tractors, beginning with an experimental model in 1908. The tractor was experimented on for the next three years, and by 1911, the Abenaque tractor had strengthened its rear wheels, as well as made improvements in the operator's platform, which now included a seat and canopy, and was offered to the public.

One of the first ones was reported in the Vermont Phoenix newspaper in October 1911: "A trackless engine belonging to the Abenaque Company passed through here Wednesday evening on its way to the Loomis Brothers farm in Putney with machinery for plowing and harvest work. It was a curiosity, the engine and machinery being as long as two freight cars."

Many testimonial letters came in for the tractor, which had a rectangular tank cooling system, three forward and one reverse speed, and moved at 3 mph.

One of the directions in the booklet that went with the tractor said, "Great care should be taken in oiling the engine while running, that the fingers or clothing are not caught in any of the moving parts. This applies especially to the governor, valve levers and belting." It is possible that this directive was included based on occurrences in the Abenaque Machine Works shop. In 1894, two men received hand injuries. In 1905, a 26-year-old worker got his

legs tangled in a belt. He was pulled around repeatedly, hitting his head each time, and died.

The Abenaque 15-hp tractor weighed 11,000 pounds, and had a massive bore and stroke of 8-5/8 x 12-1/2 inches. The drive wheels were 56 inches in diameter, exclusive of cleats, with 20-inch tires. Front wheels were 36 inches in diameter.

The 12-hp Abenaque could come with 14-inch or 20-inch tires on the driving wheels, as desired.

Abenaque also made a 25-hp tractor. The company praised the machines for its short turning radius.

The booklet that accompanied the tractor opened like this: "The advantages of the gasoline traction engines are too well known to require more than passing mention. The advantages over the steam tractors are that: They may be started up at a moment's notice, there being no fuel expense except when the traction is in operation; a licensed engineer is not required; the fireman is dispensed with entirely; the fuel cost is less than when burning coal; teams to haul water and coal are done away with; the engine may be used in barns and where a steam traction engine could not be used; a gasoline tractor can be used on steep hills where the ordinary steam traction engine would not be suitable, due to the fact that, because of the grade, the boiler tubes or fire box would be uncovered; the weight is much less than that of a steam traction engine; no attendance is required while the engine is being used for stationary work."

This 1908 Abenaque had three forward speeds, and one reverse in its sliding steel-gears transmission. When Gilbert Colgate took over the Abenaque plant, he tried to modernize it but without success, as the company folded in 1916, possibly because it was too far from tractor markets. It was a 15-hp machine and weighed 11,000 pounds. (Westminster Historical Society)

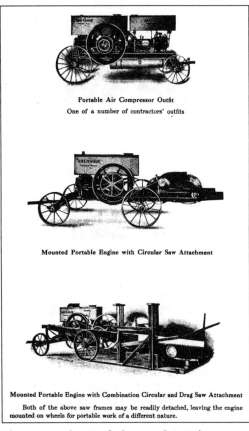

Portable Air Compressor Outfit
One of a number of contractors' outfits

Mounted Portable Engine with Circular Saw Attachment

Mounted Portable Engine with Combination Circular and Drag Saw Attachment
Both of the above saw frames may be readily detached, leaving the engine
mounted on wheels for portable work of a different nature.

These are three of the products that were made by Abenaque Machine Works of Westminster, Vermont, from the back of an Abenaque booklet. Today, any of these machines are highly prized by collectors. (Westminster Historical Society)

The booklet said the Abenaque tractor would appeal especially to farmers whose land was not level, and that it could pull three 14-inch bottom plows under favorable conditions, getting through eight acres a day. It could haul loads of 20,000 pounds.

The booklet also says, "We are advised by the road commissioners of a New York town owning and operating

This is a photograph of an Abenaque tractor pulling a disc in a field near Westminster Station, Vermont, during the second decade of the 20th century.

one of our machines, that the weekly expense when using six horses on the road machine has been $84 per week (including two-horse teams hired at the rate of $4 each per day). They state that when operating the scraper by means of the Abenaque tractor, they accomplish one third more work at a total weekly expense, including cost of gasoline, cylinder oil and operators, of $36, or a net saving of $48 per week plus one third more work." That in a nutshell could explain why tractors were becoming favored over horses at this time.

On March 5, 1904, the company registered in Keene for a foreign corporation, and shipped Abenaque products overseas until 1915.

The company went bankrupt in 1915, at which time an announcement was published (on Sept. 23):

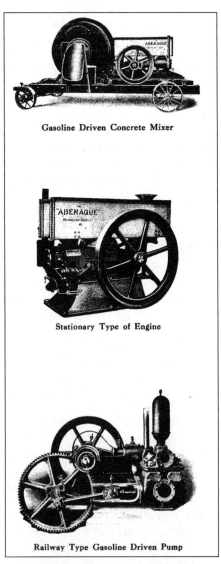

Gasoline Driven Concrete Mixer

Stationary Type of Engine

Railway Type Gasoline Driven Pump

Some of the Abenaque engines were put to different uses, like the gasoline-driven concrete mixer, shown here at the top, a stationary engine below, and a railway-type gasoline driven pump at the bottom. Abenaque Machine Works of Westminster, Vermont, made a wide variety of different gasoline and kerosene engines. (Westminster Historical Society)

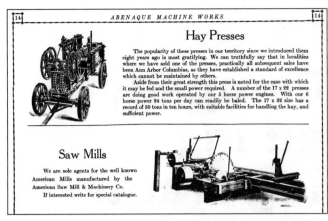

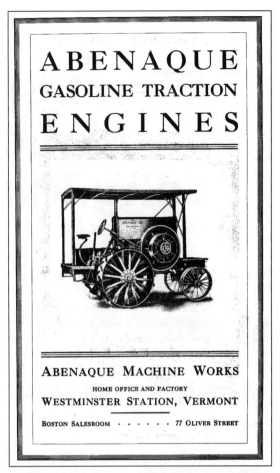

Abenaque was also representatives for different products, like the famous Doylestown Thresher manufactured by the Doylestown Agricultural Company, and shown here. (Westminster Historical Society)

"PUBLIC, ATTENTION. The business of the Abenaque Machine Works, Westminster Stations, Vt., manufacturers of the famous Abenaque Gasoline Engine and Wood Sawing Outfits was on Sept. 1, 1915, taken over by new interests and the purpose of this advertisement is to advise the public that business will be continued along the same lines as formally except under greatly improved conditions.

"Our stock of both engines and repairs is very complete and if you are considering the purchase of an outfit can assure you it will be to your advantage to get our catalogue and prices before purchasing. Write today."

The business limped on for six more years, still under the Gilbert family auspices, until it filed its final bankruptcy in 1921.

Abenaque automobile

The Abenaque automobile was built in 1900, half a dozen years before its tractors. The company built an experimental gasoline automobile in 1900, but decided not to market it so it could concentrate on its lucrative farm machinery program.

Nothing else is known about the Abenaque automobile.

This is the front cover of the Abenaque Gasoline Traction Engine booklet from Abenaque Machine Works in Westminster Station, Vermont, from 1908. (Westminster Historical Society)

Chapter 48

Blumberg Company Involved in Long-Running Fraud

The Blumberg Motor Manufacturing Company of San Antonio and Orange, Texas, is worth mentioning because many people believe the company built a tractor (the Blumberg steady pull), which it did; and two automobiles (the Blumberg custom four-cylinder; and Blumberg V-8 car for seven passengers for $3,000, from 1915-1922.)

The Blumberg steady-pull tractor

Two sizes of Blumberg steady-pull tractors were built beginning in 1918, a 3,700-pound 12-24 model that cost $1,250, and a 9-18 that weighed a mere 2,750 pounds and cost $800. Both engines were built by Blumberg, four-cylinder motors of 4- x 5-inch for the 12-24, and a 3-3/4- x 3-3/4-inch bore and stroke for the 9-18.

Blumberg automobiles

There weren't any.

Beverly Rae Kimes and Henry Austin Clark Jr. write in the second edition of the *Standard Catalog of American Cars 1805-1942*, "The Blumberg represents one of the longer-lived frauds in the history of the American automobile. Some references indicate that it was in production from 1915 to 1922, but the fact was that it was never really in proper production at all. There was a lot of stock sold, however."

A former shareholder of the company was interviewed, and he remembered well what had happened. He didn't receive any dividends, nor any correspondence, so he traveled to the San Antonio Blumberg offices, discovering they were a suite in a swanky San Antonio hotel. The factory was a deserted and long-unused shed. H. G. Blumberg wasn't at the hotel, and when the stockholder made an appointment, didn't show for it. By then he had moved on to his new venture, the Lone Star Motor Truck and Tractor Association.

Blumberg Motor Manufacturing Company of Orange, Texas, built the Blumberg Steady Pull 9-18 starting in 1918. It weighed 2,750 pounds, sold for $800, and used a 3-3/4 x 3-3/4-inch bore and stroke, until 1924.

Chapter 49

Cushman Has Long History in Gasoline Engines

Cushman Motor Works of Lincoln, Nebraska, never did make a Cushman tractor, although it did manufacture a MacDonald, which it promoted aggressively in Canada, and a Ward tractor, which it sold in the United States. It was also involved with cars and trucks.

MacDonald tractors

In 1918, Cushman went aggressively after the Canadian tractor market, manufacturing a 5,900-pound 12-24 MacDonald tractor with a four-cylinder 4-3/4- x 6-inch engine.

Before Cushman Motor Works began building tractors, it was well-known for its gasoline engines. In the bottom right-hand corner is the Cushman 8 hp–essentially a tractor–a two-cylinder that weighed 320 pounds. "This is a wonderful little powerful all-purpose engine," the advertisement says. The engine and the truck together weighed 740 pounds. "Can be pulled around anywhere by hand." (Dan Roen Collection)

Cushman made this combination thresher and sold it in Canada, among other places. "The separator has 24-inch cylinders and a 46-inch rear," advertising information says. The extension frame was made of channel iron braced with truss rod. "The separator can easily be handled with the two-cylinder, throttle-governed, non-vibrating two horsepower Cushman engine. It will thresh from 600 to 1,200 bushels a day, depending on conditions, and requires from ten to twenty gallons of gasoline a day."

Ward tractors

Cushman never did get heavily involved selling tractors in the United States–it was better known for its gasoline engines after brothers Everitt and Clinton Cushman formed the company in Lincoln, Nebraska in 1901. Its first products were two-stroke engines for boats, followed by four-stroke water-cooled engines for farm use; the company sold thousands.

Even when Cushman did get involved with tractors, its first effort, in 1912, wasn't strictly a tractor, but the Ward Tractor Plow. The manager of Cushman Motor Works announced

Cushman Motor Works of Lincoln, Nebraska, was more aggressive in the Canadian market and did better with its MacDonald tractors in Canada than it did in the United States. This 12-24 from the late teens was a four-cylinder machine with a 4-3/4 x 5-inch bore and stroke engine, and weighed just under 6,000 pounds.

Cushman was also involved with the manufacture of the Ward Tractor Plow, a 20-hp machine using a Cushman two-cylinder engine. Before Cushman got into making tractors, it had a long and respected history of making gasoline engines for the farm.

the tractor plow, and the Ward Tractor Company was organized. The tractor plow was exhibited to great interest at the National Tractor Demonstrations in Fremont, Nebraska that year, with a 20-hp, two-cylinder Cushman engine.

Cushman automobiles

Like so many manufacturing companies of the time, Cushman didn't know which kind of vehicle it wanted to make, so it experimented with all of them. In 1903, Cushman increased its capital stock to $300,000 for the purpose of manufacturing automobiles. Only $50,000 was raised, and it appears a Cushman car was never built, perhaps not even a prototype.

Cushman still makes trucks today, like this 1992 Cushman Titan. The company began making trucks in 1936 as the Cushman Motor Works, and had been founded in 1901 in Lincoln, Nebraska.

Cushman trucks

The first foray of Cushman into trucks was with a three-wheeled golf cart built in 1936. They were also used as parcel carriers and light delivery vehicles, three-wheelers with sidecars and two wheels in front. The engines were one-cylinder, with two speeds and chain drive. They were 15-cubic-inch engines that produced 4 horsepowers. They could carry up to 400 pounds, and were popular with the armed services in World War II and the Korean War.

After Cushman Motors became a division of the Outboard Marine Corporation of Lincoln, Nebraska, in 1961, larger engines were produced, and four-wheel vehicles up to one ton.

By the 1980s, Cushman had offered a vast variety of electric- and gasoline- powered models, including the Minute-Miser three-wheel Model 319 and Model 320–the first gasoline, the second electric. They have been rated at 450-pound capacity, while the Model 322 is double that.

Some other models produced by Cushman include four-wheel haulers with 1,200-pound capacity (Models 369 and 370 Gasoline GT-1 models), the 282F Thunderbolt, 325 A.B.C. Tote, and 535 Errand Master, among others.

A recent Cushman model is the ZEV (Zero Emission Vehicle) created in the 1990s to comply with on-road Federal Motor Vehicle Safety Administration standards. Top speed is almost 40 mph.

This simple drawing shows the outline of a Ward tractor Cushman Motor Works of Lincoln, Nebraska, manufactured and sold in 1913. This 15-30 used the Cushman 550 rpm engine, and had plows fixed beneath the rear of the tractor. (Dan Roen Collection)

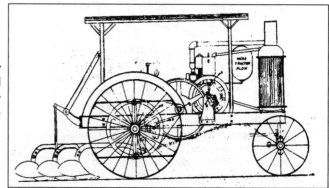

Chapter 50

Dart Starts with Bicycles and Evolves into Trucks

The Dart Truck & Tractor Corporation built tractors, trucks, and a prototype car that never was sold to the public.

The company began in Anderson, Indiana, as a bicycle manufacturer before the turn of the 20th century. Like hundreds of other companies, it decided to try automobiles, manufacturing a car engine for a few years, and then truck manufacture in 1903.

Dart tractors

A familiar name in tractor and automobile industry, William Galloway, purchased the Dart Manufacturing Company with Charles W. Hellen, and moved it from Anderson, Indiana, to Waterloo, Iowa, in 1910.

Hellen took care of the day-to-day business, while Galloway was an executive officer. (He probably spent much of his time involved with his own William Galloway Co., of Waterloo, making the Farmobile tractor, though some were probably also made in the Dart plant; he also helped bring the Maytag Company to Waterloo from Newton, Iowa for its short stint, and built automobiles).

Little is known about Dart tractors built before 1920's Dart Blue J tractor, built in 12-25 and 15-30 sizes, and selling for $1,850 and $2,000 respectively. The TY model was a three-plow outfit weighing 4,500 pounds, capable of plowing ten acres per ten-hour day. It used a Kingston 1-1/4-inch carburetor, and an Eisemann magneto ignition system.

The company went through several name changes–Dart Motor Truck Company, Dart Truck & Tractor Corporation–before it folded, probably due to the agriculture depression, in the early 1920s.

Dart automobiles

Dart Truck & Tractor Corporation's only entry in the automobile field was a car called the Dartmobile, built in 1922. This passenger-car prototype never made it past this initial stage as the company decided to keep all its resources in the commercial market area, perhaps because the tractor had not been wildly successful. The Dartmobile was powered by a four-cylinder L-head engine, and may have been built on one of Dart's truck chassis.

Peculiarly enough, the same year that the Dart Truck & Tractor Corporation moved from Anderson, Indiana, to Waterloo, Iowa, 1910, a Dart car was manufactured in Anderson, Indiana, but had nothing to do with this Dart company.

Dart trucks

Dart is best known for its trucks. The first one was built in 1903 in Anderson, Indiana, when the company was called the Dart Truck Company. The first Dart truck had a 20-hp, two-cylinder engine mounted under the floor of the half-ton high-wheeler vehicle. It weighed 1,800 pounds, and had a loading space of 45 x 78 inches. It had an open body, although a panel-type body was also available. It was a colorful affair, with a Brewster green body and maroon chassis, a blue body and yellow chassis, or blue body and maroon chassis. It cost $650 (open) or $690 (panel).

When the company moved to Waterloo in 1907, the truck was completely redesigned to a conventional layout with a four-cylinder engine and chain drive in 1/2-, 1- or 1-1/2-ton models.

In 1914, the corporate name was changed to Dart Motor Truck Company, and it started doing business with the

In 1920, Dart Truck & Tractor Company of Waterloo, Iowa, manufactured its Dart Blue J Model TY tractor, a 4,500-pound tractor with a four-cylinder Buda engine and a Kingston carburetor. The Dart tractor may have been available only this one year. Dart trucks are much better known, and emanate from the same company. (Dan Roen Collection)

Dart Truck & Tractor Company of Waterloo, Iowa, made this Dart Model B Flare Board Express truck in 1914, about ten years after it had started making trucks, and just a few years before it started its ill-fated voyage into manufacturing tractors.

U.S. Army, selling 325 of the 2-ton Model CC trucks to the U.S. Army. In 1918, the company was renamed again, to the Dart Motor Truck and Tractor Corporation, making models up to 3 tons.

Another rename in 1925 made it the Hawkeye-Dart Truck Company; it was reorganized as the Dart Truck Company later that year. It branched into making trucks for mining companies, and during World War II, it built truck tractors as tank transporters that were powered by 250-hp six-cylinder Waukesha engines. In the 1950s, after several name changes, the company began concentrating on dump trucks, and after it was bought by the parent company of Kenworth and Peterbilt in 1961, the company name changed again, to KW-Dart Truck Company, building mammoth dump trucks.

Throughout the late 1960s and 1970s, Dart also built twin-steer six-wheel fuel tankers for aircraft, as well as front-end loaders, log stackers, and snowplows.

Since the 1980s, the company has produced the Dart 4000 in four models: 120-, 130-, 150- and 160-ton articulated bottom-dump coal haulers. All of these models were fitted with Ingersoll-Rand compressed-air starting motors with tanks of 19 cubic feet capacity. Top speed was approximately 40 mph.

Over the years, the company has made a wide variety of models, and still produces Dart trucks today.

Chapter 51

Hart-Parr Company Innovates, Invents Word 'Tractor'

Besides its other contributions to the world of motor vehicles, the Hart-Parr Company of Charles City, Iowa, introduced the word "tractor" into the regular farming vocabulary when Hart-Parr's advertising manager, W. H. Williams, used the word in a 1906 advertisement to describe the Hart-Parr 30-60 "Old Reliable" tractor.

Hart-Parr was an innovative company, developing schools to educate farmers about the newer and more complicated tractors and machinery that it produced; offering health insurance for its workers; selling homes to workers on the easy-pay program, as well as lots for buildings, offering the services of a doctor at the plant, and more.

The Hart-Parr Tractor Company is inextricably tied into the University of Wisconsin in Madison. In 1896, Charles W. Hart, and Charles H. Parr, young engineering students at the U of W, founded Hart-Parr Gasoline Engine Company to build stationary engines they had designed in college.

That winter of 1896, they convinced J. H. Bowman to invest $3,000 in their manufacturing product. The business was named Hart & Parr, until April 27, 1897, when it was reorganized as the Hart-Parr Company.

About the turn of the century, space became a problem for the company, and when Hart-Parr was told by the Madison powers that its company might lessen the desirability of Madison as a place for people to live, it cast its eyes elsewhere.

Hart's father said Charles City, Iowa, would give a warmer reception to a young and growing business, and that's where the company moved.

On July 5, 1901, ground was broken for the first buildings of the Hart-Parr Company in Charles City, Iowa. The early business of Hart-Parr was based on manufacturing a line of small stationary engines, portable engines, pumping outfits, and wood-sawing outfits.

Having been farm boys themselves, the Charleses knew something about the needs of farmers, and decided it was time to manufacture traction engines.

Hart-Parr tractors

In 1903, Hart-Parr sold 15 "tractors," as they would later be called. That year also, it developed its plowing tractor and perfected the oil cooling system for tractors. Suddenly, Hart-Parr tractors were "hot." The company could not make them fast enough.

The first traction engine/tractor was a 17- to 30-hp rated machine. The 1903 version was a 22- to 45-hp engine. Flywheels weighing 1,000 pounds and tractors weighing 20,000 pounds were Hart-Parr trademarks. The tractors were driven and steered by chains and meandered at 2.3 mph. The 17-30 had a two-cylinder horizontal, four-cycle engine with a 9-inch bore and a 13-inch stroke. The engine was sparked by a low-tension generator and cooled by an oil cooling system which required five expansion bulbs. It was rated to pull a four- or five-bottom plow. This Hart-Parr No. 1 was the first successful production tractor ever built, earning Hart-Parr the recognition as "founder of the farm tractor industry."

The 22-45 tractor used a two-cylinder horizontal, oil-cooled gasoline engine operating at 280 rpm. Exhaust pipes terminated in the radiator to induce draft. No expansion bulbs were required. Forward and backward mo-

After Oliver Chilled Plow Works bought out Hart-Parr in the late 1920s, it continued to make Hart-Parr tractors, but in 1930 added the "Oliver" name, which it used until 1936, when it phased the "Hart-Parr" out entirely. This row-crop Hart-Parr was manufactured in 1936 by the Hart-Parr Tractor Division of Oliver Farm Equipment Sales Co. of Charles City, Iowa. It weighed 4,340 pounds and used its own 4-1/8 x 5-1/4-inch bore and stroke four-cylinder engine to pull two or three 14-inch plows. (Dan Roen Collection)

The First Pierce-Arrow in 1902

Both Were New in 1902

The Hart-Parr is Still Giving Service

In 1902, the year of the first Pierce-Arrow, HART-PARR founded the tractor industry by building fifteen successful gasoline traction engines. Old HART-PARR No. 3, pictured above, was sold to an Iowa farmer who has operated it continuously for twenty-three busy years. Today, it and six others of the original fifteen are still giving service on American farms.

As In the Past, HART-PARRS are Built for L-a-s-t-i-n-g Service

The modern kerosene-burning HART-PARR, while vastly improved and simplified, is still built with old-fashioned thoroughness to give enduring service. The *improved* models for 1925, with enclosed drive, disc clutch, greater power, stronger construction and *detachable power take-off*, represent a quarter of a century of knowing how. When you sell a HART-PARR you sell l-a-s-t-i-n-g satisfaction. It is not "just a tractor", but a year in and year out investment for its buyer.

HART-PARR COMPANY, 143 Lawler St., Charles City, Iowa
Founders of the Tractor Industry

KEROSENE TRACTORS · STATIONARY ENGINES · FEED MILLS
HART-PARR
FOUNDERS OF THE TRACTOR INDUSTRY
WASHING MACHINES · AIR COMPRESSORS · COMMERCIAL CASTINGS

In this advertisement, Hart-Parr teamed with Pierce-Arrow automobiles to proclaim that "Both were new in 1902," and that Old Hart-Parr No. 3, built in 1902, was still giving service ca. 1917. Hart-Parrs were made in Charles City, Iowa, having moved there from Madison, Wisconsin, when the shortsighted town fathers thought the company would be a burden rather than a blessing to their community. (Dan Roen Collection)

tion were controlled by one lever. The operating cost was half of a steam engine, and required no water, steam, gauges, boiler, flues or grates to service; no fires to endanger the fields. No seat was provided for the operator.

The visionary young men realized tractors was the way to go, and thus dropped their successful stationary engine line to devote full time to making tractors.

Soon after getting their tractor on the market, the price of gasoline jumped amid rumors regarding a diminishing supply. So Hart-Parr turned to alternative fuels, conducting experiments and perfecting its design so that its tractor would operate just as successfully with kerosene or distillate for fuel as gasoline.

Other tractors made included the 18-30, 17-30, and 22-45, before Old Reliable came on the scene. Old Reliable was powered by a 300-rpm, two-cylinder, kerosene-burning horizontal engine with low tension magneto. Five dry cells were used to start the engine with gasoline. A centrifugal pump, along with forced draft derived from exhaust pressure in the radiator, circulated oil coolant through the radiator. Old Reliable weighed ten tons.

Hart-Parr made larger and larger tractors, like the 40-80 horsepower; and a monstrous railway-locomotive-sized 60- to 100-hp prairie sodbuster reportedly weighed more than 50,000 pounds, and was in Hart-Parr's catalog only in 1911 and 1912. Wheels of this tractor were nine feet in diameter.

Hart-Parr's marketing area grew, as the company entered into contracts with a firm in Buenos Aires, Argentina, as well as Austria and Russia. Shipments were also made to Cuba, Chile, and the Philippine Islands, so that the Hart-Parr product became quite generally known throughout the world. Factories had to be expanded.

In 1914, Hart-Parr introduced its first small tractor, the peculiar tricycle rig called the 15- to 22-hp Little Red Devil.

It was propelled by its large single rear wheel, with a direct-drive reversible two-cycle two-cylinder engine. At slowest idle, the timing lever was reversed and the engine would misfire itself into running backward.

The two-cylinder, two-cycle, thermosyphon water-cooled engine of this 15- 22-hp tractor operated at 600 rpm and was unique because it had no valves, transmission and differential. Valve ports in cylinder walls were opened and closed by up-and-down movement of pistons. Reverse direction was obtained by reversing the rotation of the engine at slow idle.

In 1918, Hart-Parr introduced two practical smaller tractors, the 15-30 Type A, and the New Hart-Parr 12-25. In 1919, Charles Hart and Charles Parr sold out to their partner, C. D. Ellis, but continued working for the company.

Eventually Oliver Chilled Plow Works bought Hart-Parr, and continued producing Hart-Parr tractors. The first Oliver-Hart-Parr was introduced in 1930, the 18-28, with an upright, longitudinally mounted four-cylinder engine. Orchard and rice field versions were offered, and in 1931, an industrial version was added.

Soon the Oliver logo became larger than the Hart-Parr, and in 1938, one year after C. W. Hart died, and three years before C. H. Parr died, the name Hart-Parr disappeared forever from the name of tractors.

Hart-Parr automobiles

Unlike other tractor companies that made automobiles, Hart-Parr's automobiles were not made for the general market. It made two-cylinder runabouts for use only by its executives and traveling salesmen. Rather than buy cars, the company decided to save money and produced the cars itself in 1908. Little is known how good these cars were, how long they ran or whether any have survived.

Chapter 52

Lawter Company Makes Tractors and Cars

The only question involving the sketchy information available about Lawter tractors and cars is whether the same man or the same company made both of them. The answer: maybe.

Lawter tractors

Lawter Tractor Company of Newcastle, Indiana, began manufacturing tractors in 1913, and shortly thereafter bought the Universal Tractor Company, also of Newcastle. For some reason then, the plant relocated to St. Mary's, Ohio.

The Lawter tractor was an odd-looking thing, with a tiny back wheel and large front ones. It used a Teeter engine, and the 1916 model was rated 18-38. It weighed 6,500 pounds and sold for $1,750.

Lawter automobiles

Lawter automobiles were also built in New Castle, Indiana, and it seems too much a coincidence that the tractor and automobile concerns would not be related.

The first automobile designed by Benjamin Lawter was a 16 hp, and the second a 20 hp, both using two-cylinder engines. The wheelbases of the two machines were similar, 90 and 94 inches, respectively.

At this time, Lawter did not have a plant, so he had the Safety Shredder Company of New Castle build his cars as he tried to organize his company and get a factory. He went broke before he could do either, however.

Nonetheless, a few Lawter cars were produced by the Safety Shredder Factory, the 1909 Sixteen Baby Tonneau four-passenger model which cost $950; and the 1909 Lawter Twenty, a Touring automobile for five passengers, costing $1,350.

The Newcastle, Indiana, manufacturing company of Lawter Tractor Company made this automobile only one year, 1909, in a pair of designs. One was called the Sixteen, and the other, the Twenty, like this model. It is a two-cylinder, 20-hp five-passenger touring car that sold for $1,350.

This Lawter tractor was manufactured in Newcastle, Indiana, by Lawter Tractor Company. After the company bought its same-town rival tractor company, Universal Tractor Company, the two were combined, and relocated to St. Mary's Ohio in 1914. This 1916 model sold for $1,750 and weighed three tons. (Dan Roen Collection)

Chapter 53

Final Autos of Company Sold Door to Door

Young lawyer E. A. Myers recognized early on that there was potential in the automobile industry, so in 1901 he bought out a financially troubled machine shop in Garrett, Indiana, and moved it to Auburn, Indiana. He started a new company, named the Model Gas and Gasoline Engine Company, to manufacture gasoline engines and gasoline cars.

Like many companies of the time, expansion plans were announced regularly, sometimes without a basis in reality. A *Motor Age* magazine article from March 21, 1912 says, "E. A. Myers, general manager of the Model Gas Engine Works, Peru, Indiana, closed a deal last Saturday by which his company will at once erect a building in Pittsburgh for the manufacture of motors. Three hundred thousand dollars of Pittsburgh capital has been put in the company, giving it a total capitalization of over $500,000. The motor factory at Peru, Indiana, will continue in operation as in the past. Regarding the line of motors to be built in the future, Mr. Myers announced that nothing in the line of a cheap product will be turned out, but the entire attention directed to a high-class one. Among the Pittsburgh people who are back of the project are F. F. Nicola, W. C. Coffin, J. F. Keenan, J. G. Villsack and O. G. Villsack, all of whom visited Peru last Saturday, when the deal was finally closed. These Pittsburgh people had previously had a complete report of the situation furnished them by specialist engineers."

However, the factory never materialized.

Model tractors

In 1906, the Model Gas Engine Works of Peru, Indiana, entered the tractor field with a series of tractor models pow-ered by 16- to 60-hp engines. It was the only traction engine built at the time with two forward and reverse speeds.

Model automobiles

The first Model was a 12-hp two-cylinder machine with a small wheelbase of 72 inches, selling for $900 (two-passenger runabout) or $1,000 (five-passenger detachable tonneau). The 16-hp two-cylinder, added in 1904 in two models, cost $1,800 and $2,000.

Model cars sold well, with the only dim lights on the horizon being the closing of banks in the Auburn area, which set the company back. Eventually, Myers negotiated out of trouble, and by 1906 had produced 300 Model cars.

In 1906, he moved his company to Peru, Indiana, and divided it into two parts: the Model Automobile Company and the Model Gas Engine Works, one producing cars, the other gas engines. He soon realized his two companies were competing for the same customers, so he renamed the car.

Star automobiles

The Star, the new name for the Model automobile, was made in 1908. The models included then the Model 12, 14,

In 1906, Model Gas Engine Works of Peru, Indiana, tried to build a tractor, and the result was this traction engine with a pair of forward and reverse speeds, the only one of that design of the time.

Most Powerful and Easiest Riding Car

ON WHEELS SELLING AT

$1250

24 H. P.
100 in. wheel base
32 in. wheels

Get our Catalogue and compare specifications with others

MODEL AUTOMOBILE CO. :: :: Peru, Ind.

In 1907, Model Automobile Co. of Peru, Indiana, was selling its Model automobiles for $1,250. The 24-hp vehicles had a 100-inch wheelbase. That was the same year the name of the vehicle was changed to "Star" because owner E. A. Myers realized he was competing against the same customers with two different companies that he owned. He hoped changing the name would make the difference. Evidently it didn't, for after two years, the Model/Star was renamed Great Western. (Gary Hoonsbeen Collection)

This Great Western Touring Automobile sold for $1,600 in 1915 and was made by the Model Automobile Company of Peru, Indiana. It had been a Star Automobile renamed Great Western, but by this time, six years later, there were enough differences that a person could see how the Great Western had taken on its own identity, though there are still major similarities. (Roy Bernick Collection)

This Great Western Touring Automobile sold for $1,600 in 1915 and was made by the Model Automobile Company of Peru, Indiana. It had been a Star Automobile renamed Great Western, but by this time, six years later, there were enough differences that a person could see how the Great Western had taken on its own identity, though there are still major similarities. (Roy Bernick Collection)

16, and 18, the first two two-cylinder 24-hp machines, the latter two four-cylinder of 35 and 50 hp. In 1909, it produced the Model 24 and Model 30, selling for $1,600 each.

Great Western automobiles

In 1910, Myers decided to rename his company and automobile so there would be no more confusion. On Sept. 8, 1909, he formed the Great Western Automobile Company. He not only sold automobiles, but offered engines, transmissions, and clutches to other manufacturers.

The first Great Western was simply a Star renamed, as Star had been a Model renamed. Later models included the 1912 Great Western Forty, a four-cylinder, 40-hp machine with 114-inch wheelbase, selling for $1,600 (five-passenger touring, two-passenger torpedo roadster, or four-passenger demi-tonneau roadster); a five-passenger semi-torpedo for $1,650; and a five-passenger detachable four-door for $1,750.

Great Westerns were built in 1913-1916, although in 1913 the company started having financial difficulties. Myers made a number of mistakes, including signing a large

contract that he broke and was sued for. The press blamed the downfall of the company on faulty engines.

Ignominiously, the company ended, with the last few hand-assembled parts sold door to door.

Great Western truck

In 1911 and 1912, a Great Western truck was built by Great Western Transportation Company of Chicago. There is conflicting evidence as to whether this was in any way associated with Great Western automobiles. This Great Western truck was a 10-ton gasoline-electric truck with a 172-inch wheelbase, using solid rubber tires 48 x 12 inches front and rear.

The second "Model" car was called the Star, several different models of which are shown here. These 1908 Star cars were made by the Model Automobile Co. of Peru, Indiana, and were destined to be renamed Great Western a year later, with few changes made in the vehicles themselves. The cars included in this lineup are the Model 12 (on top), a five-passenger touring car weighing $1,800 pounds for $1,250; in the center, a five-passenger No. 14 car with removable tonneau, going for $1,350, and a five- to seven-passenger Car No. 15, weighing 2,900 pounds and selling for $3,500. (Roy Bernick Collection)

Chapter 54

Small Tractors and Small Cars Highlight Company

Little tractors and little cars were what Shaw Manufacturing Co. of Galesburg, Kansas manufactured from 1920 to the 1940s.

Stanley Shaw started in the vehicle business by motorizing bicycles in 1903, and a decade later built motorcycles.

The Shaw tractor

The first Shaw was a garden tractor in the 1930s, in several varieties. It was called the Shaw Du-All D, and came in

This advertisement shows a variety of different Shaw Speedsters, with a carrying capacity of 500 pounds. The Model 6B with battery ignition cost $138, while others ranged from $120 to $151 for the Model 6M with magneto ignition. The Shaw literature maintained, "...the Shaw Speedster is furnished with or without engine hood, with disc or wire wheels with 20 x 2-inch clincher tires. All models are strongly built and will carry two adult riders besides considerable luggage." (Roy Bernick Collection)

horsepowers of 2, 3, 4, and 5, using a pair of 32-inch diameter traction wheels, and a recommendation to pull one or two plows, depending on the horsepower size. It claimed three acres plowed in a ten-hour day. It used a Briggs & Stratton 3- x 3-1/4-inch bore-and-stroke single cylinder, four-cycle engine with B & S magneto in flywheel for ignition, Kingston carburetor, and air-cooling. The transmission was a three-speed sliding selective gear from 1/4 to 4 mph forward, and 1/4 to 1 mph in reverse. Six speeds were available, up to 15 mph. The final drive was spur gears running in grease.

In the 1940s, Shaw came out with its Du-All HY8, a larger riding tractor but still small compared to most other tractors. This one was designed for truck gardens and small farms. Production of all Shaw tractors ceased sometime in the 1940s.

The Shaw automobile

The Shaw automobile looked like a go-cart or derby racer. The car sold for $125 to $165, and looked like a toy, though Stanley Shaw insisted it was a real car. Wheelbase was 70 inches, and its engine a 2-1/2-hp Shaw and later Briggs & Stratton. The transmission was a single-speed

Shaw Manufacturing Company of Galesburg, Kansas, manufactured the Shaw DU-ALL D in 1920 in four sizes: 2, 3, 4, and 5 horsepower. The 4-hp DU-ALL shown here weighed 500 pounds when it was produced in 1936. The engine was a Briggs & Stratton one-cylinder four-cycle of 3 x 3-1/4-inch bore and stroke, more a garden tiller type of tractor than a pure tractor. One 10- or 12-inch-plow was recommended for pulling. (Dan Roen Collection)

Despite the company's claim in this advertisement that the Shaw Sport Speedster was "A Real Automobile," it was marketed to kids, as this flyer shows. The Shaw Sport Speedster was to be given away. It was painted red, while the seats, hood, and trimmings were black. It got 60 to 90 miles per gallon of gas, and motored at 4 to 25 mph. It also had electric headlights and a horn. "Will carry two adults and luggage," the information says.(Roy Bernick Collection)

chain or belt drive, although a shaft-driven model was made starting in 1926.

Buyers could also purchase the Shaw speedster in parts and put it together themselves, adhering to the Shaw slogan that "anyone who can use a hammer, screwdriver, and other ordinary tools can build the Shaw Speedster." Miles per hour were guaranteed from 25-90.

During the 1930s, Shaw Manufacturing Company of Galesburg, Kansas, made a tractor conversion kit, as shown in this photo. This Shaw Tractorized Car was intended to use a Ford Model T, or A, or Chevrolet. It could also be rein-driven, as in this photo.

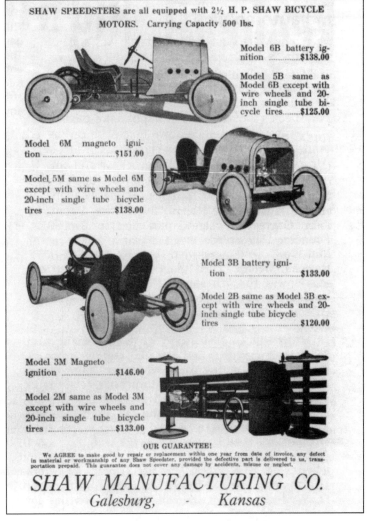

Chapter 55

Stroud Company Dogged By Fraud

Many suppositions surround the Stroud Motor Manufacturing Association of San Antonio, Texas, which supposedly built tractors, trucks, and cars.

Stroud tractors

The Stroud 16-30 All-in-One tractor was the forerunner of today's row-crop models as a tricycle-type tractor. It was manufactured in 1920 with a Climax four-cylinder engine with 5- x 6-1/2-inch bore and stroke for 3,000 pounds of drawbar pull for the 6,000-pound machine.

Stroud automobiles

Maybe some were built. There certainly was a lot of build-up in the 1919 prospectus announcing the new vehicle as the company tried to sell stock. "Statistics show there are fewer failures in the automobile manufacturing business than in the banking business," it crowed.

The prospectus showed the drawing of a five-passenger touring car with an upside-down horseshoe on the front of the radiator. (Upside-down horseshoes in superstition denote bad luck, because all the luck will run out, which is why horseshoes are almost always depicted right-side-up, which is as a "U.") The car specifications included a Continental engine, Hotchkiss drive, Stromberg carburetor, and Atwater-Kent ignition, for $1,050 in San Antonio. The company noted that a similar car built elsewhere and shipped to Texas would cost more

This is a drawing of 1919 Stroud touring car, a five-passenger vehicle with a wrong-way horseshoe on the radiator. The Stroud touring car was to be built with a Continental engine, Hotchkiss drive, Stromberg carburetor, Atwater-Kent ignition, 114-inch wheelbase, for $1,050. No Stroud automobile has ever been found so it is difficult to know if any were ever built, but it appears not.

than $400 more. "It is our aim to keep this Texas money in Texas for Texans," the company said.

If any Stroud cars were actually built, they did not survive.

Stroud trucks

No Stroud trucks have ever been found, either, though the company claimed to have built some.

The Stroud 16-30 was manufactured in 1920 by Stroud Motor Manufacturing Association, Ltd., of San Antonio, Texas. This four-wheel tractor had a pair of rear traction wheels 60 inches in diameter. The engine was a Climax four-cylinder L-head with 5 x 6-1/2-inch bore and stroke. The Stroud 16-30 weighed 5,000 pounds, (the engine 1,080), could pull four 14-inch plows, and worked at 800 rpm. The cooling system was a long tubular radiator. (Dan Roen Collection)

Chapter 56

Wharton Tractors

Wharton Motors Co. of Dallas, Texas, began selling stock in its company in 1920, and that same year built a unique three-wheel-drive tractor, the Wharton 3WD 12-22. Its Erd four-cylinder motor was a 4-inch bore and 6-inch stroke engine. It weighed 3,680 pounds, used a Split-dorf high-tension magneto with impulse started, and Hyatt and Timken bearings throughout.

It also made the Wharton FWD 20-40, a four-wheel-drive tractor built in 1920. Four-wheel-drive tractors had many problems to overcome, like excessive friction, which meant wear and breakage, a steering system that turned the vehicle easily, and more. This 20-40 was only sold for one year. Wharton also operated as Texas Truck & Tractor Company.

Wharton automobiles

Wharton Motors Company sold stock for three years before any automobiles were built in 1922. Plans called for the manufacture of seven body types on a 136-inch wheelbase chassis, and powered by a Curtiss-OX-5 aero engine of 104 hp. The body styles and prices included a touring car for $3,450, a Victoria and sport for $3,750, a sport roadster for $4,000, a sedan for $4,350, a town car for $4,650, and a Continental landaulet for $4,800. The company had a Dallas factory, along with plans for another in Johnstown, Pennsylvania. None of the four-cylinder or six-cylinder cars that were announced were ever built.

But the ambitious attempt to market a series of private cars of 4-, 6-, and 8-cylinder cars (as well as a 4-wheel drive truck, which was never built) floundered. In fact, it is probable that only one Wharton car ever was built, an OX-5 roadster, although another reference says that several were built.

After stockholders brought a suit against the company in 1924, the Wharton company disappeared.

WHARTON FWD, 20-40
Wharton Motors Company, Dallas, Texas

Wharton manufactured its Wharton FWD 20-40, a tractor with four drive wheels 51 inches in diameter with 12-inch face in the rear. The tractor weighed 4,380 pounds, was powered by a four-cylinder vertical, valve-in-head 750 rpm engine of 4-3/4 x 6-inch bore and stroke. The transmission was a special sliding gear of three speeds forward, one reverse, and was "entirely enclosed and lubricated." (Dan Roen Collection)

Wharton Motor Company of Dallas, Texas, made this Wharton 12-22 tractor in 1920, the only year it and its companion tractor, the Wharton 20-40 four-wheel-drive tractor, was made. But the business, which also made a Wharton automobile–only one prototype–failed, and so did the Wharton tractors. This 12-22 weighed 3,680 pounds and used an Erd 4 x 6-inch bore and stroke four-cylinder engine. It was an unusual design, a three-wheeled tractor with traction in all three wheels. (Dan Roen Collection)

Bibliography

Books:

Ehrich, Terry, Editor, *Hemmings' Vintage Auto Almanac*, Tenth Edition, Hemming Motor News, Bennington, Vermont, 1994.

Farm Implement News, *The Tractor Field Book, With Power Farm Equipment Specifications*, Farm Implement News, Chicago, 1929.

Georgano, G. N., Ed., *The Complete Encyclopedia of Motorcars, 1885 to Present*, George Rainbird Ltd., 1973, London.

Gray, R. F., Compiler, *The Agricultural Tractor 1855-1950*, The American Society of Agricultural Engineers, St. Joseph, Michigan, 1975.

Gunnell, John, Ed., *Standard Catalog of American Trucks*, Krause Publications, Iola, Wisconsin, 1987.

Handbook of Automobiles 1915-1916, Dover Publications, New York, 1970.

Kimes, Beverly Rae, and Henry Austin Clark Jr., *Standard Catalog of American Cars 1805-1942*, Second Edition, Krause Publications, Iola, Wisconsin, 1989.

Mroz, Albert, *The Illustrated Encyclopedia of American Trucks and Commercial Vehicles*, Krause Publications, Iola, Wisconsin, 1996

Norbeck, Jack, *Encyclopedia of American Steam Traction Engines*, Crestline Publications, Glen Ellyn, Illinois.

Purdy, Ken W., *Motorcars of the Golden Past*, Galahad Books, NYC, 1966.

Van Horn, Lloyd, *Early American Motor Trucks*, Mason City, Iowa, 1994.

Vossler, Bill, *Orphan Tractors*, Motorbooks International, Osceola, Wisconsin, 1996.

Wendel, C.H., *Encyclopedia of American Farm Tractors*, Motorbooks International, Osceola, Wisconsin, 1992.

Wendel, C.H., *150 Years of International Harvester*, Crestline Publications, Glen Ellyn, Illinois, 1981.

Wendel, C.H., *The Allis-Chalmers Story*, Crestline Publishing, Sarasota, Florida, 1988.

Wendel, C.H., *Unusual Vintage Tractors*, Krause Publications, Iola, Wisconsin, 1996.

Magazines:

American Thresherman
American Thresherman and Farm Power
Antique Automobile
Country Gentleman
Farm Power
Farm Implement News
Farm Implements and Tractors
Gas Review
Horseless Carriage
Motor Age

Index